ARMSTRONG

MATAPÉDIA

MIRAMICHI

QUEBEC CITY

TRURO

HALIFAX

MONTREAL

TORONTO

Rolling Home

A Cross-Canada
Railroad
Memoir

Rolling Home

A Cross-Canada
Railroad
Memoir

Tom Allen

PENGUIN

VIKING

VIKING

Published by the Penguin Group

Penguin Books Canada Ltd, 10 Alcorn Avenue, Toronto, Ontario, Canada M4V 3B2

Penguin Books Ltd, 80 Strand, London WC2R ORL, England

Penguin Putnam Inc., 375 Hudson Street, New York, New York 10014, U.S.A.

Penguin Books Australia Ltd, Ringwood, Victoria, Australia

Penguin Books (NZ) Ltd, cnr Rosedale and Airborne Roads, Albany, Auckland 1310,
    New Zealand

Penguin Books Ltd, Registered Offices: Harmondsworth, Middlesex, England

First published 2001

10 9 8 7 6 5 4 3 2 1

Copyright © Tom Allen, 2001
Maps © Kyle Gell Design, 2001

The author has changed some names in this book to protect privacy.

Printed and bound in Canada on acid free paper (∞)

NATIONAL LIBRARY OF CANADA CATALOGUING IN PUBLICATION DATA

Allen, Tom, 1961–
    Rolling home : a cross-Canada railroad memoir

ISBN 0-670-88473-1

1. Allen, Tom, 1961– —Journeys—Canada. 2. Allen, Tom, 1961– —Family. 3. Railroad
travel—Canada. I. Title.

FC75.A337 2001   917.104'64   C2001-901140-7
F1017.A337 2001

Visit Penguin Canada's website at **www.penguin.ca**

For
Melissa and Wesley

Contents

Thanks

Sharon Adams
Jennifer Allen
Melissa Allen
Pauline Allen
Philip Allen
Wesley Allen
Chris Barry
Mark Bothwell
Don Brown
Catherine Campbell
Terry Dean
Leone Earls
Jane Farrow
Mark Franklin
Cynthia Good
Greg Gormick
John Gotziaman
Alan Guettel
Philip Hartling

Jackie Kaiser
Catherine Kaloutsky
Sharon Kirsch
Bob Kroll
Meg Masters
Malcolm Matthews
Sandra Matthews
Michelle Melady
Anne Mercer
Joy Pennick
Phonehead
Paul Raynor
Erika Ritter
Scott Sellers
Sandra Tooze
Diane Turbide
Kenneth Welsh
Heather White

Introduction

I GREW UP DURING the echo of the last hurrah of passenger rail travel in Canada. By 1961, the year I was born, the Canadian Pacific Railway had only to admit its plans to abandon the passenger train. It wasn't making money. Some of the business was taking off on the airlines, some in affordable cars and on the improved highways. Even the mighty *Canadian,* the elegant transcontinental beauty considered one of the best trains in the world, simply couldn't turn a profit. It cost too much to operate. Even though the train was usually sold out, there was still too much of Canada, and not enough of us.

But I didn't know that. I was a kid, and the train to me was magic. The first trip I can remember was from Montreal to Toronto in 1968. We took the *Rapido,* Canadian National's corridor train. It was huge and noisy and went half as fast again as the cars we could see on the highway. I was enthralled. I was also sick. It was a Friday afternoon. The train was full of families and businessmen, and I had a red spot on my cheek. "Hey," my sister said, "maybe he's got the chicken pox." Everyone sitting within ten seats went to the lounge. I did have the chicken pox, as it turned out. I was speckled by the time we reached Scarborough.

This brings up the other side of train travel. Trains are metal boxes. Although they may be large, if the business is going to keep moving, they need to be full, and a large metal box full of humans is never a pretty thing. It doesn't matter if it's a two-car dayliner held together with duct tape or the most luxurious twenty-three-car rail cruiser. New hairdos flatten, drinks spill, clothes wrinkle, the air stales, tempers shorten and, generally speaking, travellers looking forward to a relaxed and happy arrival do not arrive happy or relaxed. They arrive tired and greasy, with at least a little of their dignity left behind and, quite possibly, with an infectious disease they didn't have when they left home.

If you were on that *Rapido* in 1968, please accept my apologies.

I've probably been paid back several times by now, anyway. I've been in a lot of metal boxes lately. From June 1999 to September 2000, I travelled by train from the Atlantic to the Pacific to Hudson Bay. I travelled by coach and by first class. I, in fact, rode a two-car dayliner held together with duct tape and a luxurious rail cruiser, a twenty-three-car sleeper train, a four-car tourist train and the first-class car of an express train that goes so fast it hurts your ears and won't stop for anything. I saw dazzling technology and depressing neglect. For some of the way I travelled with my wife and two small children, some with my father, and still other bits I travelled alone. Even then, there was always someone to talk to. I met all kinds of people: some who live by and for the railroad, and others who wouldn't care if it never ran again. I met engineers whose fathers and grandfathers had been engineers, and who would like to pass on the torch to their own children, but who aren't sure there will be any jobs left.

If there is no railroad to pass on to the next generation of engineers or passengers, I wondered what the cost of that might be, and if there is any way to find out.

Just as the Canadian railroad has been in steady decline as a passenger service in my lifetime, its image has been steadily buffed with lore and romance. Older Canadians speak mistily of the train. They talk of its spirit, and how it defined the land. For many who arrived here as immigrants and made their first journeys inland by rail, the train *was* Canada. They say it taught them pride and respect in their new land, and what it meant to be Canadian. And those same people say they wouldn't have learned that on an airplane or in a car. They say if we let the passenger train die, something in us will die, too.

On the other hand, for the farmers whose ancestors rarely lived a day without saying, "God damn the CPR!" such mistiness is exactly that. For them, and many others, the railroads didn't define the land, they defiled it. They got it cheap, sucked away the easy money and pulled out.

I figured the institution known as the Canadian Passenger Train was probably all of those things, and I went looking for what was left of it. Seeing as I'd be travelling at various times with my children, my spouse, my father and by myself, I hoped that, between the cursing, dreaming, hope and disappointment, I also might find out a few things about another part of Canadian life.

There are consequences to putting a bunch of people in a metal box on wheels. It's not just flattened hairdos and spilled drinks. The train affects relationships, as well. Some of them are new and springy. Some are old and creaky. Some are flattened, spilled and worse. Others aren't sure what they are, but as it always is between people, they certainly aren't what they were when the train started rolling.

I'll try to keep the mist and romance to a tolerable level. It's addictive, I know, but I'd like to keep the air as clear as I can. It's been getting stuffier in here since we left the station.

The power keeps cutting out and I'm not sure the air conditioning's working. Besides, there's a kid a few seats over with a runny nose. He's looking kind of pale, and I think I saw him scratching his cheek.

Rolling Home

A Cross-Canada
Railroad
Memoir

Halifax, Nova Scotia

~

GETTING UP AND GOING was the hard part.

It was a beautiful Saturday in late June and we had just spent a week's holiday in Nova Scotia. There were four of us—myself, my wife and our two children—and we were heading into Halifax to catch VIA Rail's *Ocean Limited,* westbound to Montreal.

It had been a glorious week from that very first morning—a foggy two hours on Lawrencetown Beach, complete with stone skipping, fossil hunting, lots of silent gazing and surfers. That was a treat. I knew Lawrencetown had surfers, but I'd never seen them. For that matter I'd never seen any surfers in the kind of weather we had that morning. It was a steel-grey day with a persistent wind and a black sea so cold that your knees ached if you stood in it for a minute.

Surfing is an amazing thing—just a board on the sea, with one second either way holding the difference between flying freedom and crushing defeat. It's no wonder they wait so long to make a move. You'd think surfers would be a carefree lot, surfing being a fairly organic pursuit, but surfer society is strictly regulated. They sit out there on their boards, silently jockeying like locomotives idling in the yard, staring ahead

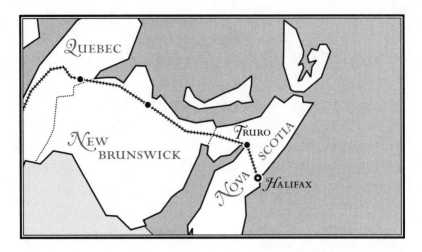

and waiting for a good wave. The wrong wave brings only shame. The glory fades quickly and the fall comes hard. But for the surfer who finds a good wave, the rewards are enormous.

That week I was pretty sure we were on to a good wave. In the Annapolis Valley, on a sunny, clear day, we arrived at Grand Pré just in time for low tide on the Bay of Fundy. The flats were so wide, and the tide so fast, that by the time we'd walked out for a look the tide had already turned and was coming back in.

There was an old dance hall by the shore, with sway-backed floorboards and a long covered porch. A van full of tourists from Louisiana arrived, and then a fiddling family from Newfoundland. Within ten minutes, they'd turned our afternoon into a non-stop blast through every tune known to eastern Canada. By the time we left, the tide had turned back the other way again and we were all toasted like marshmallows.

On our last night in Nova Scotia we stayed with family friends in Chester Basin, on the South Shore. I've known Malcolm and Sandra since I was a kid and their kids were babies. Malcolm and my father worked together in the late sixties and we visited them often. When I was there Malcolm seemed to treat me as if I were grown-up, which, compared with his tiny kids, I guess I was.

It occurred to me after we arrived on that June afternoon that I was about the age that Malcolm was when he met my dad, and that my children were about the age I was. I found myself eavesdropping all afternoon, to see if the same thing would happen again, if my kids would end up feeling grown-up.

After dinner the wind died down, along with the day's sun, but it was still warm on the veranda. I came into the house to help with the dishes, and noticed Malcolm had stayed outside and was sitting on the steps beside my son.

They sat out there for ten minutes with their backs to me, my son with my father's friend, gazing out over St. Margaret's Bay. When they finally came in, I snuck Malcolm aside and asked what they'd said. "Nothing at all," he laughed, which, when I thought about it, was perfect.

The next morning Malcolm found an old soccer ball in the shed. In no time at all a furious game was underway, which was great, except that it was time to go. At least, it was time for us to leave if we wanted to get into Halifax and catch our train with a minimum of stress, but I couldn't bring myself to call things off just yet. I loaded the car. I looked around for stuff we'd forgotten. I waited until what I thought was the very last minute.

As it turned out, the very last minute had gone by about thirty minutes earlier.

Then, once we finally got on the road, I found I wasn't exactly sure when our train was leaving. Memory told me we were boarding at one o'clock. But with the excitement of the soccer game and trying to get away in a hurry, I hadn't taken the time to check the tickets. I had taken the time, however, to put all the bags in the trunk, including the one with the tickets in it. With an hour of driving time left for exactly an hour's drive, another possibility emerged: the one in which the train was not boarding, but *leaving*, at one, which meant we couldn't stop to check or we'd miss it.

The surfer in me wobbled a bit.

Halifax has a classic Canadian train station: not really big, but still longer than it is wide and never quite sure if it's a church or a barn. It's near one of the city's container ports, too, so there are locomotives and train cars cluttered all over the place. Even there, though, it's hard to hide a nineteen-car passenger train. We could see as we wheeled around the last corner, two blocks away, that all was not completely lost. The *Ocean Limited* hadn't left. It was just idling and rumbling and looking awfully anxious to get started. As we pulled up I could see that there weren't any passengers on it yet, but that was a mixed blessing. It meant there were nineteen cars' worth of people lined up in the station—and they were all ahead of us. It also meant most of them were between the front door and the baggage counter, and we still had to check our bags.

I may as well tell you about the bags now. They are no more convenient to deal with here than they were piled up in a hotel lobby, but as I learned soon enough, avoiding them is more trouble than it's worth. So, meet the bags. There were eleven of them: four backpacks, three overnight bags and three large duffle bags, or, one bag each for the kids, four each for the adults and a laptop computer, a bonus, for me. The laptop is how I kept track of all this so I can tell it to you now. That made it a non-negotiable necessity, but that also made it solely my responsibility, and it was heavy. On days with lots of walking

I ended up with a welt from the shoulder strap. It was also dangerous. If I hoisted the rest of my load first, the last deep knee bend, for the laptop, ended up being a clean-and-jerk of Olympian proportions. If I wasn't up to it, as happened once or twice, I ended up guy-wired to the platform and had to start all over again. But if I went for the laptop first, inevitably, when I bent down for the other bags, it swung around like a three-iron and smashed into whatever was in its path—sometimes my forehead, and sometimes someone else's.

I don't remember which bag I started with on the way into the train station in Halifax. I might have been carrying all eleven. I don't know. My only memory is of leaving my wife and daughter to return the rental car, grabbing my son by the hand and charging through the doors in time to see a man in a VIA outfit closing the baggage window. I started the laptop swinging and ploughed ahead.

The baggage handler said we were supposed to have been there half an hour before departure in order to check our bags. I silently thanked him for confirming, officially, how wrong I had been. He said he would see if he could do anything and told me to wait with the bags while he checked.

That's when the other cost of the last-minute soccer game emerged. My son had to pee. He couldn't wait.

The bathrooms were across the station, on the other side of the crowd. I was opening the door to the men's room when the baggage handler came back to his post and, seeing I had left, threw his hands up in the air and stalked away. My son walked into the men's room. I ran back to the baggage counter and caught the handler just before he went out to the platform for good. He gave me a look, but he took the bags. Then my wife and daughter arrived and it was time to board.

Order is important to my wife. Monumental brushes with disorder, such as panic-stricken sprints in pursuit of possibly already-departed passenger trains, therefore, are not her favourite activity. I tell you this only to provide perspective on the family's general emotional condition, especially after my wife asked me where our son was, and I said he was in the bathroom.

"You sent a six-and-a-half-year-old boy," she said, stating what was now, too late, painfully obvious, "to the bathroom, by himself, in a train station?"

It was a good point. We were at the easternmost limit of a four-week transcontinental train trip. Our bags were packed and on the train. Our accommodations were reserved and paid for. We were going to see much of our bountiful land and meet many, many wonderful people. We were going to be better off than we had been. Everything was exactly as it should have been, except for one thing: Our son was alone in the train station bathroom.

The train station bathroom is exactly where you'd expect the one awful thing to be. Train stations have a strange relationship with their bathrooms. The station itself really is a church of a kind. It's a temple to the people that pass through it. Most places in Canada, when you get off the train and walk into that main lobby, it doesn't matter whether you are a judge with twenty years on the bench or looking at twenty years from the other side, you're as important as you can be. Train station ceilings soar above you, leaded glass bathes you in light and grand arches lead you into town. Even in a smaller centre, the train station is the front door of the community, and when you walk in, you can do so with pride.

If, however, you have to go to the bathroom before you cross that civic threshold, the jig's up. Train station bathrooms hold the ugly truth of urban life. They stink. People stagger in after using their seats as beds and their boots as pillows. They have showers in the sink and leave their fetid puddles behind. They change in the stalls and pull on suits with the ties already knotted, sordid deals in their pockets half done and, more often than not, a few of the stalls are already full, being used for other sordid deals of their own. All kinds of disreputable things happen in train station bathrooms, involving all kinds of disreputable people. But even for them, it's still a step they'd rather not take. Nobody uses a train station bathroom unless he or she really has nowhere else to go.

Remember *Witness,* the mid-eighties Harrison Ford movie about an Amish boy who sees a gruesome murder? The kid was about six years old. It happened in the train station. It happened in the bathroom.

It also happened in a Hollywood movie. That's what I told myself as I plunged into the men's room. It wasn't that dirty, to be honest, but it was soaked in the desolation of a train station men's room—full of failure and frustration and disgust, including my own, because my son wasn't there.

He wasn't in the women's either, or in the lobby, or by the baggage counter, or on the platform.

I felt my stomach churn, signalling my brain that simple distress was no longer enough of a reaction. Being "better off" was suddenly meaningless, as was the entire trip—all that remained was fear.

"Dad," came a voice behind me, "where were you?"

He was right behind me. He'd been looking for us. I hugged him, said I was sorry, that I loved him and that we had to go. Then, all in one motion, we did.

I began to relax once we were all on board, ploughing single file through the central corridor. We'd made it, after all. I still had on a couple of guy-wire shoulder straps from the bags we'd brought on board, and the laptop was, in fact, right in my lap. I was too tired to move it. But there was nothing to worry about now, I thought. We were finally on our way and had four weeks together to look forward to. I smiled at my family.

They weren't looking.

~

We had a good set-up on board.

We were in a sleeping car, for one thing. The alternative is to ride coach. In coach you get a seat, a pillow and a blanket. The *Ocean Limited* takes eighteen hours, overnight, to get from Halifax to Montreal. That's a long time to be in a space designed for sitting up, especially if you're trying to lie down.

The sleeping cars on the *Ocean Limited* were built in 1955 for the Canadian Pacific Railway by the Budd Company of Philadelphia, Pennsylvania, and refitted in 1990 by VIA Rail. Each sleeping car has berths, roomettes, bedrooms, a general-use bathroom and a shower.

We had bedrooms C and D, adjacent rooms with a movable partition between them. I went to C and waited for our service attendant to draw back the wall.

It's odd, in a way, that train travel carries an image of romance and elegance. The first few kilometres out of any major train station in Canada are enough to burst even the thickest bubble. It's all very well to be in the burnished art deco lounge car, gazing through the oversized windows or enjoying the view from the observation dome. Yet none of that helps what there is to look at. Leaving Toronto, if travelling east, one has the pleasure of viewing scrapyards, decrepit buildings, the sewage-choked Toronto harbour, and a variety of bland and deserted industrial parks. To the west, there are brickyards, piles of reclaimed tires and, behind a food terminal, several crates of rotting watermelons. Entering Winnipeg, one sees a wide selection of scrapyards. In Montreal it is much the same, but there is more graffiti.

On the way west out of Halifax, there is no rotting fruit. There is rock. The track is at the bottom of a six-metre trench cut right out of the Appalachian stone of the Halifax peninsula. Ironically, if you could see out and over the cut, the view might not be too bad. The track goes behind one of the city's more beautiful neighbourhoods, with grand old trees and brightly painted clapboard mansions. The rock does recede eventually, but by then the train has left the beautiful neighbourhood and is behind Sears—a bland white building, surrounded by a parking lot.

Unlike many other Canadian cities, though, Halifax does give its departing train travellers one truly spectacular sight while they are still within the city limits. The Bedford Basin, which lies to the north and east of the Halifax peninsula, is one of the most beautiful natural harbours in the world. It is deep and wide and accompanied, even on the most blustery days, by an almost eerie stillness. For me, that stillness comes from the knowledge that just beyond the shore the water is over fifteen metres deep, making the shoreline more like the top of a submerged cliff. During the Second World War, as with every other period of conflict the region has known, the basin was used as a holding area for battleships on their way to and from various tours of duty. Apparently, the captains of those countless vessels also considered the basin an ideal holding area for other unwanted military gear. No one knows exactly how much is down there in the murky depths, but every now and then a mine bubbles to the surface and makes sure everyone's still paying attention.

That mysterious and vaguely threatening profundity, along with the play of light across the water and the mighty MacKay Bridge soaring overhead, makes the Bedford Basin a breathtaking sight when viewed from the train. But there is a catch. Most of the time, just as your train arrives at the still shores of the Bedford Basin, it also pulls up alongside a container train. This means that, most of the time, the view consists not of dancing light and soaring bridges, but of a line of rusting metal crates painted in tasteless colours and emblazoned with cheesy corporate logos. Knowing what's in them doesn't help much, either. Statistically, those containers coming through Halifax are most likely to contain paper (189,183 metric tonnes), peat (90,129 metric tonnes),[1] inorganic chemicals (42,495 metric tonnes) or french fries (just 22,120 metric tonnes). Small potatoes, really.

At the eastern end of the Bedford Basin, one finds a container pier with the cruel name of Fairview Cove. The other container terminal, you will recall, was back behind the train station. That one is named (more predictably) Halterm.

The combined Halifax ports send containers by ship to Boston and other American ports, as well as to Newfoundland and St. Pierre and Miquelon. They also send them by truck along the Trans-Canada Highway. The majority, however,

---

1. Peat? Who knew?

somewhere in the order of 235,000 per year, end up doing exactly what we were—heading west on a train. Often, to the consternation of viewing passengers, they are doing it at precisely the same time.

Containers have become part of the visual fabric of Canadian life. We lived in Halifax for a while. During that time container ships were such common sights that we simply didn't notice them at all. One late afternoon in downtown Halifax, on a corner not far from the waterfront, with tall buildings on all sides, my wife claimed to have seen one of the buildings move. As she reached for a lamppost to steady herself, she saw that the moving "building" was, in fact, a container ship heading through the harbour to the basin. It was the largest structure in sight. In the dim light it had become part of the landscape.

Once all of those containers land in Canada, the ones that are loaded onto rail head out for the United States and Mexico. Others end up somewhere between our three coasts, and still others go right across the country to Vancouver or Prince Rupert, are loaded onto another floating building and keep right on going.

There is one more reason that container ships are like buildings. Sometimes they have people in them. One of the increasingly common, and not often reported, cargo items brought into Canada by shipping container is smuggled people. It is hard to know exactly how many immigrants are smuggled into Canada by container each year. The ones we hear about tend to be those who aren't lucky enough to arrive alive. Certainly, the skulking agents of the people-shipping business would rather keep the numbers unknown. One thing we can be sure of is that, like us, all container passengers began their journey convinced they would be better off when it was over. Given the chance to compare, any container travellers would surely ask themselves what more I and my family could possibly want.

These are sobering thoughts for passengers on a train that boasts several showers, observation domes, two dining cars and a snack bar. I tried not to feel too bad about losing my view to a container train. And to help remind me of the greatness of my wealth and privilege, as if on cue, the wall began to move. It was the partition between our bedrooms. It slowly folded away, and there, on the other side, was my family and a smiling VIA attendant named Janice.

She locked away the partition. She answered our questions about dinner and bedtime and toilets and blankets and air conditioning and when we would get there, and then she left to meet the people in bedroom B. Janice had plenty of greeting and question-answering yet to do at that point. For the next twenty-two hours she would be solely responsible for two sleeping cars' worth of train passengers, some quiet and agreeable, some not. There were call buttons in every room, in each bathroom and beside each bed, and she was expected to answer them as quickly as she could, at any time of day or night. If a passenger were the kind of person to be upset over, say, a container train blocking the view, Janice's job could be a busy one.

"Working the train is very physical," she told me. "Everything is so long, there's a lot of walking. Every time you want something it's five cars away. There are only five and a half hours of rest at night, and just the physical movement of the train makes you tired. You get train legs after a while, but I still don't have them yet. I have bruises."

Janice had only been with VIA for eight months, after ten years as a flight attendant with Air Atlantic. Air Atlantic ran out of runway in 1998. She'd been out of work for a month when VIA recruited her.

"I was flattered they called," she said. "They didn't mind that I didn't know a lot about trains. There were four weeks of training."

There were a lot of people working on that train who looked as if they'd had a lot more than four weeks' training, and a lot more than eight months on the job. Most of those people were men. I asked Janice about that.

"There are a lot more women that are being hired now, so it's not so much the old boys' club, but you still get that feeling when you're working with people," she said. "It is a real guy's job sometimes, I find. A flight attendant's felt like a woman's job. We wore pantyhose, worried about our makeup and appearances and grooming standards. On the train you don't get a shower, and you're sweaty and you're running around. Nobody cares if I wear makeup or how my hair looks. I like it this way, though. It feels like maybe you get a little more respect."

I've found, over the years, that people will say what's most important to them, one way or another, within a very short time of meeting.

With rail workers, there were two things that came up almost every time. One was what Janice was talking about: respect. I heard that word from almost everyone I spoke to, and especially among the older workers, "respect" was usually followed by a job title that I never saw written down, but it's obviously a big part of working on the train. It doesn't seem to matter if you're a porter or an engineer or a baggage handler—if you know what you're doing, and you work hard and you earn the respect of your peers, eventually you'll be "A Railroader."

Janice didn't think she was one yet.

"It's a little early in my career to think about that."

Then she said the other thing that all Canadian rail workers talk about: the future. "I don't know if I'll have the chance. I don't know that it'll be here in twenty-five years. I'm not sure there's the money to support it. This run is only six days a week now. It has to be more reliable. It'll be here a while, but I don't know about the long run."

We were rolling by the lakes and evergreens of inland Nova Scotia. There were cornfields and cattle as we approached Truro. The gravel on the roadbed was scrolling by, along with the occasional container train. I had nothing to complain about.

Ꭰ𝓣ruro,
ᏉᎥ𝓞va ᏕᏟcotia

⁓

𝓣RURO WAS ONE OF THE FIRST TOWNS in Canada to hear the sound of a distant train whistle. As early as 1839 there was a coal-burning steam locomotive working the mines of neighbouring Pictou county. It was called *Samson,* which is a questionable name for a machine in a mine, but no one seemed worried.

That was only three years after the Champlain and St. Lawrence Railroad company had run Canada's first passenger railroad along the fifteen miles of newly laid track from La Prairie to St. Jean, Quebec. For people living in Truro, the idea of getting dressed up to ride a train for an afternoon excursion, instead of down into the earth to dig for coal, must have seemed the height of fantasy.

By 1849 Canada had established the Railway Guarantee Act, which told investors that they would be sure to make money if they built a railroad. Or, put another way, if anyone lost money on a railroad, it would be the taxpayers. Not surprisingly, in the following ten years, by 1859, Canada went from having fewer than one hundred miles of track to more than two thousand.

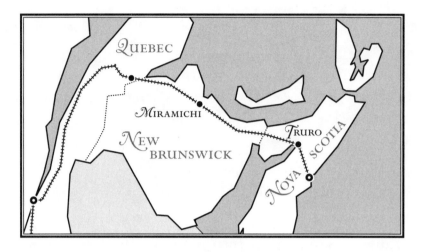

Tracks were laid over much of central Canada, from Montreal to Sarnia, and joining up with the lines criss-crossing the New England states, but none of them came to Truro.

In 1867 the Canadian government, under the British North America Act, did what it almost always did when it came to the railway, for better or for worse—it stepped in.

With the Intercolonial Railway, the government skipped the "we'll give you the money after you lose it" part and built the thing themselves. The Intercolonial put the railroad on Prince Edward Island, and linked Nova Scotia and New Brunswick with Montreal, where it joined the network of lines then owned by the Grand Trunk Railway.

The Intercolonial offered luxury Truro would have only dreamt of a generation before: Pullman Palace sleeping cars, excellent refreshment rooms, express service with no need to change cars and speedy service that could make it from Halifax to Quebec City in a mere twenty-four hours.

The Maritimes' very own railroad was paid for entirely with government money. The government just gave it to them. It would be over a century before they began to take it away.

In the meantime, Truro, because of where it sits at the top of the Bay of Fundy, was a natural focal point for the railroad in the Maritimes. As the junction point for trains heading northeast to Pictou, Prince Edward Island and Cape Breton, southwest to Windsor, south to Halifax and west to everything else, it became known as "The Hub of Nova Scotia."

These days Truro has only one passenger train, but some people still call the town the Hub. Thirteen thousand people live there. It has a small downtown, a fast-food strip, shopping malls, a daily and a weekly newspaper, and an underwear factory.

You can see the Stanfield's plant from the train as it approaches the town from the west. It's a big red-brick box of a building, where some four hundred employees make briefs and long johns, turtlenecks and T-shirts. The company name is painted right across the top of the building in white. "Stanfield's Unshrinkable Underwear," the wall said when the plant opened in 1906. By the seventies, however, the middle word was entirely painted out, leaving only the words "Stanfield's" and "Underwear," with an extra-large gap between the two.

I asked a Stanfield's spokesman about that. He told me that "Unshrinkable" was originally part of the company's brand name. With the post-war years, advertising standards became more stringent, and Stanfield's eventually had to face the fact that it is impossible to make underwear that is truly unshrinkable, so they changed the name. There's nothing new about an advertisement shrinking the truth, but to admit it so publicly and to leave such a visible legacy of honesty, well, I found that mighty refreshing. There aren't many corporate bodies that are so frank about their dirty laundry.

A Stanfield's spokesman told me nobody in Truro even notices the sign any more. I did, when I first went to Truro in July 1976, but I wasn't there for underwear. I was going to the Nova Scotia Summer Music Camp. It was my first trip without my parents. I was fifteen.

You may wonder why a kid from cosmopolitan Montreal, the birthplace of Oscar Peterson and Maynard Ferguson, and the home of the world-famous Orchestre Symphonique de Montréal, would travel to a small city boasting formerly unshrinkable underwear to study music. Many Montrealers wondered exactly that, and the answer sheds light on the differences between small-town and big-city life in Canada.

The band was a big deal where I went to school, Montreal West High. We had the usual amount of talent and a devoted, very hard-working director, Barbara Maxedon. Besides, to our way of thinking, it was natural that we should have an excellent band. Our city was the most sophisticated in the country, we were often told, and we certainly never doubted it. We'd produced Oscar and Maynard. Therefore, although we practised and rehearsed, we also spent a lot of our time hanging out in the park and lying around the pool, being sophisticated.

Not so at the CEC high school (Cobequid Educational Centre) in Truro, Nova Scotia. Our school band went on an exchange trip with theirs when I was in the eighth grade. It's not that they didn't have a park and a pool in Truro. In fact, both were a lot nicer than ours. But when faced with teenage boredom, instead of playing at sophistication, they played at music. The Truro kids played all the time.

The CEC band is one of the best in the country. Since 1970 they have won the Maritime Band Competition almost continually, with several national competitions as well. Some of the program's alumni went on to play all over the country, including—a cruel blow—with Oscar Peterson and Maynard Ferguson. When our big-city high-school band played alongside the band from the town of Truro, Nova Scotia, we were hicks.

The CEC band director was an interesting factor in all of that, too. Ron MacKay was a French horn–player. He was a strong musician and a good conductor. He was a band director and horn soloist with the Stadacona Navy Band in Halifax. He also played so many gigs with the CBC that, in Ron's words, "For a while there I didn't even bother picking up my Navy paycheque."

Above all, Ron was a great teacher. His real gift, I suspect, was that fuzzy kind of awareness that works well with teenagers. He very well might have seen you skulking about the beer store or sneaking behind the wooden backstop with your sweetheart, but he never said anything. He just looked slightly preoccupied when you passed by the next day, as if there were something he had to say to you but he either couldn't quite remember what it was or was waiting for just the right moment. We never knew if we were steps from execution or coasting down easy street.

Ron's summer band camp lasted for two weeks. It had excellent teachers and a dedicated staff. It also had three hundred high-school students living in a college dormitory, many of them away from home for the first time and doing a whole lot of stuff that Ron probably wished he'd never seen, if indeed he did. Three of us from Montreal went to Truro for the summer band camp in 1976—Jane, a trumpet player, Lynne, a trombonist, and I. We took the train.

It left Central Station in Montreal, as it still does, early in the evening, arriving in Truro the next afternoon. We travelled coach. That meant we had two double seats facing each other. The seats were hard and springy, the backs reclined, if a little stiffly, and the armrests and headrests were made of the kind of vinyl that left creases on your face. The entire car was decorated in maroon.

In 1976 we still thought of air travel as a luxury. My friends and I knew all the airplane model numbers and airline logos, even of the small private planes, but flying, except on very rare occasions, was still the stuff of fantasy.

The bus, on the other hand, was all too real. Buses were smoky and smelly and they left from terminals that moved our parents to hold on tightly to our hands as we walked through. One time, on a bus through rural Quebec, I cringed in fear as the driver pulled over, stalked back to the seat across the aisle from mine, grabbed the unfortunate passenger and shook him like a dust mop. It wasn't that the passenger was smoking on the bus, it was that he was smoking the wrong brand. Gitanes. The driver didn't like Gitanes.

The train, even with all of the vinyl, was considerably better. It was slightly more expensive, too, but that had a good side. Theatre managers will tell you that you'll never see a standing ovation for a free concert. Once folks have ponied up the extra dough for the sake of a little happiness, they're prepared to work for it. Such was the case on the eastbound train out of Montreal on that warm July evening in 1976. I was one of the first on the car. I watched the other passengers coming in. They were pumped.

The older men wore suits—hard-working Sunday suits with narrow lapels, creases like iron and shoulders the texture of burlap. They'd polished their shoes and slicked their hair, sometimes to the same shine. Their wives wore dresses as neat as the tidy steps that took them from seat to seat, consulting their tickets until they found their place. The young men had boots, and collars as wide as flatcars. And the women, all the women, young and old, had *hair*.

One woman, and in particular her hair, stay vivid in my memory. She was tall and thin and wore a loose flowered blouse and skinny pants that flared at the bottom like the Eiffel Tower, while her hair was as long and meandering as the Seine itself. It was a fountain of hair—a renewable resource. It had been teased and curled and permed and stretched until it flowed behind her like the plume of steam behind a locomotive on a January night.

My eyes followed her down the aisle, as did every pair of eyes in the car, and when she paused for a drink of water, we watched in silent awe. Getting a drink of water on the train was an event all its own. The release valve was push-button, sprung like a bear trap and loaded with enough water pressure to knock over a cow, while the small, conical paper cups were soft enough that if you squeezed them at all, they would explode all over your chest. There was no point in bringing anything with you when you went for a drink of water. You needed both hands.

The fountain of hair tossed her head and selected a cup. She slugged the button with a mighty thumb, leaving little more than surface tension between herself and aquatic disaster. Her cherry lips met the cup with tenderness, she tipped back her head, her hair cascading down, and she drank.

Several passengers sighed.

Something remarkable happens when a new person comes through a train car. The car that begins its journey as a group of strangers becomes a community with remarkable speed.

That community establishes standards and beliefs and social mores and, shortly after, an identity of sorts, often by the time the train has only just left the station. So when somebody new arrives, or an established member leaves, it is a significant thing. Human lives have become entwined.

And, I can confess, as I watched the community beauty take a drink, the idea of becoming entwined took on a new level of urgency for me. I don't think I need a theory to explain that.

No one spoke as she finished her drink. The still-empty seats among us all but cried out to her. Then, dashing hopes on both sides of the aisle, she crumpled her cup, slammed it into the trash and, her poise intact,[1] sashayed out of our world.

Things were quiet for a while. A lot of people pulled out magazines. But romance and trains have long gone together, like bandanas and boxcars, and like both boxcars and alliteration, once they get going, they're difficult to stop.

The scenery didn't help, either. The train pulled in at Lévis, across the St. Lawrence from Quebec City, just in time for us to see the Plains of Abraham glowing green in the lingering haze of a summer sunset. The Château Frontenac soared above the walls of the old town, with the ferryboats gliding across the St. Lawrence, first orange in the setting sun and then lit like lanterns against the darkening shore.

---

1. Car-to-car poise was no small achievement. In 1976, opening a train car door required a surfing stance pitch-and-haul move that was not unlike pull-starting a lawn mower. A neophyte traveller attempting to get a drink of water and take it back to another car was high entertainment, indeed. Now, on the more modern trains in VIA's fleet, the doors are sliding automatic jobs, and they are great. Each one has a large plastic button where the handle used to be. One press and the door disappears, *Star Trek* fashion, right into the wall, while you, with your flimsy, chest-soaking cone of water, and possibly your hair, can continue almost without breaking stride.

It got worse, too. Further east, the narrow strips of farmland climb away from the river in rows, just as they have for
centuries. Village lights dance against the water and disappear
into the blackening sky above. Under the circumstances, it is
possible for a fifteen-year-old boy to believe that the world is
full of magic and that every one of his life's steps has been leading him to exactly where he is at that moment: on a train, in
the dark, waiting to discover the world.

Then the conductor walked through announcing the last
stop before midnight—"Rivière du Loup." Wolf River. Rrrruff.
I decided to prowl.

Lynne, the quieter of my two fellow travellers, had just
wrapped herself in a sweatshirt and nodded off against the
window. Jane, the other one, looked up.

"Where are you going?" she asked.

I'd known Jane a while. Our families were friends, and we'd
had a moment or two. My mother had once sent me to Jane's
house with a package for her mother. It was mid-afternoon
on a Sunday. Jane answered the door in a loose sweatshirt and,
as I handed her the package, our eyes met. That was all, but
in the way of such things, it felt like there might have been
more. Then, a few months later, in a discussion of hockey
teams, she slugged me. Jane had lived in Toronto and cheered
for the Maple Leafs. That wasn't any easy position to hold in
1970s Montreal. We were walking down the school hallway
when I stated the obvious—that the Leafs sucked—and Jane
ploughed me with a left cross that would have stapled John
Ferguson.

Given that history, there weren't many moments on our
train trip east when I didn't wonder which Jane I was with:
she of the loose sweatshirt or the killer left cross.

I told Jane I was going to explore the other cars. She got up to come with me.

The *Ocean Limited* crew had switched to night-lighting. As we slipped into the next car I saw that a train car isn't just a community, it's a bedroom community. There, amid the maroon vinyl and the hard little complimentary pillows, people were down for the night.

A darkened train car feels very much like the pre-dawn hours in a city, with lingering solitude and the echoes of footsteps from the night before. That's not to say the train is quiet. There is constant clanking of the suspension, the shunting and jerking of switches, and the occasional freight thundering by. One of the mysteries of train travel is that, rather than bringing home reality and foiling romance, all of that clunk and clank just adds to the intrigue. There is the steady rocking that lulls the defences, and the hypnotic yellow of the night-lighting that, if it isn't actually humming to you, looks as if it should be. And there is, most entrancing, the siren song of the rails themselves.

On the straight sections in daylight, when the train is going full out, that song is a gallop: CHUCK-a-chuck-a-CHUCK-a-chuck-a-CHUCK-a-chuck-a, as fast as you can go. But most of the time, especially at night, it's gentler than that. There are pitching frosts and heaving bends, level crossings, tunnels and trestles, but almost all of that gets folded into the roll of the wheels. The hardest terrain brings on the most elegant sound. Most of the way across Canada by train, you hear Ca-chick, Ca-CHICK, (rest), Ca-chick, Ca-CHICK, (rest), Ca-chick, Ca-CHICK, (rest). It's a waltz and like a good waltz it's sweeping and graceful, and in no hurry whatsoever.

Jane and I strolled through the coaches, steadying ourselves as the train pitched and rolled, with more and more
passengers dropping into railroad slumber. Their necks bent
like crumpled tulips, these people weren't just napping. They
had been overwhelmed by sleep. It had pounced on them,
flung their arms across the aisle and strewn their legs in every
possible direction. They'd dropped all pretense of privacy,
and as far as I could tell, restraint was lingering very far away
in sleeping-car class and seriously thinking of getting off the
train altogether.

Now and then, as we walked, one of those waltz steps
gently rolled us to one side, Jane brushed against me from
behind, and my skin would thrill at the touch.

Then we came to a Dayniter car.

VIA no longer offers Dayniter service. It was the step between
coach class and sleeping-car class. The seats were wider than
coach, with more room in front, more space to recline, and a
foot- and legrest that turned the seat into something very close
to a bed. The car's upholstery was bright red, and a haze hung
round the ceiling. We were tiptoeing down the aisle, with the
rhythmic breathing of sleep on either side, when I saw something that stopped me in my tracks: two empty seats.

There aren't many urges that can compete with the kind
I was already feeling, but the yearning for a free upgrade has
been shown to overpower everything from laboratory rats
to broadcast executives. All I had to do was go back and get
the little ticket clipped to the baggage rack above our seats
and stick it into the clip right here. It was perfect.

"Empty seats," I murmured to Jane, my voice as close to a
growl as I could get it. "We could stay here."

Jane stood up straight and looked at me.

"Why would we do that?" she asked in a full voice imbued with the kind of incredulity that says "You're not *really* thinking what I think you're thinking, are you?"

"Umm," I said, hearing my voice shift from that of a wolf to a spaniel pup.

A large businessman in the seat across the aisle stirred.

Jane turned to stalk back. I followed, but we didn't get far. There was a tall man in a VIA outfit blocking the aisle. He had a brass pin on his chest bearing the word "Conductor."

The conversation was short:

"Where are your tickets?"

"At our seats."

"Where are your seats?"

"In our car."

"Where is your car?"

"That way."

"How far that way?"

"Um . . ."

"Better get going."

We did. He followed, too, but only as far as necessary to be sure we'd keep going, a distance he obviously knew very well. Jane and I bumped occasionally on the return, too, but by then my expectations had shifted. Part of me still hoped for an encounter with Jane of the loose sweatshirt, but I soon realized where else I had seen the look she'd just given me. It was the same one that had preceded her fabulous knock-out left cross. After that, whenever we bumped, I ducked.

None of this is to say that my first trip away from home on my own was a complete failure in the romance department. Within a few days at the camp I met a lovely percussionist from Windsor. The camp was held at the Nova Scotia Agricultural

College, which is not in Truro proper but the hamlet of Bible Hill. The name's not as imposing as it might sound. It had its hot spots, too, including a little fast-food joint with the astounding name of "Lick-a-Chick." There was also a beach by the river, grassy hills that misted over each morning and sunrise views I'll never forget.

Now and then we went to Truro, too. It was, as poetry would have it, just across the tracks from Bible Hill. The first stop after the rail underpass was King Lam, the big Chinese restaurant that was owned by the family of one of the band's drummers. Danny and I became friends, and I was lucky enough to stay at his family's place for a few weeks after camp. I was in the peak teenage growing years and ate, as you might expect, like a king. I also travelled in style. All of the men in Danny's family were car mad. Father drove a Lincoln Continental, eldest brother Kenny drove a Porsche, Danny drove a Corvette and another brother, Tony, a Trans Am. To this day, whenever I hear the low rumble of a seventies muscle car, I get hungry.

The other big treat Truro had to offer, and still offers in the summer months, is the Nova Scotia Provincial Exhibition. It was the standard summer fair of livestock, antique cars, heart attack food and nauseating death-trap rides operated by skid-row rejects with bad teeth. Despite that, there was an admission fee for the "Ex," but since the CEC band played there most days, the musicians got in free.

By my third session at the band camp, I'd adopted Truro as my summer home. I would go for the two-week camp and then stay with friends for as long as my welcome would permit, and sometimes, I've gathered since, a little longer. The great thing was that the CEC stage band lost its regular bass

trombonist to holidays for a good part of August each year, at
the time the Ex was on. That meant, if I was in town, I could
sit in.

On the surface, it wasn't much to get excited about. The
hours between shows were endless. The midway lost its shine
within the first day, while the food was so shiny it glared back
at the sun. Now and then a pig made a bolt for it, but aside
from that, the only entertainment was the magic show. There
were four every day.

"Hello, I'm Dickie Dee," the magician began each time, bowing low in his square tuxedo.

"And this . . . ," with a broad sweep to stage left, signalling
the entrance of his wife and assistant.

"Is . . . ," his voice deepening further as she achieved centre
stage.

". . . *Marge.*"

I was thrilled to be there. I ran to the fairgrounds every
single day, my bass trombone case clunking at my knees. I can
remember the route exactly: through the lumberyard, right
at the railroad ties, up the hill, over the tracks, across the road
and through the gate. Each day I ran past the cotton candy
and the games of chance, past dozens of kids my age who
wouldn't have cared if they never heard a trombone in their
lives (most of them probably still haven't) and straight to the
bandstand.

I'm still not sure why it all felt so exciting to me. We didn't
talk much about big bands in my house as I was growing up.
In fact, in those years, *nobody* did. Big band jazz was the musi-
cal embarrassment of the day, clinging to life only on TV talk
shows and Vegas routines. I was a rock 'n' roll kid who spent
hours in the basement with the stereo shaking the floorboards

above. I don't know why, but playing Count Basie tunes on the bass trombone behind a row of saxophones suddenly became the embodiment of true-life adventure. My fantasy was blasting out paint-peeling low notes in a big band with screaming trumpets soaring above, and there, for two weeks in Truro, Nova Scotia, between rows of livestock and four daily appearances of Dickie Dee and . . . *Marge,* I lived it.

On the last weekend of the summer the Nova Scotia Provincial Exhibition played host not only to the fair, but also to the pinnacle of that fantastic adventure: The Miss Nova Scotia Beauty Contest.

We played the women on and off the stage. We played "ta-dah!" chords for the emcee's intros and the requisite dainty bossa nova for the swimsuit competition. Twelve tall and slender women stepped up the stairs to our fizzing beat, their heels keeping time across the stage until they turned at centre stage and the emcee launched their names over the PA ("Miss Bridgewater—Leela!") to warm applause.

For that summer night, Truro was Vegas and I was rolling sevens.

No matter that we were playing on the floor of a horse ring, on an enormous bright-blue plastic sheet that was the only thing between us and what one would normally expect to find in the horse ring. No matter that the crowd, if we can call it that, contained not a single slender beauty in a spaghetti-strap evening gown or tuxedoed high roller, but dozens of pasty gawkers who were there because it was a place to eat funnel cakes and sleep off the excesses of the day.

The contest culminated in an impromptu public-speaking segment, in which each miss was asked to answer a question pulled from a hat. I remember two of the questions. "Name

one person you most admire and why." A tall and elegant
woman drew this. She answered that she most admired
Richard Nixon for what he had gone through in his last years
in office. She was dismissed in less than the time it took to
say "Huh?" The other question went to a dark-haired Celt
with a lovely smile. "If you could have anything in the world,
what would it be?" "Well," she said, her voice as airy as the
highlands themselves, "I guess I'd just ask for peace and love
for all the world."

There were groans from even the most deflated in the crowd.

I was oblivious. I was getting psyched for my next low C,
enthralled in a vision that was as close to a dream come true
as anything I had experienced.

Strangely enough, it was the train that snapped me out of it.

A train passed a level crossing not too far away. It was a summer freight, barrelling west with a full load of dreams and
romance and, I suppose, delusion. That lonesome whistle rang
out round the horse ring, filled the silence and disappeared.
The judges named a winner; there were screams, cheers,
flowers; we played a closer. The hands rolled up the blue plastic and we all went home, our shoes still mostly clean.

The sound of a train whistle is never far in Truro. We heard
it all night from the music camp dormitories. We heard it in
the afternoons on the lawns. We heard it the last morning of
camp as we watched the sunrise after a ripping all-night party
full of dreams and delusions all its own. I even remember hearing it as our train pulled out of town the next afternoon and
we headed back home to real life.

I should tell you that way back at the beginning of that first
trip on the way to Truro, after being turfed, if not decked, by
Jane and the conductor, I did eventually get to sleep on our

face-creasing vinyl seats for a few hours. I woke in the pre-dawn as we snaked through New Brunswick. I went for another walk.

As complete as train sleep is on the inside, it isn't kind to its subjects on the outside. It didn't take long for the toll of those few hours to register. The iron burlap suits were crinkled like paper, their spousal dresses like plastic bags. The manly young collars were folded, the boots abandoned in the aisles, and everywhere, the hair was a disaster. The collective hours of curling and perming hadn't lasted half the night—all that was left was shredded wheat.

I walked forever, surveying the effortless destruction of all that primping. Then, through one last cabin door, I found I was back in the hazy, early-morning rouge of the Dayniter. The conductor was nowhere to be seen. The seats were still empty.

I slipped into the window seat, pulled out the footrest and reclined as far as I could. It was heavenly—a firm, soft mattress of a non-vinyl fabric, with a pillow and blanket close by. I was asleep again in seconds.

I don't know how long I slept. We were still in New Brunswick when I woke again, but there's a lot of New Brunswick. It was barely light, and I sensed we were reaching the Atlantic. But it wasn't the Atlantic that woke me, it was a deep, rumbling, mammalian snoring a few seats behind. I didn't mind getting up. I was thrilled to have stolen as much real sleep as I had, and I wasn't keen on the conductor finding me there a second time. My gut told me to get out fast, while I could, but I couldn't hold down my curiosity. I needed to see what could produce such a sound.

I ventured deeper into the car, closer to the back, to the bathrooms and the drinking tap, and there she was. It was the floral-clad beauty of the day before—the fountain of hair. She was flat on her back, her tresses clumped about like trampled hay. Her forehead was lined. Her jaw was slack, and in her open mouth—I'm sorry to tell you this but I'll never forget it—in her mouth was a wad of pink chewing gum, rising and falling contentedly on the middle of her tongue.

I stayed in my seat the rest of the trip.

It was just after lunch twenty-three years later when I looked out of the window in bedroom C on the *Ocean Limited,* headed west this time, and saw Truro's sights once more. I saw the King Lam restaurant, and what used to be the Lick-a-Chick. I caught a brief glimpse of the dorms at the Agricultural College in Bible Hill, the lumberyard and even the fairground site before we pulled away. I can't say how many other passengers would have been flooded with memories of sex, romance, food, fast cars, great music and fantasy come to life by passing through what looked to be just another eastern Canadian town. Memory and fantasy being as ephemeral as they are, conjured up and dispersed by nothing more than the whistle of a passing train, I had to wonder how much I could trust those fantastic memories after all.

The underwear factory was still there, though. No question about that. There it stood as we rolled west out of town, tall and square, all the way up to the words that boomed out their message in black and white: "Stanfield's" and "Underwear," with the enormous gap between, proud and uncompromising, a solid reminder, unshrinking in the midday sun.

Miramichi, New Brunswick

~

*Y*OU CAN UNDERSTAND, when you're on a cross-Canada train trip, how the sound bite rose to prominence. Through the sound bite, the improvement, streamlining and maintenance of health care, schools, policing, welfare, new employment initiatives and virtually every other modern social concern are all reduced to "No New Taxes." The sound bite makes the enormous tiny.

On a cross-Canada train trip the enormous is never tiny. Most of the time, it is even more enormous than it was before. Heading west through southern New Brunswick, for example, you may look out of your window and see a placid ochre river meandering between banks of clay, bordered with waving fields of grass. As lovely as it is, there's no need to take a picture. There is almost no need to look. That river will be placidly meandering beside your window until you have meandered into complete placidity yourself. That river is not going away. You would have to say "No New Taxes" eighteen thousand times before it did. Given that, you'd think that most passengers wouldn't want to see any more of it. They do. The most popular spot on the train, and the big selling feature for any Canadian train trip, is the Dome.

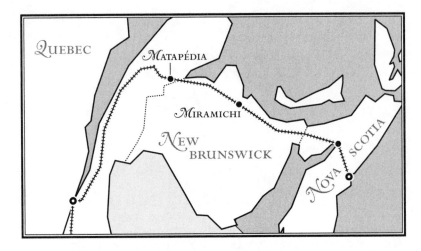

"The Dome" is the general name for the observation car. There were three observation cars on that day's edition of the *Ocean Limited*. The furthest forward was a combination lounge/snack bar/smoking room that served the coaches. Further back, for the sleeping-car passengers, there was a Skyline car with a small dining area and a lounge. The third observation car was the last one on the train: the "Park" car, each one in the VIA fleet named for a Canadian national park.

The Park car is a lovely thing. It is bright and airy with high windows and plenty of space. It is also home to the Drawing Room, the most exclusive bedroom on the train.

Passengers on board Canadian trains live in a class society. Other people in Canada do, too, to be sure, but the lines are not always so clearly drawn. On the *Ocean Limited,* exclusivity goes up with the distance from the engine—the coaches are first, followed by the sleeping cars. Accordingly, the bedroom in the Park car, the last one on the train, is considered the best of the lot.

In truth, it's no bigger than the other triple bedrooms but, as with any real estate, the real value is in its location. The

lucky passengers in the Drawing Room, if they desire a change
of scenery, do not have to go far. They are already in the most
beautiful car on the whole train. All they have to do is open
their door.

Even the Park car, however, has its dark side, and the poten-
tates living in the Drawing Room cannot escape it. Before
they can make it from their door to the Dome, they must pass
a frosted glass partition that opens onto a dark box of a room
with little light and a low ceiling. This is the smoking lounge—
the bar, the grotto. In truth, it is the Anti-Dome.

That does not mean the lounge is not a popular spot. On
our trip, there happened to be a group of grade-eight girls
from Ottawa on their way home after a week in the Maritimes.
They had no interest in the lounge, but their teachers loved
it. With its low ceiling and high windows, butts in the ashtrays
and empty Styrofoam coffee cups, the smoking lounge was a
staff room just waiting to happen. Add to that the presence of
a bar and, at least some of the time, a steward who'll pour a
Bloody Mary with no questions asked, and you've got some
people's definition of paradise.

On my first visit to the smoking lounge I noticed that everyone else in the room was silent. It was the kind of silence that
grows between people who have complained about the same
things for so long that nobody has to say anything any more.
An exhalation was a statement, and the answering drag from
across the room, a weary nod of agreement. Being a pilgrim
on his way to the Dome, I felt ill at ease. I had come for light,
for clarity, for openness of thought—and for a glass of orange
juice for my daughter.

The steward served it up, on ice, and banged the empty can
into the trash. I half expected him to slide the glass along the

bar, but he didn't. I reached for it and turned out of the lounge toward the back of the car. I felt a breeze of wry, knowing smoke rings drift out behind me.

From the smoking lounge, the next stop on a tour of the Park car is the Bullet Lounge. It is tapered toward the back, and being silver and a product of the same era as the original TV version of *The Lone Ranger,* it is said to resemble a silver bullet. It does, sort of. In other ways, though, it is the opposite. By nature, the Bullet Lounge is slow. People recline in the Bullet Lounge, and read or chat—hardly bullet-like pursuits.

It is a short climb from the Bullet Lounge to the Dome—a small staircase up. The Dome is directly above the smoking lounge, both in latitude and attitude. It is as bright as the day will allow, and is built entirely of glass, except for a strip of art deco lighting down the middle. It's shaped like an egg carton and protrudes above the rest of the train by about one metre.

The climb takes seven steps—the same number that, according to some, it is supposed to take to get to heaven. But unlike heaven, on that day anyway, the Dome was full, which made it a strange sight.

The Dome is like a small theatre. There are twenty-four seats: six rows of four, two on each side of a centre aisle. The entrance is at the back, so that when you step in, as in a theatre, you are looking at the backs of heads. Also, people in the Dome tend to whisper. This is particularly odd, because the train is very noisy. The wheels and gear below (to say nothing of the deafening irony from the lounge) create a constant and significant rumble. At times it is close to the sound of an airplane engine. Still, in the Dome, when passengers want to speak with their neighbours, they lean conspiratorially towards them and whisper. It is the unwhispered law. Although train folks are generally sociable, there is something greater in the Dome than mere fraternity at play. The people there have a unified purpose—they are watching a show.

This is where the sound bites come in. There aren't any. The show in the Dome is a continuous, sprawling epic quite unlike any other. There is no good time to get up and buy popcorn. In fact, there is no bad time either. The Dome show goes on regardless. There is a soundtrack, the ubiquitous rumble with punctuations of ca-Chuck, ca-Chuck, ca-Chuck. There are characters. Some are skilfully introduced (the Atlantic Ocean) and developed (a few bit parts near Bouctouche and Miramichi), and then flower into full, romantic leads (Baie des Chaleurs) before exiting with gentle grace (into the Matapédia River). Others appear in the opening frames, say nothing and never leave (the boreal forest). There are cameos ("Look! A moose!") and gags ("Oh. It's a cow."), action scenes (lightning at dusk), love scenes (sunset over the Gaspé) and hours and hours when it seems that something will happen, but nothing does (parts of northern New Brunswick).

It was hard at first to believe that the people in the Dome could have been the same general consumers who'd elevated the sound bite. They sat attentively as the unedited, raw truth of Canada, the director's cut, scrolled by. They sat for far longer, I'm sure, than any of them ever would watching the slickest sitcom. Comparing them to theatre-goers actually shortchanges their attention span. They were more like plants in a greenhouse, soaking in sunlight with no plan of turning away, ever. They were, in a word, content.

I brought my daughter her orange juice. She drank it and smiled, and I felt, for a moment, like I was precisely who and where I was supposed to be. But I didn't have a seat. My daughter was in the second row, with the seat beside her taken, but the one in front of her was not. At least, it appeared to be empty. When I went to sit down in it I found a book lying there. Someone was holding the seat.

It was a good seat. The front row offers great views. On curves you can see the whole train snaking out before you. It is possible to imagine, in the front row of the Dome, that you are not sitting in a glass egg carton, but out in the open air, facing the wind and—who knows—running along the tops of the cars like Indiana Jones. Indiana Jones, I told myself, wouldn't let some schmuck with a Harlequin Romance[1] claim the best seat in the house. Indiana would move the schmuck's book and sit there himself. So I did.

Before I could even begin to put the book down on a nearby ledge there was a flurry behind me. It was a tall fellow with a beard sitting three rows back. Reaching for his book, he muttered something like "Oh! Sorry . . . that's mine . . . I didn't think . . ." The universal terminology for "I was hogging the best seat and now I've been caught." He had entered the shrine of contentment, claimed the best seat and decided that he was, in fact, still not fully content unless he got one thing more—a second seat, just in case.

He wasn't the only one, either. There was a guy in the back row who had opened up a newspaper and buried himself behind it, wall-fashion, with open arms, so as to make the seat next to him not anywhere anyone would like to sit. He wasn't even looking out the window. Later in the trip I saw a woman bolt to the Dome first thing in the morning and run right to the front. She had knitting needles with her, yarn and snacks. It

---

1. It was Proust, actually, but that just made it worse.

was a beautiful day, we were entering spectacular territory, and clearly she planned on bathing herself in the beauty of her handiwork and the splendour of the wilderness all day long. When I came back to the Dome hours later, she was asleep, and by the look of it, had been for some time. Her chin was anchored to her sternum. Yarn spilled over her lap to her feet, while the glory of Canada rolled by unseen.

A piggy person can do well in Canada. We've set the place up, more or less, on the assumption that people won't act that way. The truly unscrupulous, if they're smart, too, can do pretty well for themselves.

But on the train, it really doesn't work that way. The train is too slow and Canada is too huge. There's just too much to hog.

It was time for dinner. We trooped back down the seven steps and turned the corner to head back to the front of the train, toward the dining car. After perceiving True Contentment, so closely followed by Piggery, I wasn't keen on passing by the callous sophisticates in the smoking lounge. A disciple who has seen swine in the shrine would likely be high entertainment to them—worthy of several litres of smoky smugness. But as I passed, I have to confess, their silence seemed different this time. In fact, it was exactly the same as in the Dome. Just before we stepped by, I saw one fellow blow a long, relaxed column of smoke up to the ceiling. His eyes were closed, and he wore a little smile. Clearly, he was judging no one.

We were already eating our soup when Duncan and Myra sat at the table across from ours. They were in bedroom B, the one beside us. The first thing Duncan had told me when we'd met that afternoon was that he retired in 1990 after forty-five years with Canadian National. He was on the train for the first nineteen of those years, and spent the rest at cn's Nova Scotian Hotel in Halifax, but he was a Railroader just the same.

The service manager asked if he'd like to wash his own dishes. Duncan laughed. It was an inside joke.

"That was my first job on the railroad. I started as a pantry-man. That really meant washing dishes. There wasn't time for much else. I was on the Halifax-to-Montreal run. We fed three hundred people every meal and I spent all day in the sink, from six in the morning till eleven at night, three days on, two days off. I washed the glasses, the silverware, the plates, the cups, the saucers . . ."

I was aware of dirty dishes. Our table seemed to be gener-ating a fair number on its own. That trip on the *Ocean Limited* was one of the first with buffet service in the dining cars, instead of waiters who served the dinners to each table. It was a cost-saving measure that cut down the size of the kitchen crew.

To be honest, for a young family, the buffet worked fine. It gave our kids something to do. Eating became a fun little exercise in self-directed nutrition (walk up to the buffet, stand in line, come back with two carrots, a bun, a pile of butter the size of a lemon and, five minutes later, go back for more, all on a new plate). But the Railroaders among us, both active and retired, were much less keen. It wasn't just the jobs, as it turned out, it was a matter of pride.

I was on my second serving of chowder, using a second bowl, when I asked Duncan when trains got automatic dishwashers.

"They didn't," he said. "They still don't have dishwashers. Dishwashers use too much water." Just then a crew member went by with a plastic tub full of dirty dishes. I made a note to visit the kitchen after dinner and tell them how much we enjoyed it.

Duncan was the lone dishwasher for a few months in 1945. In those days a dining car had a crew of twelve. The steward was the boss. There were five waiters, four cooks, a chef and a pantryman. Duncan had nowhere to go but up, and he did. He worked each of those jobs over a total of nineteen years, ending up as steward.

"My toughest job was third cook. I'd get up at five in the morning. I was first in the kitchen every day till the chef took over at six. I had to light the charcoal. That's all we used in the broiler, the oven and the stove. They were always hot, too: four hundred to four hundred twenty-five degrees. We cooked everything from scratch: roast beef, chickens . . . pastry, too. I made muffins, buns and pies every day."

I asked if he'd cooked at home at all before he started the job.

"Nope," he said.

Myra laughed. "He still doesn't."

We had turned north just before dinner, and saw glimpses of the Atlantic between the forest, the appetizers, the estuaries and the main course. Meals are a highly social time for passengers in the sleeping cars. For one thing, instead of being off in our own compartments, we were grouped in one room. And instead of having one window view, bracketed by the walls of our rooms, we could watch the scene go from window to window to window, all along the car. People would point things out to other tables. Socializing was easy.

"I served the Queen twice," Duncan said. "I was on two of her special trains. Once in 1947 and another after that." A few people turned around. "I also worked on Princess Margaret's train for a month, and I served Lady Diana at the Nova Scotian

Hotel. I brought her from the door to the head table. But the one I remember most was the Queen. That was the first time I met royalty. I was her waiter."

Everyone was listening.

"What did she order?" someone asked.

Duncan didn't miss a beat. "Lamb chops and small boiled potatoes."

His timing was good, too. Our own royalty, our five-year-old daughter, arrived at that very moment with yet another plate of, not lamb chops and boiled potatoes, but bread and butter. Duncan showed his training by smiling, but not saying anything.

"The dining cars were busy all summer," he went on. "But not in the winter. They put me to work as a brakeman."

A brakeman, I found out, worked on boxcars, applying the brakes. You may wonder, as I did, how it was that a boxcar would need brakes when it didn't have an engine. A boxcar didn't need an engine, Duncan explained, if it was leaving a hump yard.

It took a few minutes, to be quite honest, before the light went on for me. Railroaders, I've found, have a patois all their own when they are speaking in technical terms, and their speech tends to speed up in proportion to their terminology's distance from the rest of the world's daily language. "Well, time to head down to the hump yard," for example, wasn't a sentence I'd heard before.

I had, however, seen the occasional freight car adorned in bright blue lettering, with the words "Do Not Hump."

I'd always wondered.

A hump yard, Duncan explained, is a rail yard with a big hump that provides a gravitational push-off that allows the yardman to move cars without having to engage a locomotive. The cars are simply released off the hump and allowed to roll (or, I suppose, to hump) to their new location. Exactly *why* some cars should be humped, while others should not, I cannot say. Nor can I say why another phrase, say, "No Humping," or even "Hump at Your Own Risk," was not used instead.

Railroaders, obviously, although concerned with safety, still have a sense of humour.

Duncan did his share of humping in his time, but it didn't sound like it was particularly fun. He spent four winters in an Alberta hump yard, which must have had one heck of a hump. It was seven kilometres away from the main yard, where the boxcars were headed. If a boxcar was needed in the yard, they'd let it go off the hump and it would roll the whole way, with only Duncan to make sure it didn't get going too fast and, ultimately, that it stopped where it was supposed to.

The brake system was a wheel and chain. With it, the operator turned the wheel and that tightened a chain and engaged the brake. Some older boxcars still have this system. The wheel looks like a steering wheel that sticks right out of the top of the car at one end. That would put Duncan, or his contemporaries, about three and a half metres off the ground—not so bad if the braking system always worked, but it didn't.

"If the boxcar was full, it got going pretty quickly," Duncan said. "Sometimes fifty miles an hour. But the chain wouldn't always catch the first time. If that happened, I had to release it and try again. Sometimes it took four or five times. The car was going pretty fast by then."

After a few of those, Duncan learned that there was a point when he would have to come to the unpleasant conclusion that the brake wasn't going to work at all.

"That's when I'd use the trick the old guys taught me," he said. "I'd get down the ladder near the front of the car and kick snow in front of the wheels so the snow would slow it down." I have to admit, the idea of a boot's worth of snow slowing a runaway boxcar seemed incongruous to me. Duncan said it worked, though, and I don't suppose he would have been in any shape to tell the story if it hadn't. I never saw him without his shoes on, but he certainly walked as if both his feet were his own.

He did have one story of a mishap.

"In Halifax they used the same system. It was only about five hundred yards from hump to pier, so the distance wasn't as far, but the end was a lot less forgiving. The only thing at the end of the line was Halifax Harbour."

Duncan saw one car go over in 1951. The brakeman jumped to safety.

~

There was plenty of splashing going on in the kitchen when we dropped in after dinner. Duncan would have liked the scene. It was time to do the dishes, but it wasn't left to one person. The entire crew were involved: waiters, the chef, the service manager, all in what, in restaurant terms, would have to be called a small kitchen. I thought about Duncan again. The kitchen would have felt even smaller if there had been a two-hundred-degree-Celsius charcoal oven there, too.

"Here's where we do it all," the steward announced.

"Yup," the cook said, embarrassed. "Here's where we heat everything up."

"They don't consider this cooking," Duncan told me later on. "They're not making it all from scratch any more, even though they could. It's not the same as it was."

He told me a story that I've since heard from many old Railroaders.

The story always starts where the train runs alongside a river, but that could legitimately be almost anywhere in Canada. The train stops at a fishing camp, and a ragged-looking wild-man gets on. He's dirty and unshaven. He's been out in the woods for weeks, maybe months, prospecting and fishing and living off the land. All he's got with him is a pack of clothes and a crate of salmon on ice. He sends the fish to the baggage car, but before the porters take it away, he takes one out—a real beauty—and sends it to the chef. Then he finds his room, cleans up and gives his bush clothes to the porter to throw in the garbage. He has his shoes shined. He shaves. Half an hour later, he arrives at the dining car a new man, and eats a meal that includes salmon, cooked to perfection. It is the fish he caught himself, an hour earlier.

The look of satisfaction on the man's face is like no other.

"That's what being a Railroader is about," Duncan said.

I glanced back at the dining room as we were beginning to say good night. The crew was hustling to set up for the next sitting. They were settling bills and sweeping the carpet, and at the buffet, there was work to do. The grade-eight girls had been through the desserts. The serving tweezers were smashed into the eclairs, there were fingerprints on the brownies and all the Nanaimo bars were gone.

As it happened, a few months after our trip an eastbound *Ocean Limited* was in a serious accident about where we were, near Miramichi. A manual switch was left open and the train slammed into a pair of boxcars on a siding. Forty-one people were injured, but only one was seriously hurt—the cook. He was very badly burned.

When I first heard of that accident, I assumed the cook had been in the kitchen with several hot soups and sauces on the go. It wasn't a nice thought. The pots are big and the room is small. But the injured cook wasn't in the kitchen. He was by the buffet, which kept the food warm by steam. It was full of very hot water.

The cook's union complained that the buffet was a safety hazard. Eight months later, in March 2000, VIA announced it would be going back to waiters in the dining car on the *Ocean Limited.*

Wherever he was when he heard that, I'm sure Duncan nodded his approval.

Back in our bedroom, the bunks were down and made (Janice, our service attendant, had been working while we were at dinner) and our journey suddenly felt like bedtime on a family camping trip. Each step was a small adventure: changing, brushing teeth, climbing the ladder to the upper bunks, getting tucked in and reading stories. Then, the most drawn-out adventure of all: falling asleep.

Through it all we rolled along, through the forests of New Brunswick, with the setting sun reflecting first on the trees and then, as we edged our way along the south shore of Baie des Chaleurs,[2] on the far shore and the mountains of the Gaspé Peninsula across the bay. As the day's light faded, so did the

2. It translates to "Bay of Warmth," except that in French the word for warmth can be plural, hinting that, in French, there is more than one kind. In English there's only one—something that's not hot enough to be hot.

kids, until it was quiet, except for the blended rhythms of rolling wheels and gentle, steady breathing.

It was about that time that I noticed the day's tension had fallen away, too. My wife and I glanced at each other in what might have been a look of relief, congratulation, resignation or, most likely, all three. We hadn't missed our train. Our son had not vanished from the bathroom in the Halifax train station. He and his sister were safe in the bunks above our heads as we glided through a wooded New Brunswick corridor in a cozy cabin on wheels. It was a summer night. We were on the train. Canada was big and life was bigger, and there was no point in taking them both on at once.

Matapédia,
Quebec

~

I WAS BEGINNING TO NOD OFF when, from our bedroom window, I saw a string of lights in the distance. It was the bridge in Campbellton, New Brunswick.

Campbellton is tucked into the western corner of Baie des Chaleurs, the bay that opens onto the Atlantic between the Gaspé Peninsula and the Miramichi. It's also where the loveliest of rivers finally strolls into the sea after leaping and drifting through the northern reaches of Appalachia. The Matapédia River Valley is one of the most stunning sections of rail in the country. I first saw it on those high-school trips to Truro, slipping in and out of sleep in the pre-dawn. Seeing it while only semi-conscious gives it a special dreaminess, too—a series of slow-motion scenes nestled in the mists of sleep.

As far as I know, the only way to have that experience is to take the train either from Montreal to Halifax or Halifax to Montreal. It takes a long time, and from either direction you get there in the middle of the night. That way, you are so relaxed that your body cries for sleep while your mind struggles to stay awake and take it all in. It's a very specific pleasure.

There isn't much like that these days—non-portable pleasure. On a purely analytical level, you'd think that some

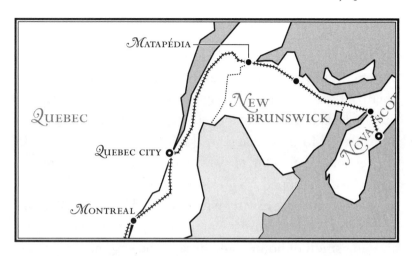

combination of high-end technology and muscle relaxants should be able bring something close to the experience of riding a train through the Matapédia River Valley in the middle of the night, even if you are, in fact, in the family room of a split-level in Don Mills at three-thirty in the afternoon. But it doesn't work that way. Riding a train through the Matapédia at night is one of the rare pleasures of life, and the only way you can get it is to get on board, drink lots of coffee and wait.

I'm not sure if it's because of all that effort, but I realized fairly early on in my acquaintance with the Matapédia that I had a sense of ownership about my experiences there. The land along the railroad might have been bought and sold, occupied and contested a thousand times in its history, but that sleepy rolling feeling, and the moonlight glistening on the rippling river, and the swoop of the train rounding the corners on the hillsides were *mine*.

For a traveller, there's an irony surrounding that ownership. I've found that the intensity of the feeling is directly related to how much the place in question is willing to ignore you.

It's like the breakfast you get on the all-night bus trip from Sault Ste. Marie to Toronto. At least, it's like the breakfast you might get. Most of the restaurants along that strip of towns north of Lake Superior have eggs like rubber, toast like smoke and smoke like grease. But there is one place, *somewhere* between the Sault and Toronto, that is breakfast heaven. My friend David Wadley told me about it. He was on that bus. In the early morning the driver stopped at a greasy spoon so everyone could eat. Dave is still not sure exactly where it was. He stumbled in and took a seat by the counter when his nose caught hold of the dizzying smell of homemade bread. The eggs had been collected that morning from a henhouse out back. They were cooked in sweet butter and served with farmer's sausage that was tasty and fresh. The bread was as perfect as his nose had imagined it, and the coffee rich and dark. Dave floated back onto the bus, wondering if he'd been dreaming.

Dave told me about that breakfast eighteen years ago. It had happened five years before that. He still remembers it. The real beauty of the place wasn't just the food, or even Dave's delight at finding it there; it was that the restaurant had its own reasons for being. It wasn't designed for Dave because of his age, education and income bracket.[1] That restaurant simply served breakfast the way the people there liked it, and Dave was lucky enough to happen along when it was ready.

The train doesn't stop anywhere for breakfast. It doesn't have to—the dining car is lovely. But the train does offer attractions that wouldn't mean anything to anyone but you, and some of the best ones involve the people who live beside the railroad track.

---

1. Sorry, Wads.

In Campbellton, the track went behind a small apartment building. There, by his open window, was a man apparently at the end of his working day. His apartment was small, just a kitchen with a table for eating, and a main room, with a bed, TV and chair. There was a rowing machine on the floor, and it looked as if he had just been working out. He was in a muscle shirt and dark pants, sitting on the edge of the bed. The TV was on in front of the rowing machine, but he wasn't watching it. He was watching us.

At least, he might have been. He was staring out the window with the kind of faraway look of a person who either has a lot on his mind or nothing at all. It was a vulnerable moment for someone in plain view of a nineteen-car passenger train. He was hiding nothing, and for my part I felt as if we weren't there at all.

That's how it is when the train goes through a small town. The train is trusted, and astoundingly, if you're on it, so are you. You're so trusted you can waltz right by inside nine hundred tonnes of steel and a guy in a muscle shirt, thinking about his love, or his pain, or his health, or his family—or maybe, who knows, just thinking about nothing at all—won't even close his curtains. Sure he's showing his secrets to anyone on the train who'd care to look. That's OK. He knows you'll be good for it.

~

We stayed a while in Campbellton. Whether we were waiting for a freight to pass or waiting so we could watch the lightning over the Gaspé mountains across the bay, I'm not sure. Either way, we were still an hour from the town of Matapédia, at the southern end of the river's most beautiful stretch, and I knew we'd likely have to wait a while there, too. Matapédia is where the *Ocean Limited* hooks up with, and usually has to wait for, the train VIA calls the *Chaleur,* on its way back to Montreal.

The *Chaleur* follows the south coast of the Gaspé Peninsula to the town of Gaspé before it turns around and comes back. I have never done the trip, but I've been on the *Ocean Limited* enough to know that there's always a wait in Matapédia. I'm not saying the *Chaleur* is unreliable exactly, but it does wind through breathtaking scenery that is teeming with the history of this country. If I ever do get to go, I don't think I'll be in much of a hurry to come back either.

Still, it was nearing midnight and the whole car was so quiet I could almost hear it breathing. For someone who was absolutely determined to stay awake, sleep was sounding better all the time. I took a walk.

The Bullet Lounge was empty, except for little piles of yesterday's newspapers and last week's magazines. If you include travel time to and from the airport in Halifax and Montreal, and the time spent sleeping in a hotel once you get there, it doesn't take much longer to take the train between the two cities than it does to fly. The difference is, once you get on the train, you may as well be going by way of Pluto. Strangely, even though airline customers actually do leave the planet's surface when they travel, as passengers they never lose touch with earthly life. They phone the office, check e-mails, are offered the latest editions of the day's papers . . . Often they are told the temperature where they're going before they even leave where they are. Rail passengers, on the other hand, although anchored to the planet by gravity and steel, lose contact with earth altogether. The papers in the Bullet Lounge might just as well be a century old as a day. Once train passengers step on board, they float off into a world that is completely their own.

The Dome at night is particularly otherworldly. It has the feeling of an intergalactic drive-in. Even so, the feature presentation hadn't begun yet, and I wasn't sure I'd make it through the trailer. Instead, I opted for bracing irony and went to the smoking lounge.

As it turned out, there wasn't a shred of irony to be found, but there was George.

George has been working the Montreal-Halifax route since 1962. If you ask him, he'll tell you about all the celebrities he's shown through the area. In the first sentence he told me about Lester B. Pearson, John Diefenbaker, Pierre Trudeau, Bing Crosby and Alfred Hitchcock.

"I started as a porter and eventually worked my way up to sleeping-car conductor. As porters, we did everything. I made my customers' beds, shined their shoes and swept them off as they got off the train. I carried a whisk with me just for that. I pressed their clothes. All our sleeping cars had a little room at the end where they kept an ironing board and an iron. We had hat bags, too. No one ever complained about my ironing or my service, even when I lost their hat! That happened now and then. Shoes, too. They'd leave them outside the door for polishing overnight. Sometimes I'd mix them up. We'd have to dream up elaborate schemes to figure out whose shoes were whose. Most of the time we got away with it. Unless someone went to sleep with dirty shoes and woke up with a new hat."

George had always worked exactly where he was when I spoke to him—in the sleeping cars, somewhere on the Canadian National line between Halifax and Montreal, for thirty-seven years and counting.

He had his own version of the fisherman-who-flags-the-train-at-the-riverside story. The Matapédia is famous for its salmon, but it wasn't the fishermen that George remembered most, it was the prospectors.

"I saw them go up and mine the Matapédia all winter long. When they got on board they'd look like something from the Wild West: all stubbled and dirty, wearing the same clothes they'd had on for months. Then, on the train, they'd transform. I'd see them go in the washroom and ring for soap or extra washcloths. They were loaded with money from cashing in their poke. They'd shave, wash, put on clean clothes, throw the old ones off onto the side of the tracks and turn up at dinner like something from a movie. Sometimes I didn't recognize them at all.

"People were used to that sort of thing then. It was a different type of service. They knew they could count on us to show up with what they needed, even if it meant handing them the tenth washcloth. They knew we were there just for them."

To be honest, at that point I wasn't sure why George felt any more "there" for his customers back in those days than he was for me that night. I certainly didn't feel put out.

I'm guessing it came down to what he believed his job to be. He wasn't just changing his passengers' sheets or pressing their wrinkled clothes. For that brief trip to Pluto and back, George made it his job to bring all his customers as close to being Trudeau, Hitchcock and Bing as he could, even if they started out looking like wild animals.

There was enough of that mission left in George that he never would have complained to a customer about his job, especially one holding a tape recorder. But he had to be honest, too.

"It was far better then. When CN trained you, you started as a porter and you stayed there for a year. You were paid as an apprentice for six months, and then your raises came up quickly. You couldn't become a conductor until you'd done all the jobs below that position for a year each. It took fifteen years. Now it takes ten days."

Gordie joined us. He'd done his fifteen years and was a conductor for eight more years after that before everything changed.

"There is no conductor any more. Supervision on the train is now done by someone like myself, a service manager. Whereas the actual stopping and starting of the train is done by one of the engineers in the cab. Before that, the engineers received orders from the conductor as to when to start and stop. The conductor ran everything."

I suppose summoning the ghosts of former prime ministers, if not film directors, puts things in perspective, but I still felt a sense of awe at one person being in charge of every aspect of the entire train. The locomotives alone are dizzyingly complicated. The conductor also had to deal with the enormous social complexities of what amounted to an entire town full of citizens and civic workers, along with three restaurants and a bar. It's incredible the position of "conductor" ever existed at all, but it did. That conductor acted as if he owned the entire train—whether that meant welcoming Mr. Trudeau aboard or pitching in to finish the dishes.

It also meant knowing, essentially, who each of his passengers was.

"The backbone of train travel is still here," Gordie told me. "Most of the dedicated passengers are along the north shore of New Brunswick—Moncton north through Miramichi,

Bathurst and Campbellton, as well as all the smaller communities in eastern Quebec. Those communities are fairly large, but they aren't serviced by airports. They rely on us.

"When we first started working for the railroad, the idea was that the only thing was being consistent. Things had to be the same trip after trip after trip. And now, of course, sometimes the customer service gets eroded. They can say that you're resistant to change but actually you just really want to be a Railroader. So we try at least to stay within the confines of being traditional about railroading but still opening our eyes to the realities of . . .," Gordie paused before finishing, his last few words just slightly tinged, "high finance."

Gordie was like George in that he'd never actually complain to a customer, but it wasn't hard to see that he was coming close.

"We've changed the services so many, many times that it's hard for the passenger, especially the ones that aren't simply tourists, who rely on us. They have trouble just keeping up with those changes."

I gathered Gordie could have done without some of those changes as well, but he surprised me.

"A Railroader is something that evolves within yourself. It's a formulation of a lot of things. It's instincts and feelings about people, general knowledge about the geography you run over, about the equipment you have. It's a sense that the buck stops with you no matter how far down the pole you are. It's acting like you own the place no matter who you are and whose decisions it is you're acting on. Sometimes it means you have to act like you're open to new things and new ideas when actually you aren't at all. That's being a Railroader."

It was an inspiring bit of professional loyalty to hear Gordie using his own code of honour against himself. I turned from the bar to see if anyone else had heard it, but there was no one there. Even George was gone. He'd stepped up into the Bullet Lounge to straighten the magazines—oldest on top. We were at the bar in the smoking lounge on a train through New Brunswick on a summer night. I'd heard jokes about bar cars since I was a kid, and most of those were about the five-hour trip to Toronto.[2] It struck me as significant that it was midnight, half a day since we'd left Halifax, and the place was empty, except for Gordie and me and a few lofty ideas.

VIA got rid of the bar cars in 1990, along with a whole bunch of regional rail lines and lots of jobs. That's also when they got rid of the conductors. It seemed more than a coincidence. If there's one person who is in charge of making sure all the engines work and the stops get made, and that same person is busy breaking up a brawl or a food fight, or even a singalong, there's going to be a problem.

Gordie remembered the bar car as "a pretty noisy and rowdy place—which had its good points and bad points. It's a bit saner now, although it's not as much fun. Not as much social interaction. Then again, I think there's been a mellowing of the public at large. So really, it works out fine. Usually people are saying that things are always getting worse, but I think as far as general rowdiness, we saw most of it in the sixties and seventies."

He paused before cracking a smile. "Mind you, that could be because I was a participant in a lot of it.

---

2. First Montrealer: What's the best bar in Toronto?
Second Montrealer: The one on the train.
First Montrealer: Where's the best place to eat, then?
Second Montrealer: At home.

"At that point I was just keeping one step ahead of everything," he said. "Sometimes I'd have to wake them up in the bar to make sure they didn't miss their stops. Some of them were so confused they couldn't tell you where they were going, anyway."

I'd heard from more than a few older employees that VIA ditched the bar car because it was too expensive, but I never thought it made much sense. Selling booze at restaurant markups to a bunch of hooligans who are bored silly and trapped for twelve hours at a time sounds like a pretty good business plan. The trouble, it seems, wasn't so much getting them to buy the booze, or even to pay for it—it was what to do with them once they drank it.

Airlines are currently wrestling with the problem, fuelled, apparently, by oxygen-poor air and limited legroom. But in any air rage case (there was one not long ago in which a British woman and an American man decided to combine their mutual legroom and disregard the limits on their behaviour as well), once the airline has made its emergency landing, it's off the hook. The ragers, or consenting adults, as the case may be, are deposited at the nearest airport in the care of the local police, and the plane continues on its way, leaving behind only vivid memories.

With the train it was not so simple. The train didn't have to land, just to stop. It could technically have done that wherever it wanted to, told the unlucky (or, in the case of the American man on the plane, very, very lucky) drinker not to forget his toothbrush, and said goodbye. The question, though, considering the drinker was so thoroughly pasted, became a moral one, especially if it was a cold winter night and the train was several hours from the nearest town. This being Canada, and VIA being the public rail network, there really wasn't much choice. No matter how vile the offending souse, VIA always called the Mounties to tell them it'd be casting off a wretch at the next level crossing. Then, this being Canada, and the Mounties being the public police force, the Mounties sent VIA a bill. If the next level crossing was a long way from the next police station, the bill was a big one—after a while, too big.

One could make an argument for VIA having saved the Mounties a pile of dough in the first place by ferrying drunkards from one municipal police jurisdiction to another—a rolling drunk tank, as it were. After all their years of service, though, no one was prepared to stand up, or even fall down, for the bar cars. Like drunks in the alley, they simply got rolled away.

For Gordie, the memory of those times was clearly bitter-sweet.

"Sometimes we got them off very close to their destination, if not the actual place," he finally said with a faraway smile. "I guess that was being a Railroader, too."

We were pulling into the town of Matapédia. George had come back. I told him how excited I was to see the valley again. He said it was one of his favourite places on the trip, too. He said that most of the dignitaries he'd brought through had gone fishing there at one time or another.

There were already canoes moored along the riverbank every kilometre, even though we weren't in the real thick of the valley yet.

"Fishing clubs," George said, and he talked about some of the prize catches he'd seen brought on board. Salmon, brook trout, rainbow . . . I loved the idea that such luxury could be right there beside the track, that it would take just a fishing pole and a net, and a request to stop the train at what looked like the perfect spot. I began to picture Trudeau out in one of those canoes, lazily casting a fly. We were still partially in Acadia—the most genuinely bilingual area of Canada. And we were on the train, the very tracks that had first opened this land. It was a stirring idea. Our most powerful leaders fishing right alongside the everyday folks, with a few Hollywood imports thrown in, all of them meeting in the dining car at the end of the day, sharing a meal of the most beautiful fish anywhere, and this perfect, democratic scene was exclusively ours. It was Canada at its finest: clear, uncluttered, beautiful and wealthy beyond imagination.

"Of course, it belongs to the Americans," George said matter-of-factly.

I sat down.

"We leased it to them centuries ago."

This turned out to be essentially true.

I contacted the Quebec tourism office when I got back home. They sent me books and maps detailing the salmon fishing that is available to Canadians on the Matapédia. They didn't say anything about the salmon fishing that is not available.

On July 24, 1880, a group of nine businessmen from Boston and New York bought and leased exclusive fishing rights to more than twenty miles of the best fishing water on the Restigouche and Matapédia Rivers. The entire Matapédia is no more than fifty miles long. They named their club the Ristigouche Salmon Club, using the ancient spelling.

The club likes things the old way. It is possibly the oldest fishing club in the world, and certainly the most exclusive. Its bylaws limit the membership to a maximum of thirty. There is a waiting list, and the only way to get from the waiting list to the club is to wait for someone to die. As to how to get on the waiting list, there aren't any rules, but the names on the club's membership roster seem to point towards a preference for fabulously wealthy and successful businessmen and their sons: Vanderbilt, Tiffany, Goodrich and Dodge are a few.

The Ristigouche Salmon Club's dues are fifty thousand per year. If you make the list, that's not going to be a problem.

The Matapédia is one of the best places in the world to fish for salmon. All of the best places in this best place belong either to the Ristigouche or to one of the other twenty-two private fishing clubs on the river. Most of the clubs are American-owned.

The story of how things came to be this way is a familiar one. In 1880 there was no shortage of fishing holes in Quebec and New Brunswick, and no sport fishing industry. The founders of the Ristigouche Salmon Club were giving farmers and prospectors what seemed like good money for something they could get anywhere for nothing.

In places where local governments hung on to their salmon waters for public use, overfishing has finished the stock. The Ristigouche Salmon Club, with all of its smug snobbery, is one of the main reasons there are any fish at all left in the Matapédia. This puts Canadians who don't happen to be giants of industry, and the guides who make their living bringing them fishing, in the uncomfortable position of owing a debt of thanks to the New York fat cats who have kept them from fishing in their own river for more than a century.

The one truly Canadian icon who got in on the selling of the Matapédia before the Americans gobbled it up turned out to be George Stephen, one of the founding barons of the Canadian Pacific Railway. It was said that his only pleasure outside of buying and selling lands and businesses was salmon fishing at his summer retreat at Causapscal on the Matapédia.

I cherish the idea that, way back then, he might have placed a perfect cast and stolen away a twenty-pound beauty that would have gone onto an American barbecue.

When I'd recovered from the knowledge that my favourite Canadian river was owned by Americans, George told me that the track we were on was American, too. That turned out to be only partly true. In the early nineties a U.S. "shortline" company bought the stretch from Mont-Joli to Matapédia, Quebec. Shortline companies are railroad companies that buy up smaller sections of track with the goal of serving them in the same way a local trucking firm might serve a pair of des-tinations a few hours apart. They maintain track and own a small amount of equipment, leasing their track back to the larger companies when they need it. In recent years, as CN and the CPR have become less interested in serving small communities, the number of shortline companies has gone up dramatically. They own track all over Canada.

It also works the other way. In the months following our trip, CN bought lines all the way to Chicago. Still, U.S. ownership and a murky prohibition on Canadians didn't do much for my vision of the most beautiful of our rivers being available to all. It was as if the Trudeau fishing beside the locals in my imagined picture had slipped on a rock and filled his hip waders.

The train finally finished hitching up with the *Chaleur* and lumbered northward out of Matapédia station. In a few min-utes we'd be in the heart of the valley. It had been cloudy ear-lier on, but now the cover was lifting. We were crossing a time zone any moment and that would give us an extra hour—a free sixty minutes in paradise. I hurried back to the bedroom and propped my pillows right up next to the window so I could lie down as we went.

It was perfect. If I lay on my back, I saw stars by the zillions. If I lay on my front, I could look down over the river and follow it curling around rocks and laughing through rapids. The train tipped gently into a corner. The river narrowed. The show was just starting and the best part was yet to come. Never mind the Americans, I thought. They might have their paws on it for the rest of my lifetime, but for this hour it's mine.

The train lurched to a stop. I saw a neon light outside a bar. The door was open and Quebec country rock pounded out into the night. There was a jacked-up old Impala parked in front with a guy bent over the fender, throwing up. A sign said we were in Amqui, Quebec, near the northern end of the valley.

I'd fallen asleep.

I missed it.

~

The door on the bar swung open and a young couple weaved out. The woman had an inviting smile and her legs were long and springy. Her boyfriend had his arm around her waist and she was leading him to a car across the road.

It was a warm night. Even the train seemed lazy. As far as I could tell there was no reason for us to be idling in a town that size, but the train didn't seem ready to leave just yet.

The woman's skin glowed in the halo of the streetlight. Flies buzzed around the bar's neon sign. A bouncer appeared in the doorway. His belly bulged out over his belt, his T-shirt cantilevered above. The boyfriend stopped to talk to him, but the woman kept going. She pulled at his arm for a while, her waist twisting so she could keep moving without losing his touch, but after a few steps she pulled away.

She laughed as she crossed the street.

Another guy had come out of the bar. He was in jeans. He was fit. He crossed the road at the same time as the woman, at first a metre apart, and then closer. They talked a while, from either side of a car. It might have been his car. The boyfriend was still across the street, talking with the bouncer. He wasn't looking. The woman and the other guy leaned close.

The train jerked ahead.

The woman threw back her head and laughed.

I leaned forward to see what would happen, but the train rolled on, and we slipped out of town and into the night.

~

I went to the Dome, hoping for some ethereal comfort for having waited twelve hours to sleep through the feature presentation. It was 2:00 a.m. There was a faint light coming from the front seat of the Dome, a greenish glow like a radar screen. A skinny man was holding something that looked like a tiny computer, with a wire leading to some kind of sensor that was attached to the Dome ceiling.

I looked at him with question marks all over my face.

"It's a GPS," he told me.

If you wouldn't have had to ask, please excuse me, but I had no idea what he was talking about. A "GPS," it turns out, is a Global Positioning Satellite receiver. That little sensor on the ceiling was blasting a signal out into the sky to a bit of expensive space junk that was orbiting the earth, which sent a signal back down telling the GPS operator where he was, exactly, on the earth's surface.

He was in the Dome car of the westbound *Ocean Limited,* north of Amqui, in Quebec. Even I knew that.

But John wasn't really worried about where he was. The GPS was a kind of entertainment for him. He watched it in the same way some people watch TV.

"I use it for flying," he told me. There was even a little digital plane on the screen, sliding diagonally over a little picture of a train track. He pointed at the plane. "That's us."

"The plane?"

"Right. It assumes you're in a plane."

There we were, flying above the little railroad tracks.

"Railroad tracks are standard landmarks. A lot of flight paths follow the railroads. They're easy to spot and they usually lead someplace. If there are any tracks around, you can find them on the GPS," said John.

It hadn't occurred to me that we might get lost. Trains have always seemed fairly inflexible that way. The track on the screen showed a curve. We began to turn. I looked far, far ahead, and I could see the locomotive's headlight piercing the night with authority. I figured we'd be all right.

John was still watching the GPS, though, just in case. I watched along for a while. The little plane moved forward and back, slid left and then right.

John said he had a Cessna four-seater back in Miami, where he lived. I was going to ask why he wasn't flying, but I didn't have to.

"I love trains," he said, hearing my question before I could ask it. "Planes get you places. Flying a plane is an adventure, but you don't live up there. A train is a home. My dad worked on the Pennsylvania Railroad in Philadelphia. Trains were where he went every day when I went to school. Every summer I fly from Miami up to Montreal and take the train east to Halifax and back. Then I go to Gaspé and back. Then out west to Vancouver, back to Jasper, then northwest to Prince Rupert, back to Prince George and south on BC Rail all the way to Vancouver. Then I switch to Amtrak and go to Seattle and Portland and Sante Fe, and then home. I've done that every year since 1986."

I think I said, "Wow."

"That's nothing," he said. "You should meet Barry."

Barry was John's travel partner, who lives in Toronto.

"He's downstairs."

"Downstairs" meant the bedroom in the Park car—the Drawing Room, the most coveted room on the train.

"Barry always books the Drawing Room. He's already got it booked for next summer. If you know you're travelling a long way in advance, you can usually get it. Barry's done the trip over a hundred times."

John said Barry was asleep. I didn't wonder.

The little plane moved across John's screen again.

"Where are we now?" I asked.

"Right there." John pointed at the screen and looked at me as if I must have been stupid.

I turned away and looked out the window.

This rail line, one of the last stretches in the country where the train was actually used by the locals in much the same way it had been since before Confederation, wasn't really ours any more. And the Matapédia, that seductive Canadian river, stocked full of the same line of salmon and trout that had fed our forefathers for centuries, had turned out to be more open to a rich American rail nut from Florida than it was to me.

I was beginning to see why John felt it necessary to keep track of things with a GPS. The GPS captures nothing of a place's natural beauty, or its history, or whatever else might have made it what it is to the people there. Those things are far too subtle to record from all the way on the other side of the atmosphere. But who owns what, well, that's easy. That's just a matter of a few keystrokes on a terminal somewhere in the Midwest, which send a signal up to the satellite, and there you go, the river that was once labelled "Canadian" isn't any more.

I had a recurring dream for the first few years after I'd moved away from home. In it, I floated high above Montreal, until the buildings all looked like cardboard boxes. They then became cardboard boxes—nameless shapes on a flat, empty plain—and began to move, to float around the plain, joining other boxes and splitting off into groups.

I placed a lot on the identity of the city I'd grown up in. We were taught not simply to say "I'm from Montreal," but "I'm a Montrealer," and we believed we were.

That's what made the dream so frightening—it exposed the truth that these cities and neighbourhoods are absolutely random in their placement. Yes, there are physical reasons why the city thrived and grew: the river, the mountain—but now there really isn't any reason for Montreal to be where it is, short of sentimentality and convenience. If it were just a collection of cardboard boxes, it might be a lot better off a few days' slide in any direction.

It was a horrible thought that all of those streets, for me so full of meaning and memory, could be any street in any city, even a dusty flat between cardboard boxes.

The only sight that got me through those dreams was the Champlain Bridge.

The Champlain is one of three bridges that link the downtown area with the South Shore. It is a huge bridge, elegant
and arching. I often pictured escaping out over it and into the
great beyond.

In the dream, the bridge acted as a kind of tether to the
city. Instead of linking the island of Montreal with the South
Shore, it kept the boxes from drifting too far away.

Once I saw the bridge, I was able to get back to earth and
wander between the boxes, getting the occasional glimpse of
a high steel arch, until I found it again. Then I'd wake up.

John switched off the GPS and excused himself to retire to
the Drawing Room.

I sat alone for a minute, and then decided to turn in myself.

The Bullet Lounge was empty, and so was the smoking
lounge. I thought of Gordie again. I had no doubt that things
would have been considerably livelier in the days of the bar
car. I also wondered who, in the absence of a conductor-
bouncer, would be the one to tell the patrons where to get
off, either figuratively or literally.

At one bedroom there was a note taped to the door. It was
a paper napkin from the dining car with a few words scrawled
in black marker. "Pls. wk up Rimouski"—another monumental
act of trust. I'd been walking back and forth on the train for
an hour and hadn't seen a single porter or service manager.
There was no reason to think anyone would be around to wake
this passenger up. But clearly, judging from the serenity of the
car as we chugged along, whoever was asleep in that bedroom
wasn't concerned.

Back in my room I lamented missing my own wake-up call
earlier on. The Matapédia River was long gone and had widened
into a lake. As we rounded a bend the moon appeared from

behind a hill and spread light all over the water. It was as still as glass. It wasn't what I'd hoped for, but there was no mistaking it for anything it wasn't, and I decided it was worth owning just the same. Either way, I was tired, and lay down to go to sleep. Even if the boxes started drifting, I figured, I'd find the bridge eventually.

~

"Dad," one of the kids asked from the top bunk, "are we backing up?"

We were.

There's a lot of jostling in a night on the train, but there's a logic to it, and your body learns that quickly enough. There's the rocking side to side, the slam of the passing freights, the jolting and jerking when the train stops, or starts, or slows down. There's a lot of jostling. Some people have trouble sleeping at first, but most don't. The hum of the wheels and the steady rocking eventually triumph over all. For some, a night on the train is the best sleep there is.

But by the same physical logic, when the train backs up, it's just wrong.

Both kids were awake. I heard voices in the hall. An American woman in a bathrobe leaned into the corridor and asked, full voice, to no one in particular, if we were backing up.

My wife woke up.

"Are we . . . ?"

"Yes," I answered.

We were all backing up. We were all awake.

VIA's sleeping cars have showers. It is not uncommon on the train, no matter how expensive your accommodation, to wake up feeling like the inside of a garbage can. Most people on the train end up feeling this way, and the train's water supply is not unlimited, so it's best not to wait too long in the morning for a shower, no matter how early it is.

"What time is it?" my wife asked.

It was 4:55 a.m.

"Time for a shower," I said, and gathered the kids.

We were third, fourth and fifth in line.

My wife went back to sleep.

By the time we were showered and back in the room, the train had finished backing up. We were in the station at Charny, just outside Quebec City.

"Hey, kids," I said, "look! Charny is where Winston Churchill arrived in 1943 on his way to the Quebec Conference!"

They looked out the window. The station Churchill stepped into is long gone. The new one is a dull, flat 1960s affair.

"Just imagine," I soldiered on, "twelve thousand whooping troops coming home after the war in twenty-seven special trains!"

We began to move, this time forward, and rolled by a doughnut shop.

"When's breakfast?" my daughter asked.

My wife opened one eye. "Not soon enough," she said.

She was right. It arrived several archaeological epochs later in the Bullet Lounge—a modest cold buffet. I hesitate before calling it "continental," as there was a great deal more movement than one would expect of a continent. It was much more like an oceanic breakfast. We lined up, choosing our little cereal box, muffin and fruit as the train rocked back and forth, and we rocked forth and back, balancing cups of steaming hot

coffee and the urge to take yet another danish against the ter-
rifying possibility of a pileup.

We seemed to have chosen to eat along with the most inde-
cisive passengers on the train. The entire buffet table was only
a metre long, but each of the ten people ahead of me covered
it at least three times before falling into a seat.

Then, as sometimes happens, a hush filled the car. The crowd
moved apart as if guided by some unseen studio director. They
stood expectantly around a child. The child threw up.

None of us ate much.

Back in the room, our stories were dull, our games point-
less, our candies finished, and the minutes endless.

Hours later, we went to the Dome.

John was there, with his GPS.

I wondered if boredom and crankiness and selfishness and
general familial torpor would register on his little screen at
all. A blinking red light might come on as a warning, perhaps—the possibility of a social tailspin, with advice to crank
on the flaps, fly low and look for a landing.

We were drifting through a small town that was halfway to
becoming a suburb. The track went behind a series of back-
yards that displayed a broad continuum of landscaping values.
Once again, the people in the yards ignored us. Here there
was a rock garden bursting with perennials, with water fea-
tures and a birdbath, the owner, chin in hand, sizing up the
peonies. The next was a dirt farm littered with motorcycle
parts and empty beer cases. A man in coveralls was holding a
spanner and scowling at a lawn mower. He threw the wrench
onto the patio, kicked over a lawn chair and stalked inside.

"Oh," John said, "here we are." I looked at his GPS, but it
was blank. He'd turned it off and was gazing off to his right,

waiting for a break in the trees. A break did come in a minute or so more, and there it was arching out of the gloom—the Champlain Bridge.

Montreal,
Quebec

~

My FAMILY STAYED IN MONTREAL a few days. I went on to
Toronto alone.

I travelled *VIA One*, the first-class service. This meant I could
wait for my departure in the executive lounge in Montreal's
Central Station. It offered free coffee and juice, a quiet reading
environment, free magazines and newspapers and a plug-in for
my laptop.

In short, it changed my life.

A train car full of people becomes a community with
remarkable speed. That's because, in part, the people involved
start jockeying for roles in that community long before they
get on board.

Take a look at the line that forms before a train departure.
You will see them all in various numbers: the Noble Patriarch,
the Watch-It-Buddy Career Woman, the Den Mother, the Jock,
the Babe, the Bon Vivant, the Aesthete, the Loser, the Brain,
the Cynic, the Fool. Sometimes there may be many individ-
uals competing for the lead of a given role. The Den Mothers
parade their matching luggage, their designer coats, their
scarves, preening for the top spot. The Patriarchs open their
briefcases for their reading glasses and peruse their business
papers, pausing occasionally to peer at the rabble below. The

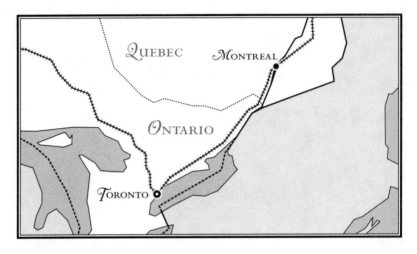

Jocks hoist their backpacks. The Babes adjust their hair. The Bons Vivants (and Bonnes Vivantes) throw back their heads and laugh, their cackles bouncing off the cathedral ceiling and scattering like birds.

When I travelled with my children, my role was cemented from the moment we stepped into the station. I was the Dad. That's about all one can do. It may be possible, when caring for young children, to play the Bon Vivant or the Noble Patriarch, but not for long. Children sense the importance of shattering their parents' illusions about themselves. The Bon Vivant buys his darlings a soda from the vending machine and the children cheer with glee. Two minutes later there is a squabble over whose Coke is whose. A tug of war ensues and both drinks are dumped into a variety of laps, including that of the nearby clergyman, who was reading of Holy Works when the Great Flood arrived.

The children, who were never trying to be any more than children in the first place, are secure in their role. But the Bon Vivant is now forced to become either the Loser or the Fool, and usually opts for a new role: the Despot.

This gives the Den Mothers ample opportunity to preen their luggage with varying levels of superiority.

Having mastered many of these latent parental roles (that is, mastered them in the sense of being, for example, as foolish or despotic as one could hope to be), I was keen to try something new. Stepping into the *VIA One* lounge immediately distanced me from my previous fatherly roles. That was exciting. It also, however, increased the competition for the remaining male positions. Jock was out. There were several who were much younger, stronger and hipper than I. Any effort in that direction would have instantly been credited to my standing as Fool. Brain and Cynic were both taken by prof-type intellectuals with pipes and books and copies of *Harper's*. Noble Patriarch was right out. There were so many stern grey heads that the place looked like the showroom at a pewter foundry.

I gave up on finding a role and took out my tape recorder to take some notes on my own hopelessness. Bingo. The gear was the key. I have this nifty-looking little tape recorder. As soon as I began muttering into it, they all looked up, although, in the case of the Noble Patriarchs, rather deliberately. Still, I knew right away I'd found my place—I was the Artist.[1]

Happily, no actual artists were on the train that day. At least, if there were any, they were dressed as something else.

I didn't write anything during my tenure as *VIA One* Lounge Resident Artist, but I played the part. The complimentary coffee steeped my muse, and I found my cross-legged Thoughtful Pose gained considerable impact as well. I gazed about, taking

---

1. The specific role label is contingent on who is doing the labelling. To the Den Mothers I was the Creative Guy; to the Noble Patriarchs and the Watch-It-Buddy Career Women I was the Mild Irritant; to the Babes, I still didn't actually exist; and to the Jocks, I was the Fruit.

notes, thinking, creating, genius fulminating in my brain. If I needed a place to sit, I merely had to stroll in the direction of the nearest Noble Patriarch, looking as if I might ask a few questions, and he would bolt sedately across the room.

Bolting, as it turned out, was right in character for the train we'd all be taking that day.

It was the *Metropolis*. It stopped once after leaving Montreal, in suburban Dorval (further increasing the Noble Patriarch population and also adding a new sector: the Soccer Mom), and then roared all the way to Toronto without stopping.

Montreal was Canada's Noble Patriarch at one time, along with just about every other role a city could play. It had a huge influence on Canada's economy and government, but mostly it controlled the railroad, and as a consequence controlled the other two as well.

When the Canadian Pacific Railway built the railroad that linked the country and took the first steps towards Confederation, it began in Montreal. There were railroads to the east of Montreal at the time. Heck, there were *cities,* but you'd never know it to look at the publicity materials of the day. A train trip across Canada meant Montreal to Vancouver. You can almost see Donald Smith and George Stephen, the CPR's founding fathers, standing on Mount Royal, looking east and wondering how all of that other stuff got in the way of their waving to London.

That's not to say that Montreal had any great regard for whatever lay to the west, either. To those folks it was one big land grant, anyway, except for the Canadian Shield, the Rocky Mountains and the Fraser River Canyon, which were all, collectively, one big pain in the ass.

That attitude wasn't sustainable in the long term. Today's Montrealer knows too well what's in Toronto: the folks who used to live next door. That change hasn't been an easy one. The snobbery that held the population together didn't wear well once things began to change. The city went from being Canada's Patriarch, Babe, Brain and even, in the case of the hockey team, Jock, to being, at best, Cynic, Aesthete and, in the case of the hockey team, Fruit. To the rest of the country, not surprisingly, Montreal's role has never been in doubt. It's the Pain in the Ass.

I can say all of this. I grew up there. We heard about relatives in Ontario who turned the cereal box around in the pantry so they didn't have to read the French side. We laughed at the hapless Leafs, the boring Blue Jays, the pathetic attempts at sophistication by all of those flatlanders out in the wheat fields and the stuffed shirts in Victoria, tending their roses and drinking their tea. Ha! Losers! We've got EXPO! We've got the Olympic Stadium! We've got the Habs! We've got culture and *joie de vivre* and crippling taxes and fascist language laws and biker gangs and a provincial police force that makes the L.A. cops look like the Campfire Girls and cigarette smoke all over the place and the Habs haven't won in almost a decade and . . . Hey, where are you going?

Maybe that's why the *Metropolis* was in such a hurry.

It's hard to know for sure, though. No matter what happened to its hometown, that train is still a diehard Montrealer. Just like the cities it travels between and the people on board, the *Metropolis* has a distinct place in the community of Canadian trains. It's pig-headed, arrogant, self-important and cold-hearted, and if you don't like it, you can bite.

I took a while to decide on an appropriate label for the role the *Metropolis* has in the VIA lineup. Well, no, I didn't. I knew what I was trying to say; the character I was trying to describe has a label that's all too familiar—the Asshole. But after seeing it in print a few times, I started wondering if there was a word that would be as accurate but with a little more . . . I don't know . . . Considering I was posing as Artist, I thought I should be able to find something with a little more pedigree.

I thought Shakespeare might be able to help.

I called Kenneth Welsh, a very good actor. Between Ken and the Bard, I figured, I might find a salty little insult that would still give the appearance of taste.

I was right about Ken. He came up with a great one, but it didn't come from Shakespeare. It came from Gerry Wilke, Ken's friend, who didn't write *Romeo and Juliet,* but with an insult like "flagitious poltroon," he almost doesn't have to.

A "poltroon" is a worthless wretch. A poltroon who is "flagitious" is a worthless wretch who is wicked and shameless. It's not a perfect fit, but it's close and it's fun to say. Why not try it yourself? Next time some lout in an suv cuts you off to make his exit, roll down your window and let it fly. Chances are he won't have read this and will have no idea what you really mean.

But I wouldn't try saying it to the *Metropolis.*

Trains, the lore tells us, are polite and old-fashioned. Engineers tip caps at friendly farmers. Children run to wave as the train passes and they are never disappointed.

If children run when the *Metropolis* goes by, it's in the other direction. Once it leaves Dorval it cranks up to the top of the speedometer. The run I was on got up to 160 kilometres per hour. For so many tonnes of hurtling steel, that's fast enough to make a wind so hard it hurts your ears when it rips by. If you're the straw-chewing farmer lugging your hay wagon over the level crossing and that bell starts to ring, you'd better hope it's the local.

For the passenger, you don't notice that speed and relent-lessness right away. The first hour out of Montreal is mostly farmland, anyway. But once you cross the Ontario border and the *Metropolis* starts to treat entire towns as if they're not there, it's not like any other train trip, and (Have I said this yet?) it's great.

Shredding Kingston is particularly satisfying. Not that I have any unfinished business with Kingston. I've spent many fine summers there, but, from the flagitious poltroon-on-rails point of view, it's a smug little lakeside burg with noise bylaws, speed limits, faux-British old world ambience and rip-off hotel all-you-can-eat rubber waffle breakfast buffets.

"Heh, heh," the *Metropolis* chuckles as it rounds the bend along the Cataraqui River, just out of town, "watch this."

People on the platform move for their bags as they see the headlamp approaching. They think it's their train. They begin their goodbyes, hugging loved ones, but half-heartedly. Something isn't quite right about the way the locomotive is bobbing in the distance.

It's less than a kilometre away now. The roar begins to sweep ahead along the tracks. The platform trembles. People put their bags back down and back away towards the station. The engine bears down. Parents grab their children. Dust blows up like surf and crashes on the pavement and all in a rush the train tears through like a chisel through a dinner plate.

The flatfoots on the platform barely get a glimpse of the people on board. It's a blur of business papers and deadpan faces. "You don't have to say anything," the Metropolitains are saying to the slack jaws staring in disbelief, "we know"—and Kingston is left looking for its hat and its composure, won-dering what it did wrong.

Privileged arrogance has long been part of the Montreal-Toronto run. In the 1920s Canadian National's *Inter-City Limited* had a barber shop on board, radio and telephone service, and a dining car in exotic hardwood panelling. The CPR's Montreal-Toronto train set a world speed record in 1930. There are stories about it trying to make up time near Cornwall and going so fast that it redistributed the gravel under the tracks.

Some of the train's luxury suffered during the Depression, but the *Inter-City* never lost its speed. In 1957 CN switched the power from steam to diesel. In 1965 it replaced the *Inter-City* with the *Rapido,* and soon after, made room in the schedule for something even better.

It was a time of great promise. Men had broken the sound barrier, orbited the earth and would soon be stepping onto the moon. Old-world elegance and stately speed just wouldn't cut it any more. CN decided that Canadians wanted more—more speed, more style. We wanted *sexy.*

In 1966 CN showed us the train that would give it to us.

The *Turbo* promised to blast passengers from Toronto to Montreal in an unheard-of three hours and fifty-nine minutes. It was all white with a raised cockpit—an earthbound missile with, dig it, a club-car smoking lounge staffed by hostesses in miniskirts and go-go boots.

Montreal Locomotive Works took a contract to build five *Turbos* and lease them to CN. The new service was to go into effect April 29, 1967, just in time for EXPO.

It didn't. Safety and reliability testing delayed the launch. The start date was reset for July 1, 1967. The *Turbo* wasn't ready for the first of July. In fact, it wasn't ready for EXPO at all, or for the following summer. It carried its first passengers from Montreal to Toronto on December 12, 1968, in four hours and ten minutes—only one year, seven months, thirteen days and eleven minutes later than originally promised.

One month later it was withdrawn for more modifications. Three of the promised five trains had been built by then, but the next summer a switch engine at the Locomotive Works factory got tired of all the waiting around and ploughed right through two of them, leaving one. It stayed at the factory for another year, until miniskirts in the club car were quickly going out of style.

The *Turbo* was pulled out of service again in 1971, put back in 1973 and after that, off and on, with a fair amount of off, the train functioned reasonably well.

In 1976 Montreal was gearing up for another big, world-class event—the Olympic Games. It was EXPO all over again—optimism, youth, idealism and excellence—and this time the *Turbo* would be part of it. That spring, while athletes went into their final time trials, CN did, too. On April 22, 1976, between two Ontario towns that couldn't have been more aptly named for a transportation milestone—Galop and Crysler—with the corporation's top brass all looking on with pride, the *Turbo* fulfilled its long-heralded promise and hit the stunning speed of 226.2 kilometres per hour.

Then the optimism, youth, idealism and excellence of the Montreal Olympics turned out to be cynicism, decay, corruption and incompetence. Soon after, the train of the future, which had never really left the present, became a thing of the past.

On October 31, 1982, it was finally decided that tricks weren't worth the treats. Maintenance was costly, the suspension never worked and the thing just wasn't worth the

trouble. The *Turbo* had spent eight years slowly zipping into
service and, after another eight, it rolled out of service and
into obscurity.

~

There was one group of Railroaders who might have been able
to tell the CN brass they were wasting their time by going for
high-speed zip instead of consistent efficiency. By the late 1970s
they'd seen almost every side of the rail business and knew the
city of Montreal in all of its roles better than anyone.

Not that the bosses *did* ask them. In fact, it's safe to say that,
until Canada's Black sleeping-car porters turned to the Canada
Fair Employment Practices Act to change their lot, the railroad bosses didn't ask them anything. Any communication
from, what were, after all, the city's Noble Patriarchs did not
come in the form of a question or anything close to it. The
words were orders, usually delivered with an insult and a
threat—not particularly noble.

The sleeping-car porters put up with that, with almost
unbelievable grace, for close to eighty-five years.

The practice of hiring exclusively Black men as sleeping-
car porters began in the United States with the Pullman Palace
Railway Company. The Pullman name was synonymous with
the height of luxury in rail travel. Any railroad that wanted to
compete with Pullman had to have Black porters, too.

For Canada's Blacks this was a mixed blessing. The first
sleeping-car porter jobs north of the border appeared in the
early 1880s. For Blacks in Halifax and Truro, in Winnipeg and,
especially, in Montreal, working the railroad was a real opportunity. It was steady work. It provided instant and lasting

friendships, both at home and at layover stops along the line. It brought tremendous respect from within the Black neighbourhoods, giving those men power and prominence in their communities.

It also meant they worked twenty hours every day they were on the train. Many of the sleeping-car porters came to the job with far more education than they would ever use changing linens, hauling bags, cleaning out spittoons and shining shoes. On top of the menial work, most put up with varying levels of racism from their customers, which ran from the occasional condescending remark to out-and-out abuse, both verbal and physical. Either way, the porters were permitted only one response: deference, respect and kindness. If they said anything other than "Yes, sir" or "Yes, ma'am," with a smile, no less, to people whom most of us would have liked to drill through a steel bulkhead, they were let go. On top of that, being too friendly with a customer was equally offensive in the eyes of the railway management.

In the late 1920s porters at the CPR tried to organize a union to change the working conditions. They were replaced with imported American workers.

Even when the Order of Sleeping-Car Porters finally came into being as Canada's first all-Black railway union, its very existence codified another kind of restriction within the larger unions themselves. No matter how well he knew the railroad, no matter how much skill and knowledge he could bring to the company, a Black porter would never be anything higher than a porter. There were no Black waiters, cooks, engineers or maintenance workers, and the Black porters' white union "brothers"—out of protectionism, racism or both—made sure it stayed that way.

Still, very few sleeping-car porters quit the railroad voluntarily. The job was hard, the pay was poor, but there wasn't any other place to go. A Black man with a university degree couldn't even expect to drive a cab. From the 1920s on, if you were Black and you held a job in Montreal, there was a 90 percent chance you worked on the railroad. Aside from labouring jobs like bootblacking and shovelling coal, being a sleeping-car porter was the best, and often the only, job in town.

That began to change in 1955. That's when the Order of Sleeping-Car Porters and the Toronto Labour Committee for Human Rights challenged the CPR. They used the 1953 Canada Fair Employment Practices Act to force the CPR to permit a porter to be promoted to the position of sleeping-car conductor.

CN followed, reluctantly. In 1964 the porters' local of the Canadian Brotherhood of Railway Transport and General Workers amalgamated with the same union's dining-car local, and the position of Black sleeping-car porter disappeared.

The men who'd worked as porters didn't. Those who stayed on finally began to move up through the ranks of the organization. Progress was slow, and for most of the porters who'd seen the worst of the discrimination the changes were too little, too late: Most were already retired. Among the porters who were younger or resilient enough to have stayed on, many moved up to positions of conductors and engineers. If it's true that the best revenge is living well, there must have been some well-earned smiles among the employees who'd worked so hard for so long.

In 1999 at Montreal's Windsor Station, a small effort was made to bring the Black porter's recognition from the community up where his self-respect had always been. That year, in February, the CPR unveiled a plaque to honour the city's Black porters. It is at the back of the station, beside the only door porters were permitted to use.

Owen Rowe was a redcap in Montreal, who was quoted in the Montreal *Gazette*: "Sure, at times it was rough. Men with families would carry bags and make beds and shine shoes and they would get called 'boy'. . . . I'm not one of those people who says the white man is the root of all evil. But I'm not Uncle Tom either. The fact is, Montreal's Black community is now the offspring of the railway porters. They are doctors and lawyers."

Joe Sealy, the Toronto-based film composer and jazz pianist, grew up in Halifax with a father who worked as a sleeping-car porter. In Selwyn Jacobs's 1996 film on the porters, *The Road Taken,* Sealy describes being a schoolboy when his father took him on the run to Fort William (now Thunder Bay).

"I was nine or ten by then. I actually got to stay on the train overnight. He made up my bunk for me and told me I should put my shoes out and in the morning they'd be polished and everything. I watched him work and he brought me food and refreshments, and I really got to see what he did because he basically gave me the full treatment."

A few years later, Joe Sealy took the train again with his dad—this time to Montreal to see a touring edition of Norman Granz's Jazz at the Philharmonic. The JATP shows were the biggest big-ticket concerts of the day. There were big bands and big names from every corner of the jazz world, but the biggest name on the show that night came from right around the corner. He was JATP's big discovery—the young Montrealer with a left hand like a locomotive and more swing in his right than you could fit in a boxcar. He was also the son of a sleeping-car porter, Daniel Peterson.

Daniel Peterson was born on the island of Tortola. He served with the Merchant Marines in the Great War. He had always wanted to play the piano, but a sailor's life, where a bunk and a duffle bag were all a man could expect, made having his own Steinway out of the question. So he had a portable organ made for himself. It folded up to fit into a suitcase. He brought it with him wherever he went and taught himself to play, until, by most accounts, he became a fairly accomplished musician. Daniel Peterson was a very determined man.

Peterson arrived, suitcase organ in hand, in Halifax in 1917. He made his way to Montreal, and by 1919 he was sailing the stone sea of the Canadian Shield as a sleeping-car porter.

Oscar was the fourth of Daniel's five children. Daniel made it very clear he wanted each of them to learn to play the piano. He wanted to be sure that his children would have more than one way to support themselves when their time came. He created a system that reflected the efficiency he had learned on the rails. He taught his oldest child, Fred, and charged him with teaching the next, and so on. Oscar Peterson has always said that his oldest brother, Fred, was the best player in the family. Fred died of tuberculosis at the age of fifteen.

Daisy, the second child, was Oscar's teacher. By all accounts she was not to be trifled with. Oliver Jones is another prominent jazz pianist from Montreal who studied with Daisy. In Gene Lees's biography of Oscar Peterson, *The Will to Swing,* Jones described her as pleasant, "but stern. If you didn't practise, she let you know it."

By most accounts, getting Oscar to practise was not difficult. As a child, he played piano all day. Still, there are plenty of musicians who spent the many hours of their child-hood at a piano, but there aren't many who ended up sound-ing like Oscar.

As the blues great Jay McShann so eloquently put it, sitting at the piano: "Oscar's the boss of this box." Oscar's technique is phenomenal. His supply of ideas is endless, and he plays many, many notes, all of them going somewhere—thousands of notes alive with urgency and purpose. That's where, you might speculate, Daniel Peterson came into the picture.

He was a very strong presence. In *The Will to Swing,* Gene Lees quotes Oscar's childhood friend Lou Braithwaite: "I remember running with friends past the Peterson door. Mr. Peterson would be sitting there. You didn't want to stop every time you went by. But you did. He had that overwhelming quality about him, and you stopped, every time. And he never said a word to you."

A man with that kind of power, who spends his working days smiling and nodding and saying "Yes, sir" twenty hours out of twenty-four, is going to have a lot of unacknowledged authority left over when he gets home. Daniel Peterson worked the Montreal to Vancouver line. He would have been away for ten days at a time, and in that time he would have travelled six thousand miles. He would have known every one of those six thousand miles intimately, answered six thou-sand questions and, likely, over the course of his career with the railroad, shined six thousand shoes. Each one would have hardened his resolve that his children should do better.

When Daniel Peterson got home, he'd want to hear his children play. He would sit silently, waiting.

Listen to an Oscar Peterson recording some time. He *knows* urgency.

Oscar Peterson is the most famous, but he's still only one of the many people who brought great life to Montreal and who lived there because of their connection to the community that was the railway porters.

That community meshed with all of the city's roles, got into its pockets and its heart and its pants, and gave it a swagger and an impulsive groove that Canada hasn't seen since.

~

I remember my first trips to Windsor Station. I went with my dad.

Now and then, on weekends when he had to catch up on something, Dad took me in to his office with him. The office was empty, with endless corners of industry to explore and wonderful toys. The electric pencil sharpener and the IBM electric typewriter and, my favourite, the bowls full of paper clips that I could snake together, surprising the secretary the next day when she reached for one and got thirty-seven.

The other thing I loved about going to my father's office was playing at being a grown-up. It's odd to look at it coldly now—not at what I thought being a grown-up meant, I was quite clear on that. I spoke insistently on the phone, furrowed my brow, looked sternly down my nose at the newspaper, sometimes put my face in my hands. The odd thing to me now is how much fun it was. On the special Saturday when I got to bring a friend along to the office, playing at being adults was all the more convincing. We'd each suffer several strokes and buy and sell New York five or six times, all before lunch.

Dad took the train to work. It came in from the West Island of Montreal, stopped in Montreal West, rolled through

Westmount and then into Windsor Station. The train was the other highlight of going to the office with Dad. One time shines brightly in my memory. It was just before Christmas.

The commuter train, as a vehicle, had none of the arrogance of the *Metropolis*. It stopped all the time. It was cheap. Anyone could get on. But there was still a headlong character about the thing. It was full of people, mostly men, who believed, just as we did when we were playing at being them, that they had very important things to do. They sat, steely-jawed, boring holes through their financial papers with a focus that said very clearly that if they weren't so busy eating the competition, they'd eat you.

The arrival at Windsor Station was an even greater celebration of single-minded arrogance. The doors opened on the trains and out they'd stream, columns of men in fedoras and topcoats, stepping smartly ahead, leaning with determination and never, ever looking back.

The arches that led from the platform into the station had the feeling of the entrance to a coliseum. I held my dad's hand and ran to keep up as we swished through the doors and the marble ceiling unfolded above us. The percussion of footsteps flew about the room. Looking up and slightly dizzy, I walked squarely into a business-suited backside and wound up with a face full of worsted wool overcoat. I'd walked into the man in front of me. I cringed, waiting for the reprisal, but nothing happened. Dad didn't notice, and neither did the guy I'd walked into. He was looking ahead past the man in front of him at a display. They all were. It was a train set.

They stood, a forest of hardened adults, watching the little train go around. It was a Christmas display put out by the management. There was a little village, a rail yard with boxcars, a level crossing with toy cars backed up and waiting, a Saran Wrap lake and a mountain with a tunnel for the train to go through.

I don't know how long we watched. No one was speaking, which, given the nature of the crowd, was hardly new, but this silence was different. It wasn't going anywhere. It was the kind of silence that surrounds an eight-year-old who has an office to himself with nothing to do but join together paper clips and play.

~

The train can still turn executives into children, but these days it's a little more expensive. It happens when you travel first class. There are attendants to cater to your every selfish whim, and anything from a soggy bun at lunch to the lack of a window seat is reason for a tantrum.

This was where the other step I took on my trip aboard the *Metropolis* kicked in. To make certain I was ditching my Dad-Fool-Despot role to fully embrace that of Artist, I travelled *VIA One*. That's what VIA calls its business-class service on the trains that run the corridor from Quebec City to Windsor, Ontario. There are meals, which are included in your fare, as well as all the booze you'd care to drink,[2] and it's all brought right to your seat. That, combined with the inherent fun of ploughing through hapless towns, makes for a mighty fine afternoon's entertainment.

---

2. I didn't hear of any rail rage on the *Metropolis*. As a group of travellers, the *VIA One* crowd certainly fit the profile, so I think the lack of incidents must be due to the run's latent inhibitors. One would be that getting thrown off a train going 145 kilometres per hour, even if you're plastered, wouldn't be nice. The other might be that even if the train did slow down to let you out, assuming it took you a couple of hours to get that drunk, you wouldn't be let off in the wilds of New Brunswick—you'd be in Brockville.

If the *Metropolis* is the flagitious poltroon of the VIA fleet, then the *VIA One* car is that squared, which is strange, because it's not at the back of the train, it's at the front. The *VIA One* car is right behind the locomotive.

I don't know if that is so VIA can assure its first-class passengers that they are guaranteed to be the absolute-first paying passengers to arrive at their destination. It's the kind of thing that would occur to a few of us up here.

It's also an interesting philosophical point. The idea is that experience, and the perception of it, can be compared to a passing train. Let's say the train goes through, what the heck, Kingston. It seems to be an event that all of the people involved perceive in a generally similar way. It happens at a given time. Those who are there, even if they end up running for their hats across the parking lot, all generally agree on what happened and when.

On closer examination, it is apparent that the train does not blast through Kingston all at once, but over time. There is a moment, however brief, when the first car is at the platform, flattening hairdos, drilling dust particles into corduroy blazers, while the last car is still just beginning its approach.

The result is that the people in the last car have an experience fundamentally different from the people at the front. The shock those at the back inflict is diminished. The hats they blow away have already begun to fly.

Further, within the *VIA One* car itself, there has to be a broad range of experience, all the way from the bigwig in the first seat to the loser in the back. That bigwig, although he may believe he is lustily enjoying the freshest infliction of dust particles available, is not. His seat is a full three metres from the front of the car. Even the engineer driving the train is not at the precise instant of perception. The air he or she passes through has already been shattered by the mass of rubber, steel and Plexiglas that is the train's hulking snout.

The passing train idea can also be an allegory for living. In the journey of life, it might go, it is possible to be standing on the front coupling, leaning into the wind, with your nose slicing the very atoms of time and space. That kind of awareness, and the struggle to maintain it, is a choice, just as it is a choice to take a seat in the Bullet Lounge of life, looking aft and sipping port.

There is actually an account of just that in Canada's rail history, and it involves a bigwig politician, a person at the very front of the train and another at the very back.

In 1886 Sir John A. Macdonald, prime minister of Canada, finally rode on his nation's brand-new railroad, the very one he'd spent most of his political life (and a whole lot of taxpayer dollars) trying to build. His wife, Lady Agnes Macdonald, came along and, as a good public wife would be expected to do, rode in the plush car at the back, suitably awed by her husband's great works. In Calgary, however, she grew restless and, much to the dismay of company officials, rode in the cab of the locomotive to Lake Louise (then called Laggan), just shy of the Continental Divide (1,625 metres above sea level). That's when Lady Agnes decided there was no point in living at the front of the train unless you were really going to be at the front of the train. From Lake Louise on, Lady Agnes sat on a candle-box perched above the cowcatcher at the very forward edge of the CPR Steam Engine No. 374.

This was no ordinary section of rail. Just on the other side of the Continental Divide lay what became known as the Big Hill, running between the towns of Stephen and Field. The grade on the Big Hill was 4.4 percent, twice that of any other hill on any railroad in the country. The first train to descend the Big Hill consisted of two locomotives and three boxcars. Its brakes were overwhelmed and it slid like a toboggan until it flipped on a curve and plunged into the Kicking Horse River. Three men died. The second train on the Big Hill skipped a newly installed safety switch and ran out of control into a tunnel where sixty men were working. The train derailed and stopped just in time.

By the time Lady Agnes took on the Big Hill, many more safety precautions were in place, and many more men had died. It was still the most feared section of rail on the line.[3]

Lady Agnes stayed on the cowcatcher all the way to the coast, 1,000 kilometres away. Some accounts say Sir John rode with her up there, which, given the image a national leader seeking re-election within the year might like to convey, is an understandable exercise in spin doctoring. According to Lady Agnes herself, however, the nation's First Husband did nothing of the sort. He sat at the *back* of the train that day, on the rear platform of the last car, in a low chair, with a rug over his knees.[4] There was a man with her on the cowcatcher, however. He was a CP official she refers to only as Mr. E_____, horror-stricken, no doubt, at the thought of what might happen and whose fault it would be.

---

3. It stayed that way until 1907, when the CPR began building the spiral tunnels, reducing the grade to 2.2 percent, but made for a much less exciting ride for prime ministers and their wives.

4. She didn't say he was sipping port, but we now know he more than likely was, anyway. We also know that for a while, Sir John's private secretary, Joseph Pope, rode alongside Lady Agnes. Pope decided he'd had enough near Nicomen, British Columbia, after the train hit a pig that had wandered onto the tracks. The pig was launched up and over the cowcatcher and hit Pope in the head.

Here is some of what she wrote about the trip.

Behold me now, enthroned on the candle-box, with a
soft felt hat well over my eyes, and a linen carriage-cover
tucked round me from waist to foot. Mr. E_____ had
seated himself on the other side of the headlight. He had
succumbed to the inevitable, disclaimed all responsibility,
and, like the jewel of a Superintendent he was, had decided
on sharing my peril! I turn to him, peeping round the headlight, with my best smile. "This is lovely," I triumphantly
announce . . .

   With a mighty snort, a terribly big throb and a shrieking
whistle, No. 374 moved slowly forward . . . For a moment
I feel a thrill that is very like fear; but it is gone at once. I can
think of nothing but the novelty, the excitement and fun of
this mad ride in glorious sunshine and intoxicating air, with
magnificent mountains before and around me, their lofty
peaks smiling down on us, and never a frown on their grand
faces!

   Another moment and a strange silence has fallen round
us. With steam shut off and brakes down, the 60 ton engine,
by its own weight and impetus alone, glides into the pass of
the Kicking Horse River, and begins a descent of 2,800 feet
in twelve miles. The river grows white with dashing foam.
Sunlight flashes on glaciers. Towering masses of rock rise all
around us. Breathless, almost awe-stricken, but with a wild
triumph in my heart, I look from farthest mountain peak,
lifted high before me, to the shining pebbles at my feet! With
a firm right hand grasping the iron stanchion, and my feet
planted on the buffer beam, there was not a yard of that
descent in which I faltered for a moment.

There is glory of brightness and beauty everywhere,
and I laugh aloud on the cowcatcher, just because it is all
so delightful![5]

～

I wasn't on the cowcatcher when I took the *Metropolis*. Granted,
there wasn't one, but the *VIA One* car was as close as I could
get. Still, I didn't hear anyone laughing out loud.

I did hear a lot of phlegm. There was a fifty-ish couple across
the aisle from me, with their twenty-ish son—all quite large.
They were strong evidence for the hereditary nature of aller-
gies. All of them had been sneezing and wheezing regularly
since we'd left. These were big, *VIA One* sneezes. They came
without warning, lots of "Ah" and lots of "Choo." There was
even one that went "Choo-Choo."

Then they fell asleep, all three of them, heads back, open-
mouthed and snoring like, well, like trains.

I tried to remember how I'd classified this family back in
the *VIA One* lounge in Montreal. They might have been Nobles,
but certainly didn't look so now. The train had done its civic
duty once again, creating a democracy by lowering all of us
to the same basement-level role of Mere Human.

It was true all over the car. The Soccer Moms and the Den
Mothers were squished into sameness, as were the Fools and
the Brains, the Cynics and the Bons Vivants . . . you couldn't
tell who was who. Somewhere between Crysler and Galop
we'd all had our covers blown across the parking lot, and we
were all arriving in Toronto that way whether we liked it or not.

5. Agnes Macdonald, "By Car and by Cowcatcher," *Murray's Magazine* (Jan.–June
1887): 215–35.

There was one man, though . . . He was several rows behind me, speaking on a cellphone, but I could still hear most of what he said. He made dozens of short calls. He said, "Hey, ya old dog!" and "Ha, ha!" in every one. He told an off-colour joke, usually the same joke, in every one. He said he had great deals to show them and would only be in town the next day. He did this off and on for the last ninety minutes of our trip to Toronto. Most of us in the car, even the phlegmatics, I'm sure, would have gladly called his entire list ahead of time if we could have gotten the phone away from him for a moment, just to warn them.

On the *Metropolis,* only two managed to cling to their identities: our train, the flagitious poltroon of the fleet, and its spokesperson, the Cellphone Man, a backside riding in the front of the train.

~

Our *Metropolis* community dissolved as soon as we stepped off in Toronto's Union Station. Most people had managed to bring everything they needed on board and were, by virtue of that decision, newly anointed as Brains, no matter how dumb they looked. It meant that they could walk out through the station's majestic lobby, flag a cab or catch the subway, and escape.

Those of us who'd checked our bags were all instantly Fools. We had arrived, it turned out, within minutes of the east-bound *Canadian,* VIA's train No. 2, just in from Vancouver— twenty-one cars of relaxed happiness in no hurry at all.

We met in the baggage room, where, apparently, the staff were in no hurry either.

I waited an hour and a half for my bags.

When I finally trudged out to Front Street, it was raining and my pants were glued to my legs. I saw a cab and waved like an idiot. The driver noticed me at the last minute and swerved across, stopping a few parking spots ahead. I bent for my bags, slowly, and stood up to see the Cellphone Man on the sidewalk shaking hands with a prospect, likely his second or third since he'd arrived. Then he made another call, looked at me and took my cab.

Order had prevailed. I was still a Dad, and he was still a F . . . well, no, he was an Asshole.

Toronto, Ontario

~

*T*HE BUSIEST PASSENGER RAILROAD in Canada is almost invisible from the street. It employs close to ten thousand people. Those ten thousand run 798 cars and eighty-three trains carrying two million passengers every day. At rush hour the trains are three minutes apart. It is the subway system of the Toronto Transit Commission.

It's true that, technically, the Toronto subway is not part of a cross-Canada train trip, but it's an important cultural study. Besides, geographically speaking, you almost can't avoid it, anyway. The subway runs out of Union Station, where the *Metropolis* drops you off and the *Canadian* picks you up. It's also the natural outflow for the enormous GO[1] train system that brings another 130,000 commuters into Union Station every working day. In fact, if your Montreal train arrives at the same time as a GO train or, say, as a hockey game crowd is emptying out of the Air Canada Centre just down the street, you may very likely visit the subway system through no choice of your own. At peak times, the ridership going through the

---

1. "GO" is short for government of Ontario. Although it is a very effective commuter train system, if you've had any dealings with any Canadian government body, you'll see the irony in the name.

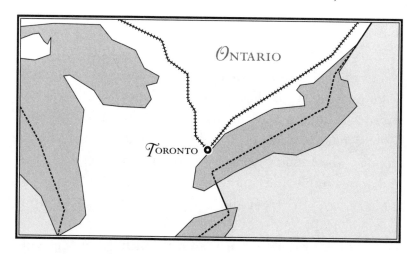

terminal is a tide of humanity that will deposit you on the platform without so much as a "hello."

This is no accident. There aren't many "hellos" on the Toronto subway. Canadians spend a great deal of time talking about what it means to be Canadian. On the Toronto subway, there is almost no talking at all, and being Canadian becomes a very active pursuit. Canadians, we are told, are quiet, polite and make room for others. This is generally true unless, when a group of Canadians are on the Toronto subway, one of them quietly refuses to move very far from the doors because he or she doesn't want to have to fight through all the other Canadians when getting off. That is when Canadians behave like true Canadians and clump by the door, ignoring all the other Canadians trying to get in. At that point, a Toronto subway car is a microcosm of Canada itself, with wide, unpopulated acres in the middle and millions jammed about the entranceways, and nobody talking about it.

I suspect most subway systems reflect the larger society of their cities in much the same way. Montreal's metro is modern, sleek, stylish and heavily subsidized with taxpayer dollars. Vancouver's is clean, relaxed and four and a half metres off the ground.

I lived in New York City for a short time, and as the song recommends, I took the A train. It is a north-south line that runs from the top of Manhattan to the bottom and beyond. More significantly, though, it is also a cultural express. Without stopping, the A train will take you from 125th Street in Harlem and, for example, the famous and raunchy Apollo Theatre, all the way to 59th Street and Columbus Circle, steps from Carnegie Hall.

Most of its riders, though, aren't shuttling between cultural venues. Most of them are going to or coming from work. Either they're cranky because it's the start of another day, or they're cranky because they've been cranky all day and now it's time to go home. Either way, all of that crankiness only really matters on the long blast from 125th to Columbus, when the train rattles and lurches for three minutes without a break. New York being New York and full of New Yorkers, there are no wide open spaces in the middle of the cars. At rush hour, every inch of every train is stuffed.

One morning, leaving 125th Street, one last passenger managed to press himself between the closing doors just before the train began to roll south. This created a domino effect among the dozens of passengers clustered around the door, which culminated in the woman in the seat next to me becoming uncomfortably intimate with the backside of the large woman standing in front of her. The large woman kept her balance, but only just. Each time the train rattled side to side, which it did often, the seated woman was once again given the opportunity of becoming much more familiar with the standing woman's buttocks, than, it is likely, she had ever been with her own. After five or six of those brushes with greatness, the seated woman blew up.

"Get your ASS out of my FACE!" she roared, and pounded the standing woman's considerable caboose. The standing woman wheeled around with alarming agility, yelled "Bitch!" and the fight was on.

There was a lot of shrieking and swinging, but they didn't get very far. With peacekeeping skills that would have embarrassed the Canadian military, the many other New Yorkers sharing that particular small space pulled them apart. That was fine, but "apart," under those circumstances, must be taken as a relative term. They still had, at most, less than a metre between them, and we had only just passed 96th Street. There was a long way to go.

Now, on the Toronto subway system, it would have been easy for two people to ignore each other for the length of the city. In Toronto, one could put forward a cogent philosophical argument that, unless acknowledged, the person less than a metre away didn't actually exist. But this was New York, where silence is as rare as a small sandwich, and reticence moves to New Jersey. The two American gladiators simply had to face each other.

At first, they glared, which was a poor choice. Glaring only really works when it precedes a highly visual exit and the slam of a door, both out of the question. This left the women with two options: ignore each other, something they had already shown little aptitude for, or talk.

They talked. It began with the seated woman. "You had your ass in my face," she said, still miffed. At this point the other passengers became a factor. Despite the rattling and the lurching and the constant rumble of the New York subway,

the train grew practically silent. Every ear in the car was waiting for the larger woman's response. We were lucky. She was
a born performer.

"So?" she said, cocking her head. "Best ass in town."

The crowd cheered. The slighted woman bristled, but soon
saw she'd been bettered and began to laugh. The air softened,
lighthearted conversation sprang up all around and at
Columbus Circle the two women left the car arm in arm, with
the rest of us murmuring happily in their wake.

I've never seen that happen on the Toronto subway.

But the Toronto subway does have its nether regions, and
I myself was lucky enough to see them, on the mighty thin
excuse that I was writing this book.

I first heard of the "secret subway stations" through a zine
called *Infiltration*. "The Zine," the masthead boasts, "About
Going Places You're Not Supposed to Go." I can admit to being
very keen on this idea. There is something very attractive about
getting under Toronto's clean and brittle surface. The subway
system is full of pleas from well-meaning charities and admo-
nitions from the management to be polite, stay away from the
edge of the platform and never, ever drop the first piece of
litter. That one, along with all of those silent, repressed
Canadians, is enough to make an even slightly devious person
scream. So, when I discovered there was a secret group of
"infiltrators," meeting in small guerrilla-style units to scurry
about the subway tunnels, climbing ventilation shafts and crawl-
ing under platforms, I was keen.

The only problem with exploring the subway tunnels on
foot, as far as I could tell, was that they were not designed for
pedestrians. They were designed for hurtling death-traps that
would happily shred a careless middle-aged man like a heel

of provolone. Ninjalicious, *Infiltration*'s intrepid editor, is quite clear on that point. The introduction to the issue on subway tunnel-running is titled "You Probably Won't Die," while acknowledging that, in fact, you very well might. Ninjalicious cautions the prospective explorer always to be aware of the subway's electrified third rail. "The last thing I need," he writes, "is some subway inspector finding a fried corpse lying across the tracks with its charred hand grasping a smoking copy of *Infiltration*."

That was enough to stop me from deciding to leap over the security gate, but the idea wouldn't quite leave me, either. The most tempting destinations, to me, were what *Infiltration* called the "secret stations." There are two.

One was excavated and built, platform and all, in the early 1950s, before the TTC changed its mind and never built the rest of the line. It sounds attractive, but is really just a sealed cement box under Queen Street. There are no tracks, there's no chance of any streetcar hurtling out of the blackness to kill you, and therefore, it's not really worth seeing unless you have to do something outrageously life-threatening to get there.

The other secret station is a working subway stop that has been abandoned since 1966. That one is below the Bay Street station, at the heart of Toronto's tony Yorkville shopping district.

The stores in Yorkville sell shoes for hundreds of dollars and suits for thousands. It's the neighbourhood where you'd expect people to keep an extra subway station around just in case.

The station was built in the early years of the system as a link between the north-south and east-west lines. It allowed passengers to change lines without having to change trains.

The system proved confusing, however, because it meant that, from the same platform, a train might be heading south or west, for example, with only the signs in the window to distinguish the difference. Torontonians didn't like it. Especially when they found they were going the wrong way and had either to squish back through the crowd to get out or ask another Canadian where they were. The TTC closed the station after just seven months. It's only used now for film shoots, equipment storage and as a shortcut for trains needing to switch lines. If you go to Bay Street station now, you can see where the passage to Lower Bay used to be. The tiles are noticeably newer, and in one of those walls, there is an unmarked door that leads to the staircase down.

Once I looked, I discovered that my regular subway travelling took me by the switch to Lower Bay almost every day, on my way home from work. It's not much to look at, just a tunnel that curves off to the east, but knowing it led somewhere made it suddenly interesting. I kept thinking of the description I'd read in *Infiltration*:

> The three of us then intrepidly hiked down the centre tunnel, striding along the small trackside ledge as fast as we dared while keeping a careful eye on the electrified third rail. We were grateful whenever we found some dark corridor, maintenance area or ventilation room where we could stop and calm ourselves for a moment or two.

I can't say what it is about the danger of trains. The advertising materials about train travel sell a product that is quite the opposite. Trains are stately, safe and elegant. Trains, if you are a prospective tourist, are not fuming, unstoppable monsters, they are rolling country inns. Rolling inns are attractive, but, somehow, so are fuming monsters.

There are times, standing on the platform as the subway is approaching, that I feel a kind of pull towards the tracks. I'm certainly not alone in this. There are plenty of people who succumb to that pull every year. I can only guess how many don't.

Speaking personally, my intrigue isn't a response to any overwhelming despair. It's not a roaring death wish, just a passing thought, a seductive call from some buried little synapse in the back of my brain. It would be so easy. My world may be spinning far beyond my control while I try hopelessly to bring some order to my being and some sense to my life, but there's one thing I can do about it—a little veto button that's all mine, and it's only steps away.

As kids, we all felt the lure of the tracks. There were two sets in town. To the north were the Canadian National tracks—the town's main street, Westminster Avenue, crossed the CN tracks via a steep little bridge, which, interestingly enough, was known as "The Hump." At the other end of town was a level crossing, where Westminster Avenue, Sherbrooke Street and the Canadian Pacific Railway tracks all met. It was also where we crossed the tracks each day to get to the high school. When a morning train came by, it was sport among the boys to sneak under the gate and feign fearlessness by getting as close as possible. At some point in our genetic past, this kind of behaviour might have served some purpose, but as wiser folks were no doubt predicting, one day a grade-nine boy got too close. He was looking east when a dayliner came from the west. It sent him four and a half metres.

Even that failed to dim the call of the tracks, especially the CN line. In addition to the Hump, it had a creek bed, a swamp, was home to rats and snakes and, most important, was a short-cut to the golf course.

Golf was not big among the boys of our town, but to be seen climbing through the hole in the fence onto the tracks with a golf bag was. It meant you were going to sneak onto the course and elude the groundskeepers and, more important, it meant you were going to cross the trestle.

The trestle was of classic design: no sides, a floor made only of awkwardly spaced railroad ties and just long enough to scare the living Jesus out of any boy who thought that there might be a train coming once he started across.

There was always a train coming. We heard and felt them at all times of day from anywhere in town.

I don't remember where I said I was going the day I crossed the trestle. I didn't own a golf bag, so I know it wasn't that. All I really remember is the sight of each foot landing on the blackened ties and the intermittent views of the creek. I didn't look back, I only looked down, as my heart thudded and my ears peeled the air for the merest distant rumble. My foot landed on the other bank and I felt instantly joyous, foolish, relieved and terrified. Now I would have to cross back over again to get home.

I wasn't consciously thinking of the trestle when I pressed my face against the subway window, waiting to see the switch and the tunnel leading to Lower Bay. Nor was I when I lingered by the north end of the platform, sneaking looks down the tunnel, or timing myself from the nearest pillar to the "Danger—Do Not Enter" gate that leads to the tracks. I opened the gate. I saw where the tile of the platform gave way to the black soot of the other side. I began to step when I remembered a friend of my wife's named Owen.

Owen is a very cautious and methodical person who would never think of doing anything as impulsive as sneaking up a subway tunnel. If he wanted to see Lower Bay, he would go to that unmarked door at the top of the abandoned stairway and open it. Owen is an engineer for the TTC. He has a key.

"Sure," Owen said, when I asked if he'd show me Lower Bay. We met on a weekday mid-morning. He was waiting by the unmarked door. He opened it, and we stepped through a doorway, down some dirty stairs and into 1966.

The lights above the platform were single-bulbed, hanging from single wires. The tile work on the walls was unchanged, all grey and dull. It was clear that no public passenger had stepped into a train from the platform for decades, but everywhere, coming and going in waves, was the rumble of passing trains. There were places where the wall had been painted for use as a film set. With the amount of film production going on in Canada these days, if you see a Hollywood movie with a subway scene in it, chances are you're seeing Lower Bay. The station also serves as a storage area for work crew machinery. There were shelves of soot-covered mechanical gadgets at the eastern end of the platform behind a floor-to-ceiling chain-link fence as if they might try to get away.

Once I'd seen all of that, though, and taken in the oddness of a totally private place that was steps away from a totally public one, there wasn't much to it. I wasn't sure whether I should feel glad I hadn't risked my life in the tunnels to get there, or disappointed that I'd skipped the most exciting part.

"What's that?" I asked Owen, pointing to a gadget beside the tracks in the tunnel. I stepped towards it and realized that there was no "Danger—Do Not Enter" gate separating the tracks from the platform. All I had to do was walk down a skinny set of stairs and I'd be in the tunnel.

I started that way and Owen became noticeably nervous. The TTC has a special training session for those who work on the tracks, so they can be aware of exactly how much searing power they're messing with. Owen said no one was supposed to be at the track level unless they'd been through that training. I decided not to tell him I'd read *Infiltration* and already knew all there was to know. We were standing in the gloom of the tunnel right beside the tracks, and I half expected a lightning bolt to leap off the third rail and fry me.

The tunnel was a surprisingly cavernous space. The ceiling was quite high and it was very, very noisy. The rumbling of trains was all around us, even though not a single train was in sight. Then one arrived at Upper Bay, just above us. The scary thing was that I didn't realize where the sound was coming from until it was literally on top of me.

There was a switch just ahead of us, and then, three metres farther into the tunnel, the bit of machinery I'd noticed from the platform. I walked towards it.

"That's a trip mechanism. It's a safety feature in case the driver fails to stop the train," Owen said.

My mind went back to the summer of 1995, when a driver on the TTC did fail to stop on a Friday afternoon at rush hour. Three people died.

"Isn't that the kind of trip mechanism that . . ."

"Yes," said Owen. "We've done some work on them since then."

The runaway train, with an intern driver alone at the helm, blasted through three of those trip mechanisms and three red lights before it rounded a bend just north of Dupont Station and hammered into the back of another train that was waiting in the tunnel there. The speeding train rammed the standing train forward ten metres, and penetrated the last car of the standing train by five and a half metres. The impact was so immense that the two cars ballooned out to fill the entire diameter of the tunnel.

The passengers killed were in the last car of that standing train. That could be because the passengers in the first car of the speeding train had a few seconds to prepare for the crash. Once they saw their driver come out of his little booth and run, literally, towards the back of the car, it was clear something was up. The driver managed to put about six metres between himself and the front of his train before the impact.

In addition to the deaths, there were thirty serious injuries. One man lost two limbs. There were also other kinds of casualties: Several people lost their jobs over the incident, and many of the TTC's safety practices were reviewed and subsequently changed.

The TTC concluded that there were three main causes of the crash. One was the inexperienced driver. Another was a manufacturing problem with the trip mechanisms, meaning they were faulty when they were installed. The last problem was a maintenance issue. Each trip mechanism relied on a bar that was supposed to rise up and catch a lever to engage a manual emergency brake system on the underside of the train's wheel assembly. Somewhere along the way, a bolt had been replaced and the new bolt head was big enough to block the trip bar from hooking the lever. The trip bar went partway up, but the bolt head pushed it far enough back down that the emergency brake went untouched.

Owen told me it takes at least 152 metres to stop a train under the best of circumstances, potentially longer if it's full, or travelling at full speed, or on a hill and on a corner, all of which the train in question was. That's why the first two red lights the driver ran through were so important. Even if the last trip mechanism had worked, by the time the train had gone that far, that fast, it was going to crash.

For the first few years after the accident, the TTC kept the pulverized cars absolutely as they were, until all of the resulting legal claims were settled. I went to Greenwood Yards, where Owen told me they were stored, but I was too late. They'd been rolled away to an unnamed location, mangled and charred, full of awful stories that no one will ever tell.

There are still people in Toronto who will ride only in the middle of the train, never in the first or last cars.

Owen told me that while we stood next to the tracks in the tunnel off Lower Bay. Another train pulled in and pulled out again above us. I started wanting to pull out, too.

"The trains aren't the most dangerous part," Owen said, seeing my nervousness. "They're reasonably predictable. It's the electricity you have to watch."

He took me to a substation. The TTC has substations every couple of subway stops. They are usually medium-sized brick houses. Some actually have shutters in the windows and picket fences, as if people live in them. People don't, though. Substations are holding tanks for a constant and raging river of electricity that comes in at 13,800 volts, and is scaled down to a manageable 600. Then it's distributed along sections of rail to power the train.

The substation Owen brought me to was built in 1953. Walking in felt like climbing inside the back of one of the old radios or turntables I used to take apart as a kid. There were columns of wires and cables all bedecked with switches and meters; the hum of power was constant, and got louder when a train went by. Basically it was a bungalow full of electricity— a powerhouse.

Owen told me not to touch anything. I said I wouldn't. But just inside the door, we came to a column of copper slabs all bolted together next to dials—something like a set of inter-connected mechanical levers. I wanted to see what they were supposed to pull. I got closer.

"You know that's live, right?" Owen asked.

I almost said, "Oh, sure," and touched them anyway, when what he was telling me sank in. The copper "levers" I'd been tempted to pull were, in fact, what he called "busses"—chunks of copper with a goodly portion of that 13,800 volts scream-ing right through them. Once I knew, I could see exactly where the line went. It entered the complex through a giant (about the diameter of a can of tennis balls) cable, through a rack of fuses as big as a clothes iron, over a track by the ceiling and down to near my feet, where it was bolted to the buss, a flat plank of copper about the width of a downhill ski.

I was used to electricity looking menacing—wires and cables and great racks of coil that were snake-like. In the safety commercials of my youth, they came alive with gleaming teeth and delighted in the piquant taste of curious boys. These busses looked about as threatening as a stack of wood.

But the room was full of them, and not one of them was covered. There was no glass cover, no insulating layer or filing cabinet to keep them in, just hundreds of things to touch, lean on, brush against, fall into, poke—and each of them would kill you in seconds.

They also might kill you even if you didn't touch them. Owen told me how all of the equipment could "arc" at any time. That much power going through the cable or the buss will do a lot to get where it wants to go. If you're between where it is and where it would like to be, you're fair game.

Most of the floor in the substation was covered in rubber tile, but in places it was painted concrete. It was wet in places, too, just to make it a little more interesting.

I could see why average workers would make sure they didn't spend all that much time waiting to get fried. The gear was awfully intimidating. There were switches the size of toboggans, the kind of giant switches mad scientists throw late at night to bring their subjects to life. There were relays with miles of copper coil and circuit breakers as big as furniture.

Circuit breakers are what will shut off the electricity when something goes wrong. You'd think they'd be allies, but Owen made it clear they couldn't be trusted on their own. The current is not keen on having its circuit broken, and might just leap out into the room in a sickening cackle, looking for something, or someone, to pour itself into. The TTC helpfully has a set of "chutes" on the top of those circuit breakers that will literally channel the electricity away. So unless you're over 2.4 metres tall, you might get by with just a tanning session and a perm.

Owen said the more modern substations have all of their gear encased in glossy, efficient-looking cabinets. This wasn't one of them. Still, many of the people who work with the subway's awesome power prefer the old, everything-can-cook-you-like-a-french-fry kind.

"These old ones are no more dangerous, really," Owen said. "When it's in a filing cabinet it doesn't look so nasty, and you can get complacent. There could be a loose connection in there and you wouldn't know till you tried to open it up and got cooked. A lot of us just like to be reminded of that."

Owen did have a story about people who weren't reminded quite often enough, and frighteningly it wasn't the people who work by the electro-blasting copper planks, it was the ones telling the other people what to do.

The TTC has a Transit Control Centre. It's in a nondescript building well away from the subway line—a big, open room that looks like a stock trading floor, except that, instead of stock prices on the front wall, there is a giant electronic map. It is probably twelve metres across, in little pixels that keep track of each track and train in the whole TTC system. Every section of track is on the display, every substation, every power source, every switch to every line and spur, and it's all, literally, controlled in that room. It looks like the bridge of a television starship. There is a captain-like person who sits in a big chair, and many lieutenant types who sit at desks equipped with computers and telephones. When the captain says "Engage!" a train in Scarborough changes tracks and several hundred Canadians go where he wants them to.

The captain looks as though he enjoys his work.

Owen and I visited the morning after a fire in one of the tunnels. The overnight work train, essentially a garbage truck on rails, had caught fire and melted a coupling or two. The eastern half of the line was shut down. It had snowed, too, that morning, so traffic was hellish, but in Transit Control, it was clear that everyone waited for days just like this. They were walking smartly and with purpose from one control centre to another, discussing, giving orders, standing arms akimbo and surveying the light board. This was *it*.

Owen and I tried to stay out of the way. You don't want to distract these people.

Back in the summer of 1995, mere weeks after the crash, Transit Control had a meltdown of its own that never made the papers. There'd been an electrical short on the northbound Yonge Line. It was on a long section of track between stations. The short was nothing serious—just some insulation along the third rail that had worn thin—but nobody knew that yet, and the smoke was so thick the driver had no idea what was ahead of him.

He stopped and called Transit Control.

The light display in Transit Control looks pretty cool, but it's not terrifically accurate when it comes to saying exactly where each train is. It's based on sensors on the track that are relatively far apart, so it's more an indication of a range of track than a precise location of each train.

When the driver saw a tunnel full of thick black smoke ahead of him and realized that there could have easily been another train stopped in that cloud or a chunk of track missing or a raging inferno, he called Transit Control and asked what to do. They told him it was no big deal and, essentially, to close his eyes and blast right through the smoke. They knew the fire was out. What could happen?

The driver had been driving for long enough to know that you never know what can happen, and most of the time it's best not to find out. He refused to move. Transit Control told him to go. He was holding up the system. They threatened disciplinary action. The driver didn't budge.

It came down to Transit Control deciding to put the speed of the system ahead of the certainty of the passengers' safety. Later, after the TTC brass had heard about it, they decided they liked the train driver's idea: better to be certain that the passenger will arrive in one piece and a few minutes late than not at all. The driver was not disciplined, but five people at Transit Control were. They lost their positions.

I could see how they could have told the driver what they did, though. In Transit Control, they weren't looking at actual people on that nifty system map, just a bunch of lights moving this way and that. I could imagine how the stress of the work would begin to wear on a controller, and how it might be a defence mechanism to think of those trains as little lights on a display, rather than cars full of real people. I could imagine how, if things started getting tense, a controller might just want to move one set of those lights past another, if only to get things going again.

I just wouldn't want to be on the train.

Later, on another night, in another nondescript building in Toronto, I actually saw the guy in charge force a train past a switch that wasn't working. He was in the Transit Control Centre, flipping the malfunctioning switch on and off, on and off, and muttering to himself as the train refused to move.

"Oh, well," he said, "I guess we'll have to cheat." And he walked out of Transit Control along the track until he was right up beside the General Motors diesel switching engine. Then he pushed it where he wanted it to go.

No one was hurt.

I was visiting the Central Ontario Railway (COR). It is a huge, O-gauge model train set, built into a former shooting range downstairs in a post-war industrial park, and run by the Model

Railroad Club of Toronto. Dave agreed to show me and my kids around that night. He was the one who'd moved the engine, but there was no shame involved. If you didn't count the hundreds of little plastic figures walking the streets of the towns, waiting for the train, working the freight yards or climbing the rock face on the mountainside, nobody but us saw him do it.

The layout takes up 409 square metres. It uses 1,524 metres of track; each tie was individually placed by club members and spiked with a single, tiny tack. There are some 750 engines and cars that run between the two main settlements: Ebertville and Lilleyburg. They are named, as everything on the COR is, for prominent members of the club—in this case, two of the founders, Harry Ebert and Borden Lilley. Both have now died but, Dave assured me, they live on in a legacy of model freight yards, turntables, suspension and box girder bridges, tunnels, rivers, a mountain range and a harbour.

The COR is a scale railway in every sense. The trains, the buildings, the track—everything about it—is an accurate reproduction of the real thing at $1/48$th the actual size. It also exists in scale time. There are clocks around the layout that run at triple speed—a twenty-four-hour day takes eight hours. That way, a member can put a commuter on the *Lilleyburg Express* in Ebertville in the "morning," have him or her travel the sixteen "kilometres" to get there, do a day's worth of work and catch the local back home, all in an evening's session at the club.

That little plastic passenger had better not be late, though. The trains operate on a printed schedule and they leave on time no matter what.

The same is true for the freight trains. They have work to do. There are a number of businesses that rely on them for supplies: a brewery, a furniture factory, an ice factory, a strip mine, a logging operation, a port. Each freight car has a serial number and a waybill. Every time the railway runs, those freight cars are assigned destinations and are expected to make their deliveries on schedule. The folks at Sharp's Brewery aren't going to care if their hops are in the middle of a sixty-car freight train that's backed up in the yard behind a coal train. They've got beer to make.

Even so, if there is a problem, they are just going to have to wait. No one is going to walk over to Ebertville, pick up the grain car and carry it to the other side of the room. That would be cheating.

The club was founded in 1938 in Borden Lilley's basement. It soon outgrew the space and had to be moved to a spare room in Union Station, where it stayed until the current room became available in 1946. The space really was a firing range. It was the testing facility for the wartime munitions factory upstairs.

Now there's a printing press upstairs. The night I went they were running off thousands of covers for a Harlequin Romance historical series. Love, not war. How times change.

Times don't change downstairs on the COR. The layout is frozen in an era when steam and diesel engines both worked side by side, when passenger trains were the only way to get from one town to another, and everything ran right on time: 1955.[2]

---

2. One lovely irony about this is the bizarre fact that the world's largest manufacturer of O-gauge model trains is the Lionel Model Train Corporation of Chesterfield, Michigan. It is a solid, old-fashioned American company, founded by the original Lionel, Joshua, in 1900, and fashioned on good old American family values. It also now has a prominent Canadian as its part owner—someone whose public image has little in common with American family values or the ruling aesthetics of 1905, and *especially* not with those of 1955. Neil Young, the rock star, bought a big chunk of Lionel in 1995, along with a New York investment company called Wellspring Associates.

There really was a Central Ontario Railway at one time. It started up as part of the late nineteenth-century railroad boom, running north from Picton, on the shores of Lake Ontario in Prince Edward County, through Trenton, Coe Hill and Bancroft. Its financiers intended it to continue north and join up with the Grand Trunk's Ottawa–Parry Sound route, but they ran out of money just eight miles short. The tracks of the COR never had the chance to bring their wares to the rest of the country.

At least, not until the railway was shrunk to ¼8th scale. One of the later additions at the club was a second main line, which runs the complete length of the layout under everything else. There are no sets or fancy station stops, but it's important. It's the CN line. Now, instead of being restricted to the industries between Ebertville and Lilleyburg, the trains on the COR can make freight destinations anywhere in Canada.

Dave had to explain that a couple times before I got it. Let's say there's a load of dinettes from Francesco DuBerri's Italian provincial furniture factory in Mount Batten, just south of Lilleyburg (named not for Lord Mountbatten, but John Batten, a club member). The boxcar has a waybill that says it's going to Saskatoon, a known hotbed of Italian provincial furniture lovers. The boxcar goes around the layout until it reaches the switch for the CN line, then disappears under a plaster mountain and goes around the underground line until enough time has passed for it to have delivered the load. I don't know how long it takes to get from Lilleyburg to Saskatoon in one-third-scale time, but however long it takes, that's how long the train stays circling the layout under the plaster mountains. Then it comes back.

The members of the Model Railroad Club of Toronto make sure things happen exactly that way every month, on the first

Wednesday. The twenty or so members meet in the evening and run the railway. One of them is stationmaster for the night, and sits in the Rail Traffic Control booth. The others are responsible for driving the various trains. The station-master starts the clocks. The trains all start to hum and away they go—passengers to Lilleyburg, hops to the brewery, dinettes to Saskatoon. At "9:05 p.m." the *Lilleyburg Express* leaves Ebertville, just like it says on the printed schedule. If there is a coal freight blocking its way by the harbour, the sig-nal light will be red, and the guy driving the train has to wait until the freight has moved off to a siding and the light turns green. It's possible his plastic passengers aren't going to get to Lilleyburg on time. He's likely to be upset. Sometimes, according to Dave, very upset.

Some club members spend hours and hours there every week. When it's their turn to be stationmaster (and wear a special hat?), it's a big deal.

"My dad was a member. He brought me in 1970 and I've been here ever since. But I'm one of the calmer guys," Dave said. "Sometimes when things go wrong and trains are late, I have to tell the other guys to take it easy. They're just *toys*, remember?"

At one point Dave called it a game. There are rules. You can bend them, but you still have to play.

I believed Dave when he said he was one of the calmer ones, but even he went slightly red when that switch engine wouldn't go where he wanted it to. He tried it several times. It was starting to get under his skin. If two children hadn't been present, there might have been a more colourful dis-play. There was also a conspiratorial air about the way he used the word "toys." I don't think he really would have said that on a Wednesday night with the whole club there and the ghosts of Harry Ebert and Borden Lilley lurking in the sidings. Between the two of them, they spent some eighty years making sure the little bell would go "ding, ding, ding" at the level crossing, the boxcars would get to the brewery, the passengers to Lilleyburg, and everything would be just right.

After eighty years, is it too much to ask that a train get there when the schedule says it will?

～

The night after my visit to the COR, I passed through Toronto's Union Station on the way to the subway. It was quiet in the main hall. The ticket wickets were closing up. A train heading back to Montreal was just about to leave. An electronic voice came over the PA, announcing each of the main stops. It finished up with a lifeless "All aboard," and after a pause, unbelievable for a command uttered in the imperative, "please."

I wandered down to the departure gates in time to see the service manager on the Montreal train watching for any last-minute arrivals. He surveyed the empty lobby as if he was staring down an unruly crowd, and seeing nothing further to worry about, disappeared up the stairs.

The guys in Ebertville would have been proud.

I had a few moments before my subway arrived. I wandered around the station, watching for the coal-black mice that scurry around the rails. It's a family game—looking for subway mice. They're fun to watch because the trains mean nothing at all to them. They can be right under the track when the train passes and be in no danger. It's amazing for me to see a living thing so close to getting flattened and so confident that nothing will ever go wrong. As it happened, I saw a mouse that night and was watching it so intently as I followed that I didn't notice where I was on the platform. When the train pulled to a stop, I saw I was about to get on the first car.

It's hard to admit that I actually thought of moving to a middle car at the next stop just in case. A few days earlier I'd been seriously considering running through the tunnel between trains and breaking into mysterious, lost subway stations just for fun. So, I made the best of it. I got on and sat looking out the train's front window into the tunnel ahead. Just before we got to the switch that led to Lower Bay, another fellow walked up and watched out the window, too. I saw his eyes peer down the curving tunnel. He leaned as far as he could to see what was down there, and even after we'd passed it, he had a gleam in his eye.

He might have noticed the same thing in me, but we didn't talk about it.

Armstrong, *Ontario*

～

*L*EAVING TORONTO AND HEADING WEST, I was a family traveller again. The four of us, and our bags, took the subway downtown mid-morning on a beautiful summer day, primed for a cross-country adventure. Union Station hummed with purpose. Now old pros, we stepped smartly through the crowd and right onto VIA's train No. 1 with nary a mishap.

The train was huge, with twenty-three cars, including two engines and four Domes. It pulled out on time, at exactly 11:00 a.m., and with the first westward lurch, inertia was banished from our company. We were going across Canada. We'd be on this train two whole days before getting off in Jasper, Alberta, and then continuing to the Pacific—two whole days on the mighty westbound *Canadian.* Exciting things were happening, and we were part of them.

Twelve minutes later the children were fidgeting.

We noticed right away that the crowd was different on this train. It wasn't that we were surrounded by geezers, which, I'll confess, was my initial fear. Some, in fact, were not old at all, but they were sedate. Our children, while wonderfully behaved, were not. They were fidgeting. They were active. Thus at lunch, ours was the most exciting table. We had drink spills,

minor food flings and plenty of noise. The next-most-exciting table was beside us, at which a trio of German tourists and an American neurologist quietly discussed train travel around the world and how much better life is "when one can speak Polish."

Our children were doing their best, which was better than most, but meals were hard. Restaurants, with service and manners and abundant cutlery, are an adult world. Being a child in an adult world is tiring. My kids were tired of it already, almost as tired as the macaroni and cheese.

That's when we met Duffy.

Duffy sat behind us at lunch. He was a quizzical fellow with a long grey beard and a twinkle in his eye. He had a lightness about him, although I was at a loss to say exactly why. Once I'd heard about his trip so far, I was amazed he had any lightness left.

Duffy's real name was Edwin, but he liked to be called Duffy. He and two friends had booked their trip a year in advance through a travel agent. They were to fly the two hours to Toronto from their home in Richmond, Virginia, ride the *Canadian* in sleeping-car class to Vancouver and fly home.

On their way to Toronto, their plane had flown into a storm. The two-hour flight took seven. Then, after a few days in Toronto, they'd arrived at the station to find that instead of the three single bedrooms they had reserved and paid for, they had one.

"One," Duffy said, smiling as he puffed his pipe. At the time, we were ploughing through the moonscape north of Sudbury. It was raining comet-sized drops that pounded the Dome. "One bed. That's it. I squabbled with them all morning and they finally gave us a second one. I was steamed. We paid a lot and were very disappointed."

I'm aware that I might be giving VIA a rougher ride here than is fair. I think it sometimes happens that the best story-tellers make the most of their disasters, and authors have a way of finding the best storytellers when they're on the train. None of those sedate folks in the dining car had any such complaints. Satisfaction was, far and away, the general rule. Had it been otherwise, no one would have been talking about the benefits of speaking Polish. They'd have been cursing in Polish, to be sure, and several other languages, until they got what they wanted.

Complaining as a general activity is, I have found, strangely favoured by the tourist crowd. They love the trip. They love the train. They love where they are, but it could always be better, and since there's plenty of time, they might just as well tell you all the reasons it could be better, right now. It's one of the things I love least about travelling with train tourists, and I'd complain about it here, except that I'm writing about Duffy.

When Duffy complained, it was a joy. Duffy's misadventures were serious enough, but he related them with an arched-eyebrow quality that gave them an odd attraction. He could have been reeling off the itinerary of his ten-day back-packing trip through hell, the Hell-and-Back Package, but somehow left you wishing you'd gone along, too.

"I don't really like the train," Duffy told me. "It's only marginally pleasant. I think it's tiring and very confining."

"Really?" I said. "That's great."

Then the service manager announced we were stopping in Capreol. Duffy lifted his cane, said, "Here we go!" and skipped down the car to the door with a laugh.

Capreol is a railroad town. There are more train cars than houses and the playground has a caboose and an old steam engine tucked in beside the slide and the swings. We passed through the rail yard on the way in to the station, and every track was full. There were odd-shaped, extraterrestrial maintenance vehicles with ploughs and arms sticking out in every direction, rail welders like robotic praying mantises, and savage-looking rail-grinders with multiple saw blades and face-like fronts that could have come from a 1950s comic book.

There was also a jacking pad. At least, that's what the sign said. After learning what "Do Not Hump" was about, I thought it might be worth looking into. It's a lift for tank cars that have stuff they need to get off their chests. That's all.

In Capreol, every vehicle in the parking lot was a pickup, and every pickup was a Hi-railer. Hi-railers are cars and trucks that have retractable rail wheels, as well as conventional wheels and tires for the highway. Maintenance crews use them to get to a railroad worksite not accessible by road. To me, to be able to pull off the highway and drive off into the sunset on a railroad track in your own car would be freedom of the finest kind, which, of course, it's not. Rail traffic is carefully controlled. If I ever did up and hotwire a Hi-railer, climb on the main line and head west, I'd be much more likely to drive into an oncoming freight than anything else, and the only sunset I'd see would be my own.

The train stopped in Capreol for a thirty-minute break. A few families waited for arrivals. Crew members went into the station to make calls. Paul, the service attendant for our car, helped us down and wandered up the track to a van parked at a level crossing about ninety metres away.

For the sedate among us, thirty minutes' break meant strolling the length of the train, marvelling at the power of the locomotive, gazing across the town at the true face of rural Canada and drawing well-hewn conclusions. For the rest of us, the unsedated, it meant a thirty-minute sprint. We played tag. We had races. A cloudburst had been through town just before us. We hopped over, around and right through the black puddles left on the platform. We were well on our way to flinging away the entire break without a break when Duffy took his pipe from his lips and with a grin, silently pointed to the sky in the east.

The storm had moved off, with blue sky spreading out behind it. The afternoon sun was low, and there, across Capreol, over the Hi-railers and the praying mantis cars and the jacking pad, spanned the most perfect rainbow I have ever seen. Red, orange, yellow, green, blue, indigo, violet—each clearly visible—a full, complete arc right across the horizon, with a partial second bow starting in the sky above that.

Paul returned from his visit with the folks in the van down the tracks, and it was clear they must have come from somewhere very close to the end of the rainbow. They were selling blueberries. Paul bought a couple of litres. As we climbed back on the train, he gave them to us by the handful. They

were big wild berries, oozing with flavour and sweet enough
to make your tongue bounce. The kids carried theirs in cupped
hands down the car toward the Dome. It was the slowest they'd
walked all day. Peace began to settle.

At first my wife resisted. She chose, instead, to focus on
the vast potential presented by blueberries, summer clothes,
children and the absence of laundry facilities, but above us
the treetops were golden with dusk, and below us was a series
of clear and glassy lakes. Slowly, even for our fidget-focused
family, the Dome became the theatre of contentment once
again. We saw two beavers and watched in silence as a teenager
at a fishing camp climbed into a runabout, bailed it out in seconds, started the motor on the first pull and bolted off around
the point, leaving a perfect wake.

"This must be a movie," someone joked. "Where's all the
swearing and cursing and finally giving up to row?"

We rolled the last of our blueberries into our mouths and
sighed.

The kids were excited to get to their beds. They pulled on
their pajamas and bounced for two hours, till a brilliant half
moon rose where the rainbow had been, and finally, bounced
out, they slept. The Canadian Shield rolled by and by and by
as though it was just getting started, which, in fact, it was.

As for me, eleven hours of our trip had gone by and I was
feeling it. I lay down with the room gently rocking, and before
I knew it, another seven had gone by, too.

~

I woke to find my daughter at the foot of my bed. The train
was stopped. It was 6:30 a.m. She wanted to know if we could

go out and get some more blueberries. We were in Ferland, at a level crossing. There was a small wooden church facing the track. The sign read "St. Joseph's." I didn't see anyone selling blueberries.

I was impressed, though, that the taste of those berries had stayed with her that way. My guess is, with all the rush of information bombarding the brain of a five-year-old, if a memory lasts overnight on a train, after a double rainbow, it will probably last a while.

At breakfast we sat with a couple from Oregon who'd already been all the way from Vancouver to Halifax on the train and were now on their way back. They were more or less neutral about the experience.

"We said we'd do it," he said, "and now we almost have."

I got the feeling that the space in their memories might not be as easily accessed as my daughter's.

It was my first encounter with what I came to think of as the "cruise" mentality. The Cruisers on board were not dissimilar from the Complainers we'd met the day before. It wasn't that they were unhappy or that anything was wrong with the trip, exactly. They were just following the itinerary. If Hornepayne was supposed to have a big mill that makes wooden poles, well then, the Cruiser reasons, let's see it. Bring it on. We want poles.

There is a pole-producing mill in Hornepayne. It goes by in a few seconds.

"There it is," the Cruiser will say.

"Right," says another, "we saw that last time."

For the Cruiser, it doesn't matter if it's worth remembering. Remembering that you remember is enough.

There is an archaeologist and chemist at the University of London named Don Robins who has put forward a theory that he calls "stone memory." He suggests that stone contains the magnetic energy to literally record the echoes of its time—that the sounds of an era, the vibrations of sound waves through space, are magnetically recorded in the stone they've passed over and preserved indefinitely in that stone. He has some pretty convincing arguments for the idea, including the one called "magnetic slip resonance," which I won't try to explain. He had enough trouble doing that himself, to be honest, and he has a Ph.D. in solid state chemistry. But the idea of stone being able to hold the memory of the sound that has gone around and through it is attractive. Especially on a train winding through the Canadian Shield.

The Canadian Shield is the ocean of stone that covers half the land area of the country. It is made up of some of the most ancient stone on earth, some being upwards of two billion years old. It descends from the shores of Hudson Bay, east well into Quebec, south to the U.S. border and, as any Canadian train traveller knows, west almost to the Manitoba border. The Shield may not have the peaks of the west, the sky of the prairies or the beaches of the Maritimes, but it is not worried. In the small town that is Canada, the Shield is the tough old buzzard who holds court in the coffee shop every morning—full of character and even handsome in a rugged way, but also difficult, uncompromising, stubborn and really, really hard to get around.

Canadians go to some trouble to nurture and preserve their cultural identity. We have grant programs, the Canadian Broadcasting Corporation, museums and kilometres of government hallways leading to rooms full of reports that nobody reads. Still, if stones can record sound, and I must say, I haven't *really* tried listening to them yet, any of the thousands of jagged rock faces that line the railroad north of Lake Superior would have the very oral history of Canada stored in its vaults.

There'd probably be a lot of cursing in there.

It wasn't easy to get across the Canadian Shield before there was a railway. In those days the only way to get to the prairies through Canada was by water. For the coureurs du bois who canoed the route, bringing furs for trade through the Great Lakes and up through the river systems to Hudson Bay, the trip was dangerous but understood. For early Canadian homesteaders it was almost impossible. Many of them decided they'd rather stop being Canadian. With this side of the border consisting of 1,500 kilometres of granite, no matter how articulate, the Midwest of the United States couldn't help but shine by comparison.

Getting as far as the lakehead (now Thunder Bay) was not so difficult—steamers ran regularly, if not particularly smoothly. From there, though, it was another story. As of 1872 the way of choice to Winnipeg, and, in fact, the only choice, was a mishmash of lakes, rivers and portages called the Dawson Route. It was named after the man who first charted the route, Simon Dawson, later an MP with the nickname "Smooth Bore." He got the name for his cool and calm demeanour. He was likely the only person ever to travel the Dawson Route to be described in that way. The travellers went by tug, steamboat, horse and wagon, and over miles of treacherous and exhausting portage trails by foot. On top of that, most of the time they were over a week late.

The trip was only supposed to take ten days, but twenty wasn't uncommon. There were several very good natural reasons for this, and one of them was certainly the Canadian Shield. But there was also the matter of the people involved. The contractors who operated the Dawson Route made money on freight and were subsidized by the government to transport passengers. That subsidy came up front, in a chunk. The trouble was, under the terms of the deal, they were supposed to get the passengers there in ten days, but could take twenty with the freight. They had almost no reason, except the preservation of their own integrity, to get the passengers there on time, if at all. Certainly, once the contractors had the subsidy in their pockets, they weren't going to say anything, and they resented mightily the few passengers they did end up bringing along. Most homesteaders were left feeling they'd done something wrong simply because they couldn't be thrown into the hold and forgotten. Sometimes they were, anyway.

But the real action stories held in the stone of the Canadian Shield got there the hard way: through explosives.

The Canadian Pacific Railway spent $7.5 million in explosives blasting its way through the Shield north of Lake Superior. Most of that was spent on a liquid explosive that would take off a person's limb with a mistake the size of a coffee spill. It often did. Nitroglycerine was too unstable to be carried by wagon. So the unlucky workers blasting through the Shield for the CPR carried the explosive in ten-gallon barrels strapped to their backs. Any sharp movement—the merest impact—and it would ignite, taking along what or whoever was close by. A certain fatalism settled on the workforce—as it would if you spent every day with your own gravestone strapped to your back, watching fellow workers blow themselves up despite their best efforts. They slopped the stuff around with less and less care, convinced it was going to kill them anyway. Often they were right. Sometimes workers died because of nothing more than the puddles left by their colleagues. And— it's hard to believe no one considered this, given where they were working—nitroglycerine is even more unstable when it is cold.

The cuts and tunnels that recorded those many blasts are still there, but we didn't go by them on our trip. They are on the CPR route, Canada's first transcontinental railroad. Since 1990, VIA Rail has travelled on the Canadian National track, which goes much further north through Ontario before arcing south again to run alongside the CPR track in Winnipeg.

There have been plenty of complaints about that change. The CPR route goes through more and larger communities. Thunder Bay is on that line, as are Kenora and Dryden—towns that were built to service the railroad and still do. They are also towns that would use a passenger service. From Kenora, a town of seventeen thousand, the closest major airport is four hours away, in Winnipeg. The train would be a reasonable alternative, but it now uses the CN line. So to get the train from Kenora, passengers first have to take a two-hour bus ride north to Armstrong. Then, according to the current schedule, they can either catch the *Canadian* at midnight, if they're heading west, or if heading east, at dawn.

I made several trips through the area in the course of writing this book, and have met precisely no one from Kenora while on the train.

I do know several people from the Kenora area who now live elsewhere—people who grew up there when it was still a stop on the train line. They are full of train memories. Mention the train to a displaced Kenorite and you will immediately be regaled with stories. There was the grain-car derailment in the early sixties outside the Five Roses flour mill in Keewatin. My source remembered running out there with a bunch of kids and diving off the rails into the heaps of grain piled in the ditch. ("It was like swimming in hot water.") That same mill caught fire in 1967 and burned flat in an evening. Half the town watched the fire from the train track. ("It went up in no time and took my summer job with it. Great fire, though.") And virtually all of my Kenora sources have memories of trips home from Toronto with a sweetheart, dazzled by the nighttime views of the lake.

Well, OK, they weren't just dazzled by the nighttime views of the lake. As you may guess, the views of the lake were not really, according to my research, the chief memory of overnight trips home with sweethearts. You've heard of trainspotting. Kenora, and the northwest in general, it seems, bred an entire generation especially keen on train, um, coupling (that's *on* a train, not *with* a train), particularly in the Dome—a quaint, Central Time variation on the Mile High Club. Given the obvious Freudian link between trains and sex, the stories weren't hard to believe, but it was mostly from Kenora guys that I heard these tales. I suspected a certain amount of bravado at play. So when I met a service manager[1] who'd worked on the Winnipeg-Toronto route during the years VIA stopped in Kenora, I asked. "There isn't a lot I haven't found people doing up there," she said. "It's dark and there's no one else around . . . What can I say?"

I'm sure the stone of the Canadian Shield would have plenty to say about that, too.

The other problem with the CN track is that, for VIA's current cash crop of Cruisers and Complainers, it is not ideal. They, as a rule, take what one might call a "tour brochure" approach to travel. There is not much between Parry Sound

---

1. An unfortunate job title, given the subject matter, I know.

and Armstrong that would set a tour brochure writer's heart even mildly aflutter. Disney is not planning on opening anything in Foleyet in the near future. The train trip through the Shield on the CN route is approximately sixteen hours of stone, interspersed with bogs, lakes and trees, and a pole-producing plant in Hornepayne. If the train is a cruise, then the Shield is the open sea. There are sunrises, sunsets, lots of rocking back and forth, plenty of time to eat, but when the cruise stops, it's not in Aruba, it's in Armstrong.

You may well wonder, as many passengers do, why VIA now travels the CN track, with its short-lived views of pole-producing plants, and not the CPR track, with its spectacular views of the largest inland body of fresh water in the world.

There is an answer to that question. It's just very, very hard to find.

I asked VIA, and they said that Brian Mulroney's then-ruling Progressive Conservatives had made that decision for them in 1990 when they cut the life right out of passenger rail in Canada. Well, they didn't say exactly that, but they said it wasn't their idea.

I could list all of the other answers from all of the other official bodies I asked, but they all said what VIA said— "It wasn't our idea."

I did speak to one rail industry veteran who was willing to answer the question, but only if I didn't say who he was, so I won't. That also means that what he says can only be taken so seriously. Given the choices, I'm including it.

He gave me two explanations. The official one was that the smaller and more remote communities on the CN line were in greater danger of being "underserviced" by the 1990 cuts, so they were allowed to keep their passenger trains. In other words, if there's no train to Kenora, people are still going to go there, even if they don't get to have sex in the Dome on the way. But if there weren't a train to Hornepayne, no one would ever go there, not even to see the pole-producing plant. Hornepayne needed the train more.

The unofficial explanation was that the CN route goes through more towns that voted for Mulroney. Also, Harvey André, the Cabinet minister who represented Calgary in 1990, didn't care if he never saw a train again in his life and was fairly public about it. Calgary is on the CPR line. You lose Calgary, and there goes Kenora. The last unofficial, and in-no-way substantial, reason for the change was that the CN line goes through Edmonton and the very loyal Tory riding of Yellowhead, where, if voters weren't voting for Mulroney, they were voting for their long-time champion, Conservative stalwart Joe Clark.

But that's not an official explanation, and since the guy who told me doesn't even want me saying who he is, if I were you and I were writing my own passenger train book, I'd go with the official explanation.

Besides, regardless of the occasional lake view, neither route is a piece of cake. This is an age in which it's possible to fly from New York to London in not enough time to eat a meal and watch a movie. By comparison, getting across the western end of the Canadian Shield is, in relative terms, about as difficult as it always was—it's the modern version of the Dawson Route.

There have been a few improvements since 1875. The operators still make much more money on freight than they would on passengers, but the food is much better. The trip is extremely comfortable and the service excellent. There is virtually no chance you'll be thrown into the hold and forgotten. There is the rhythm of the ride and the Zen-like buzz of being neither where you were, nor where you are going. There is also one attraction that would never make it into a tour brochure, or a Disney theme park, but which is full of drama and laughs and is, generally speaking, a whole lot of fun—storytelling.

This is my gift to via Rail. I'm telling them now that they're sitting on a gold mine. Let's call it "narratourism." If Professor Don Robins ever manages to mass-market his theory of talking rocks, then what I'm offering will be worthless, assuming the rocks have any personality. For now, though, train travellers don't need to ask the inside of a train tunnel the story of Canada, anyway. They only have to ask the person next to them in the lounge.

On the northern route that we travelled, through towns like Capreol, Foleyet and Armstrong, there is a kind of train passenger that is neither Cruiser nor Complainer. This passenger is not crossing the Shield to tick off the items on the itinerary. Nor is he or she crossing it to get to the prairies, en route to the Rockies. Passengers of this kind live on the Shield, and they are on the train because they are going home. They live in the small railroad towns along the way, and most of them, if they don't still work for the railroad, either did at one time or have been living with and alongside it for their entire lives. This means—and this is going to sound like a leap as big as the Shield itself—it means, almost without exception, that they are natural storytellers.

The trick is to ask. Most people who have spent their lives in a remote railroad town have learned not to launch into tales of the old days without being asked. So, like the stone of the Shield, with the soundtrack of Canada embedded into it and playing continuously, they sit, quiet and solid, waiting for someone to ask.

I asked because of that church I'd seen when I first woke up in Ferland. I remembered it when I noticed another one just outside Allenwater Bridge. There isn't much *in* Allenwater Bridge, let alone outside, so it caught my eye. The sign read "St. Barnabas Church." It was a low, squat building, a cabin with a stubby steeple. It was built of greying wood and sat completely alone alongside the track. There was no road leading up to it. There was no river or lake close by, as far as I could see. Like the earlier church, it appeared that the only way to get to it was by train.

I was in the smoking lounge.

"Why would there be a church out here?" I asked out loud.

Jim and Colleen were beside me. Jim was an engineer for VIA, and Colleen had just retired from teaching school. They'd lived in Hornepayne for years, Jim for most of his life.

"There are a few churches like that," he said. "We stop there very seldom now, but we used to quite often. The padre came in on the train and held services in the church for whoever would show up. He had his bag with his accoutrements, and his robes. He'd tell us where he was going and we'd stop the train for him. Then, two weeks later, we'd pick him up again and take him down the line to the next church, while a different padre took his place at the first one. The same building held different churches—Protestants, Catholics . . . they worked shifts."

It was a Sunday morning when we passed by, but if there was a padre or any congregants in St. Barnabas that day, they were keeping a low profile. The place looked abandoned, and very far from anywhere else.

"It was a flag stop," said Jim. "We still do those. You can just get off. We get all kinds of campers and fishermen doing that. They tell the train they'll be getting on at such-and-such a spot where we cross such-and-such a river. We pull in and there they are."

The train also stopped between towns in the not-too-distant past to deliver schoolteachers. A woman from Ottawa told me about answering an ad in 1959 for a teaching position. The job was to teach in a series of settlement schoolhouses along the railroad in northwestern Ontario and, like the padre Jim described, move from place to place every couple of weeks. She took the train to Armstrong for the job interview, which she understood was to happen as soon as she got there. As it was, she got there at midnight. The district principal met her at the station and brought her directly to the local band chief's house.

At the house, the chief and his family were playing Scrabble. The principal and the potential teacher joined in. An hour later, she began to wonder what had happened to her job interview. She wondered what she'd done wrong and why no one had said anything. She decided they must have written her off and were just passing time until they could put her back on the train. They played Scrabble for two more hours, and considering her anguish, she remembered doing not too badly, until, well after 3:00 a.m., the chief stood up.

"OK," he said, "when can you start?"

"I guess they found out what they wanted to know," she said. "That I could spell, I could hold my own and I wasn't a jerk."

"I'll bet she met Dr. Guest after that," Colleen said.

"God help her," Jim said.

Dr. Guest, it turned out, was Hornepayne's dentist when Jim was a child. He was also the dentist for Armstrong and just about every other town on the train line. He had his own train car. Half of the car was his office, along with his dental chair and what must have been considered instruments of pain and unpleasantness, to say the least. The other half of the train car was his home, where he lived with his wife, the either very charitable or, we can assume, much-beleaguered Mrs. Guest.

Dr. Guest came through for a month at a time. Jim described having a toothache and being sent down to the rail yard to take care of it. His mother marched him down there and Dr. Guest put him in the chair. The good doctor took a look in his mouth, tut-tutted a couple of times and pulled out the tooth. "Word got around when the train was bringing him in," Jim said. "None of us was ever very happy to see him."

Dr. Guest's train practice in Hornepayne dried up sometime around 1957, when the highway, if you can call it that, finally reached the town.

"That was a real turkey trail," Jim remembered. "You needed a bulldozer to get anywhere."

It occurred to me that any road, good or bad, wouldn't have mattered much to a town that had lived perfectly well by the train for all those years. Until a car culture could be built up, a road south shouldn't have made any difference.

"Oh, no," Jim said, "we had cars. Hornepayne had its own GM dealership years before there was anywhere to drive."

A General Motors dealer? In a town days by train from the nearest city, with no road access and almost no roads?

It turned out Jim wasn't the only one with a vivid memory of a GM dealer from Hornepayne. Later on, when I happened to mention my conversation with Jim to my mother, she started laughing before I even got to the part about the road.

"I remember that GM dealer," she said.

Mom worked for GM at their office in Oshawa, Ontario, in the late fifties. "Each dealer had a quota of cars to sell each year," she told me. "If a dealer didn't reach us before the deadline, the company would send them a standard order of sedans and they'd just have to take it or pay to send it back."

The standard order was not designed to suit dealers in, say, Hornepayne.

"The zone office sent the dealer in Hornepayne a telegram. It said that, because he hadn't contacted them, he was under obligation to sell the order and the telegram was his contract. He was upset. He phoned a number of times. And then one day he walked right into the office in Oshawa. He had that telegram clutched in his hand and was already red in the face."

Edith, the switchboard operator, told Mom to step aside.

The switchboard was behind a ceiling-high protective glass like those in banks in major American cities. This was 1957, when people left their babies sleeping in carriages outside the department store. It makes you wonder how many other GM dealers were sent something other than what they expected. It also makes you wonder about the nature of GM dealers.

"He asked to see Mr. Hearn first," Mom said. "He was the manager."

Mr. Hearn was at lunch. Or he might have been. Edith, apparently, had a certain amount of editorial licence in such matters, because Mr. Hearn's assistant wasn't there either, nor *his* assistant.

"Bunch of crooks," the dealer said, as Edith continued checking names, the buck sliding further away by the minute.

But this dealer was made of thicker stuff than that. He had a reputation to protect. Hornepayne wasn't going to go for a bunch of white-walled, fruit-belt sedans. He'd have been

laughed all the way to Kapuskasing. So what did the resource-
ful frontier merchant do with the stink of humiliation right
there in front of his nose?

He used it. He raised that telegram with two hands until
it was cupped like a tissue around his sturdy northern snout,
and he blew his nose right into the telegram with all the force
of a blizzard on a January night. Then he threw the soiled contract down to the floor in disgust and stamped on it.

Edith found a manager. Mom didn't remember who it was,
but we can only hope he had a sturdy constitution and plenty
of tissues. Edith took her lunch break after that and Mom filled
in for the hour. No one blew his or her nose into a telegram
for the rest of the day.

The road to Hornepayne is still no picnic in winter, but it
isn't the main reason behind the town's isolation any more.
I asked Jim how many of his friends' parents worked for the
railroad when he was growing up.

"It's easier to tell you the ones who didn't," he said. "There
were two: One guy's dad was the teacher and another ran the
grocery store.

"At one time we had 137 men working just on steam engines
in the car department. That was when everything was made
of cast iron. Wings on the spreaders would break, and to fix
them you'd have to heat them for hours. That place was humming day and night."

It turned out Jim's dad worked in the car department.
Jim had memories of going down the tracks with his friends
to meet him and, naturally, of hanging around places they
shouldn't have been.

"It was the CN cops you had to watch out for. We had town
cops, but they didn't do much." He remembered clambering
on a line of steam engines in 1960.

"We weren't supposed to be there," he said, "but we loved poking around on them—all grease and soot and coal."

He thought for a minute, and then he remembered why all those steam engines were there.

"They were lined up for scrap. CN was moving to diesel."

The diesel engines could go much farther and the railroads didn't need as many stops, as many maintenance people or as many towns.

"That's when Hornepayne started shrinking," Jim continued. "It just wasn't necessary. Since then we've lost twenty families with every new system."

I checked our map. We were west of Sioux Lookout, nearing Minaki and the Lake of the Woods. Another two hours and we'd be out of the Canadian Shield. The service manager gave the first call for lunch in the dining car, and a new parade started up on board. A stream of Cruisers came downstairs from the Dome and moved slowly forward though the cars. I joined in and heard various accounts of the morning's memories. One person had seen a moose, one had seen a beaver swimming beside its lodge, but most of them were complaining. One elderly gentleman from New York City, wearing a cardigan and tartan slacks, said, "I saw seven million trees and that was six million, nine hundred ninety-nine thousand too many. When I get back to New York I'm not going to go near a tree for a month." His fellow Cruisers laughed.

I was still thinking that I'd missed some of the coolest stuff because I didn't know it was there. I wanted to turn around and look for some sign of Dr. Guest and his wife, guests both by name and social position for most of their adult lives. I wanted to stay up late enough to look a lot closer at Hornepayne. The train stops there for half an hour in the middle of the night. I wanted to walk by the GM dealership and bring a hanky.

And, oh, all right, I was hoping I'd get a chance to go to Kenora at night sometime, too.

It was going to be a hard sell to the rest of the train, even with the Kenora part. The talk in the dining car was decidedly goal-oriented: out with the Shield, on with the prairies—we want something worth remembering.

The train began to slow down. We were in the middle of a cut in the stone, with a path leading down to a river further ahead. There were no buildings in sight, but as we stopped, I saw something green being hoisted up towards the train. It was a canoe. There were five more of them laid out along the track, with about thirty teenagers and a few adults milling around.

They were Ontario Rangers.

The Ontario Rangers is a summer program for high-school students. Every summer the Ontario Ministry of Natural Resources randomly selects approximately four hundred people from the one thousand that apply. The only criterion is turning seventeen at some point that year.

The idea is to give the province's youth a chance to develop leadership skills by hacking their way through the savage bush of the Canadian Shield for weeks at a time.

This group had worked near Foleyet on Little Lake Winnebagen. They'd been clearing bush, cleaning up after a tornado and cutting portage trails. They'd done three kilometres of that so far. Three kilometres is a monstrous distance in the woods of the Shield. The bugs are merciless. The bears are big. The bush is so dense that you can lose sight of a person who is three metres away.

The Rangers had been there eight weeks.

They were thrilled.

They'd completely taken over the coach. The smell of clothes soaked in wood smoke stung my nostrils as soon as I walked in. Their packs bulged out of the overheads and boots cluttered the aisle. The car bustled with the kind of buoyant conversation that you might expect after a trip to the big city for a concert—not six weeks of hard labour in the bush.

"It's been the best summer of my life," Ian told me. "I didn't know anyone when I started and now I've made friends I'll never forget."

They were hugging and holding hands, rarely spending a few seconds without touching each other. It was an entrancing sight, so much so that I was looking right at him before I noticed the one person in the crowd who wasn't an Ontario Ranger and wasn't seventeen. It was Duffy. He was sitting on the arm of a chair, at the edge of a circle of Rangers, grinning.

I asked how he and his friends had got around their bed problem the night before.

"What problem?" he asked, and then his eyes brightened. "Oh, right. I slept in the Dome."

"Alone?" I asked. We were just north of Kenora at the time.

"Just me and two pillows," he said. "I laid my head on the tray table. I couldn't lean forward, couldn't lean back . . . It was awful, but I did OK. I was awake between two and three when the train stopped for an hour. That was good. I got to smoke my pipe out the door in, um, what's that place?"

"I don't know," I said. "I was asleep."

"Oh, yeah," he said. "I looked at the sign on the station for an hour. Let me think. It might have started with an 'L.'"

"Longlac?"

"Right. I'm not good with towns. I can't even remember where we're going."

"Where *are* you going?"

"Um," he grinned, "give me a minute."

Everybody on this train knew where he or she was going. "Where are you going?" was the most often asked question on the train. It was even more elementary than "Where are you from?"—the standard conversation-starter in a community that did little more than converse.

"Someplace with lots of mountains and rivers and a national park," he said after a while.

"Jasper?" I asked.

"It could be that. Yes. That's it. Jasper."

To be on the westbound *Canadian* and forget Jasper is like going to France and forgetting Paris. It's not only unusual, it's almost impossible. I guess I looked confused.

"I had a car accident when I was twenty," Duffy explained. "It gave me a short-term memory deficit. I tried to keep on working, but it was difficult. I ended up taking early retirement on long-term disability."

A group of Cruisers came through the car, single file, at arm's length. Near the end of the line was the gentleman from New York who had seen more trees than he'd wanted to. Trees hadn't been on the itinerary. Nor was rock. It turned out he'd seen enough rock, too.

"That's where I'm different," Duffy said. "Unless I take a lot of video I won't remember this. I won't remember the towns I've been to. But I'll remember a pleasant time with friends and that's satisfactory. I do get frustrated with myself some-times, but I can enjoy each moment to the fullest. I don't have to grab hold of one part and claim it. That's what's great about this for me . . . I mean, the bedroom business was a problem, but, well . . . I don't really . . . I mean . . . oh, well," he shrugged and grinned again. "I forgot what I was saying."

The Rangers were singing. They swayed, arms locked on shoulders, up and down the car. Duffy beamed, and for that moment, it was easy to forget I'd heard a complaint at all in the previous twenty-four hours. I noticed he didn't have a camera. For him, this moment was enjoying its only showing.

He probably doesn't remember it, but I do.

Churchill, *Manitoba*

⁓

*F*OR MY TRIP TO CHURCHILL, I stopped trying to play the role of Dad and brought along a real one: *my* dad.

Dad was approaching his seventieth birthday. He'd spent most of those years in Canada, after he arrived here from England by ship in 1950. One of the first things he did once here was get on a train. It was called a boat train. His ship docked in Halifax. The passengers trooped through Pier One and into Canada and, before they could think any further, got on a train. Two days later he was in Toronto. Four days after that he had a job on a farm in Milton, Ontario, and Canada was home. He didn't go back to England until four years later, when his father died at seventy-six. My dad never got to take a long train journey with his father. When I invited him to come along with me to Churchill, he said yes immediately. In fact, now that I think of it, he probably invited himself.

There are many reasons to go to Churchill, even if you're not travelling with your father. In October, the reason is the polar bears. They come right into town, some years by the dozen. Once winter settles in and the bay freezes up, they hunt seals out on the ice. But before that, they come into town. So do the ecotourists. Churchill is packed every October.

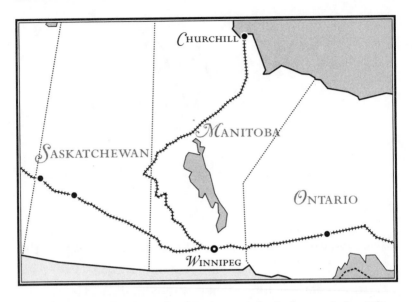

In late summer the big attraction is the beluga whales. They come to the mouth of the Churchill River to feed on caplin. Belugas are gentle and friendly creatures. They'll swim beside your canoe, five or six at a time, watching you as you watch them. The locals say you can stroke their heads as you would a friendly dog's.

Birders come to Churchill, too, in the late spring and summer, to see the annual migration. Churchill is built on a strip of land between the Churchill River and Hudson Bay. The birds flock by the thousands to the beach, and the birders do, too. They stay in the motels along Kelsey Avenue, places with names like the Polar Bear Inn and Polar Hotel. They eat in the restaurants, they buy the souvenirs and they provide enough work almost to double the town's population: from six hundred to twelve hundred.

We went in March. There are no polar bears in Churchill in March. There are no beluga whales and the only birds are crows. There are almost no tourists.

I'd been told that the northern lights were spectacular. I was looking forward to sitting in the Dome under the dancing skies.

Our train had no Dome.

Including the crew, fourteen of us got on the night the *Hudson Bay* left Winnipeg for Churchill. There were two engineers, a service manager, a porter and a cook. There was a retired couple from Louisiana. There was a young French couple on their honeymoon. There was a tall fellow with salt-and-pepper hair who was travelling on his own. There was a rough-and-ready Bushman and his wife. The Bushman had skin the texture of boot leather. There was my father, and there was me. With two engines, a baggage car, two coaches, a dining car and a sleeping car, we were averaging two people per car.

We pulled out of Winnipeg at 8:45 p.m. The *Hudson Bay* did not offer the same linen tablecloth service as the trains on the east-west line. The food was simple—soups, stews, sandwiches and burgers, but it was fresh and good, and the coffee was plentiful, even if it was served in disposable cups.

The good thing about that more modest service was the dining car itself. It was divided into an eating area and a kind of common room, a smoking area with tables and chairs. It had the feeling of a big kitchen that was always open, where friends could drop by. When I first arrived the Bushman was there, sitting across from the Salt-and-Pepper Man. The Bushman was nodding and smiling as the other talked of his days in the NHL with the Calgary Flames, and of his qualifications as an engineer, which had gone unrecognized by the authorities who built the Confederation Bridge, the fixed link to Prince Edward Island. He spoke of problems with the police in Quebec. He spoke in French and English and several Native dialects, switching language mid-sentence and gesticulating wildly. He spoke without pause. He was completely delusional. It was thirty-six hours to Churchill, one thousand kilometres straight north from Winnipeg. There were fourteen of us on board, and one of us was nuts. The Bushman smiled and nodded and sipped his coffee. I went back to my room.

Outside, the black prairie stretched out into nothingness, with service station signs and the occasional street lamp dotting the horizon. I looked up, hoping for northern lights. It was cloudy.

The next morning began with a spectacular dawn. A pillar of red shot into the sky from pink cloud that spread across the prairie like breaking surf. The dining car was washed in light. We ordered eggs and bacon, an indulgence, and I was flooded with memories of family camping trips. One crunch of bacon and I could see Dad squinting at the smoke and holding a cast-iron frying pan over the fire, serving up the family joke that, even then, we all knew by heart: "Sunny side up or broken?"

The couple from Louisiana sat at the table across from ours. They'd come all the way north by train and had maps and schedules laid out on the table between their coffee and toast. They were keeners.

I asked where we were.

"Hudson Bay, Saskatchewan, I think," she said.

As it goes north, the *Hudson Bay* veers west out of Manitoba for a short time to get around the big lakes at the centre of the province, Winnipeg, Cedar and Winnipegosis. We'd made that detour overnight, but there were so few landmarks that it was hard to tell if we'd come back across the provincial border yet.

There were skinny spruce trees on both sides of the train. There was snow. There were no hills.

"Looks like Saskatchewan," I said.

We all laughed.

That's when the illusion of camping disappeared. The Bushman was eating breakfast, too. He hadn't laughed. I sensed immediately that what I saw as empty bush was nothing of the sort to him. This was his home—as varied and interesting to him as a downtown street would be to me. There was an entire nation and several days' drive between my home and that of the Louisiana couple beside us, but to the Bushman we were exactly the same. We were Southerners, and he was not.

The Honeymooners came in. She was tall and handsome, with broad shoulders. He was boyish, with a grin, a ponytail and a video camera that he hadn't been without since they'd climbed on the night before. He filmed their walk through the corridor to their room and, with one hand and some difficulty, he filmed the shunting and lugging to get their bags inside. Now he was filming his new bride sitting down to breakfast. She was looking out the window.

The morning turned into a bright, clear day. The train rocked north. We went for hours past trees and snow. Now and then we passed a lake blown solid by the wind, or a silent, winding river. It occurred to me that if I'd picked a point in the forest as we went by, counted for thirty seconds while we steamed along and then picked another point, I would have marked off a huge piece of territory. That chunk of land would surely have been teeming with life, with history and adventure, and it would have represented only thirty seconds of a thirty-six-hour trip.

We stopped in The Pas, Manitoba, for an hour while the train took on water. The Pas is about halfway to Churchill. It's a flat, square town of about six thousand, bordered by an Indian reserve, a provincial park and the Saskatchewan River. The

Bushman and his wife stayed on board, but the rest of us, the seven southerners, set out to see the sights.

We didn't go as a group. No one said so, but I think each southern subset wanted to feel like an independent unit. Dad and I went west. I wanted to find the movie theatre where I'd been to a Hallowe'en-night Stephen King film festival years before. It was all I remembered of my last stay in The Pas. The theatre had been packed—with teenagers who roared and screamed throughout, regardless of what was on the screen. The kids had been more frightening than the movies. It was horrible. Nonetheless, the theatre was a point of reference for me, so we found it, The Lido, in about five minutes. The Honeymooners were already there. He was filming.

Next we came to a bank, which reminded Dad he'd wanted to get some cash from the machine. This was an odd moment. Except for glimpses of our fellow southerners, we had been walking by scenes that could only be part of a northern town. There were Ski-Doos parked in driveways, dogs guarding chain saws in the back of pickup trucks and a case of beer frozen into the ice outside an ice-fishing shack on the river. But once we opened the bank door and found the machine, we could have been anywhere. The ritual was exactly the same as it would have been in a city of three million, two days away by train.

We all got back to the train early. Two new people had boarded with us, both young travellers—a woman from Madrid and a man from Nagoya, Japan. She wore the look of someone using a second language and, while determined, was barely clinging to comprehension. The Salt-and-Pepper Man was telling her about local trade customs on the north shore of Quebec, and about a windmill installation he'd been involved in and why it was like a train. She was leaning forward and listening intently.

I spent the afternoon in the dining car. The steady roll of the train and kilometre after kilometre of spruce forest brought a gentle peace that settled in for the rest of the day. Now and then we'd pass a hunting cabin or a lakeside camp, some lit, with smoke coming out of the chimney. Some had paths leading to the train—clearly the only way in. In one such camp three sled dogs trotted out to meet us. They were already halfway out to the train when we stopped. They walked directly to a window off the kitchen of the dining car and looked up. An unseen hand threw them some scraps, and the train pulled out.

At mid-afternoon we came into Thicket Portage, a little collection of houses with a log-cabin post office, a shed or two, a church, a few cars and logging trucks, and a school. We'd arrived just in time for afternoon recess. A group of about ten kids ran for the swings and the slide. They threw snowballs, something you'd learn to do quite well in Thicket Portage. Just as in the towns of New Brunswick, it was as if the train weren't there. They paid no attention to us at all. I found myself smiling a long time.

A slow groove settled on the car. The afternoon sun was warm. People came and went, or bought coffee and stayed. The cook was taking a break. I asked if she'd been the one feeding the dogs, and she said yes, she always does. "It's just one of my duties."

Jan started cooking for VIA in 1986. She works different routes, but when she's on this one she does a lot more than cook. She also makes beds in the sleeping car, cleans up the rooms and the bathrooms, takes orders in the dining car and looks after anything else that's not getting done. She works six-teen to eighteen hours a day. "I didn't really know what I was getting into when I took this job," she laughed.

Jan grew up in Vietnam. She came to Canada in 1977 after two years in the Philippines. She was sixteen.

"We left Vietnam on the last day before the Communists took over. We weren't sure if we were going or not. My mother sent a friend to get me in school. We grabbed everything we could and left. We had no plan. We flew in a U.S. military plane with no seats, on the floor, on the fuselage."

Jan's family arrived in Winnipeg on August 24, 1977. I asked what she remembered most about her first moments in Canada. She didn't hesitate.

"Cold," she said. "My knees were knocking together, and that was in August! People tried to explain to us what snow was. We'd never seen it before. We couldn't imagine it until we felt it for ourselves. The first time the ground froze over, I stepped out the back door and fell flat on my backside. I didn't know how to walk on ice. I had no idea."

We'd just stopped on a trestle over a raging river, boiling with chunks of ice. We hadn't passed a settlement in hours. It was sunny and warm on the train now, but Jan had told me stories of having to move an entire kitchen's worth of food from one train to another in the middle of a January night.

At the other end of the trestle was a solitary camp with smoke coming out of the chimney and a small signpost next to the track: "Mile 13 Train Station," it read, "Population 1." A fellow looked out the window. Jan waved, and he waved back.

We stopped for an hour in Thompson. Dad and I spent twenty minutes walking along a dirt road leading to the Inco Ltd. mine before we realized we were walking away from town. After that, all we had time to do was reach the GM dealership at the edge of town. I have a picture of Dad in front of it, blowing his nose. We almost had to run to get back in time. When we did, we found things had changed.

The coaches were full. There were kids, teenagers, adults. They were noisily putting things away, talking and laughing. We went to eat dinner and found the dining car was almost full, too. The other of the seven southerners, perhaps sensing some sort of *coup d'état,* had eaten quickly and left.

Almost everyone else on the train was from Churchill. The kids and a few of the adults had been to hockey tournaments, the boys in Snow Lake, the girls in Wabowden. There were others, as well. One young family had been shopping in Thompson. A mother was bringing her daughter back from a basketball camp in Dauphin. Another had been on a course. They all knew each other. They called jokes back and forth between the tables. The teenagers were all piled into the booths in the corner. After almost twenty-four hours of solitude, we'd stumbled into the party train.

Amazingly we, the southerners, the outcasts, were invited.

All I did was ask someone where everybody came from, and I'd started a conversation that was to last well into the night. The guy I asked turned out to be Pete, the father of the young family at the table across from us. Pete looked like he had a twelve-year-old inside that never quite left—the kind who'd play ball hockey with his pals long after the street lights came on. It was Pete who'd taught Kevin, his three-year-old, the knock-knock joke that he told to almost every person in the car. Valerie was Pete's wife, and mother to Kevin and eighteen-month-old Braden. She was fit and pretty, with a kind face, and full of energy—the sort who can keep a conversation going while steering a wiggly eighteen-month-old through a train car so he doesn't whack his head on the edge of the tables. He did, anyway, but he was OK.

They came to Churchill with Pete's job. Valerie was home with the kids. They'd met in Winnipeg and saw Churchill as an adventure. They figured they'd stay a little longer.

"I hope so!" roared Frank from the table behind us. "You guys are my best customers!" Frank had the belly of a baker and the voice of a fight referee. "Hey!" Frank called to the waiter. "Get my friend Pete, here, a beer. Pete, you want a beer?"

Pete did.

"Have a beer," Frank said, full voiced. "Have a beer. Pete, you want a beer? Have a beer."

The waiter brought the beer.

I sat beside Frank, across from Dennis, a social worker, and Fred, who looked up from his hand-held electronic blackjack game every five minutes to say "Huh?" Next to Fred was Shelley. She was petite and full of wit, and was clearly loved by the whole crowd. She wouldn't say what she did for a living.

"I wear many hats," she said.

"I'll tell you what *I* do," boomed Frank. "Go on, ask me! I love my job!"

Frank, as it turned out, ran a restaurant in Churchill. When he found out I'd grown up in Montreal, he invited Dad and me to dinner the next night at his place. "I lived in Montreal, too, but now I live in Churchill and I have a great restaurant. It's the best place in town." His daughter walked by. "Angela—the best place, right?"

"Right, Dad."

"That's my daughter. Her team won two games. And so did my son's. He's half the size of the other guys. He's only thirteen, playing against eighteen-, nineteen-year-olds, but he still won the first star! He deserved it, right? Right, Dennis?"

Dennis, the social worker, had also been the coach. It had fallen to him to name the Most Valuable Player.

"I hesitated," Dennis said. "There are a pretty small group of families with teens up here. I didn't want the other parents to get the wrong idea. He was the best player, but with Frank having come all the way from Churchill, I didn't want it to look like I was showing favourites."

"Did you see that pass, right through those two big guys?" Frank beamed. "They were so mad! I saw them thinking, 'How did that little shit get away with that?'"

Frank, it turned out, hadn't been officially involved. He'd just come along for a trip south.

"March Break," he said.

Thompson, apparently, is the Florida of northern Manitoba.

Kevin climbed into Frank's lap to tell him another knock-knock joke. Frank roared.

Frank proved to be as generous as he was omnipresent. He started with a round of red wine for the table. With the wine came stories, and the favourite topic turned out to be a question that must have been asked countless times on that train: "How did you end up in Churchill?"

Shelley had a good answer: "I was living at home in southern Ontario, taking my first trip west to the Rockies. I bought a train ticket and was going to get on and off. It was summer, the high season, and I had hotels booked and paid for all the way across. Then the train had some kind of screw-up and it was delayed by two days. All my reservations were lost. I had no place to stay anywhere and the whole thing fell through. I went after VIA, but they wouldn't pay for my hotels. All they offered was another trip west. 'But, I can't go now,' I said. 'I have nowhere to stay!' They said I could go the same distance anywhere else they went. 'Where else do you go?' I asked . . ."

The whole gang chimed in for the answer, their voices heavy with resignation.

"Churchill."

"Right," said Shelley. "I came for two days. That was twelve years ago."

Dennis had come to Canada from Ireland. He worked in Regina for thirty years, then on Native reserves in Alberta, before finally heading north.

There is no road to Churchill. You can fly, and flights aren't cheap, or take the train. From Thompson north, the track is laid on muskeg. The road engineers depended on the perma-frost. As it is, there are enormous heaves every summer. The track ends up dished like a shallow roller coaster. Maintenance is tricky. There are only a few weeks to straighten things out before winter returns. That's why the track has thermal cool-ers. You can see them alongside the track—tall white pipes stuck into the ground with a grill around the middle, like the grill on the back of a fridge. It seems cruel that in a land petrified by winter there should be any reason to forcibly cool anything, but that's what they're for. They keep the rail bed frozen and stable in the case of a sudden thaw. At least they're supposed to. Either way, once it leaves Thompson, the *Hudson Bay* never gets above forty-eight kilometres per hour. It takes all night to get there.

"Even then," Dennis said, "it's been two days late. And once I came by and saw two passenger cars in the ditch."

That wasn't a comforting thought for me, but no one else looked particularly worried. The Young Travellers had joined us. They were playing cards with a couple of guys from the Churchill curling team on their way home from a tournament in Thompson. I asked how they did.

"Not so good," the skip said. "We got knocked out after two games."

"Curling?" the Young Traveller from Nagoya asked.

The skip began to explain.

"You sweep the ice?" the Young Traveller asked after a while.

"Right."

"But not too much."

"Right."

"Or the rock goes right through the . . . the . . ."

"The house."

"Right." The Young Traveller nodded, completely baffled.

The Salt-and-Pepper Man sat down to help clarify things. The Spanish Young Traveller moved to another table.

Outside, the night was pitch-black. The train rolled quietly north over the muskeg. The thaw that had us walking with our jackets open in The Pas was quickly heading south. Here they were calling for temperatures of minus thirty degrees Celsius, and that was without the wind. The wind matters in Churchill. There are no trees or hills to slow it down. If it's coming from the west, it comes halfway across the continent from the Mackenzie Mountains. From the east, it has all Hudson Bay as a windup, and from the north . . . well, from the north, it can start from the other side of the pole if it wants to.

Frank was holding forth on a favourite topic: VIA's service in the dining car.

"They should be happy to serve us. I have a restaurant. I know. This is a business. These people should carry the kind of food we want at times like this. Waiter! Bring us some cheese, please. Have you got some brie, what about a nice brie?"

"No, I don't think so."

"Camembert?"

"Just cheddar or Swiss."

Frank made a face that said the waiter might just as well have answered, "Goodyear or Dunlop." He begrudgingly ordered more wine anyway, but it turned out this was a well-practised dance. Frank needed to ask about the cheese so he could bring out his own.

"Now we'll have a party," he said under his breath, and he sent Dennis for his cooler.

Dennis came back, muttering about getting into trouble and being here as a teacher and a chaperone, but Frank wouldn't hear of it. He stuffed the cooler under the table and pulled forth a bountiful harvest: brie, Camembert and chèvre, cold cuts and sausage and, just for the hell of it, more beer.

"Pete!"

"Thanks, Frank."

I hadn't noticed Pete was back until that moment, but there he was. His wife was back in the berth and his kids were asleep.

Frank's kids, however, and all their friends, were not.

"Ask my kids about Churchill," Frank said. "Hey, Angela! The man's writing a book. Tell him about Churchill."

"It sucks."

"See? My kids are honest."

Frank's oldest, a son, is one of the partners in the business, but the other two are teens. They'd been moved from Montreal only four years before, at the peak of their adolescence, from a cultural centre to an Arctic seaport.

"They hated it," Frank said, shrugging, "but it was an opportunity."

Over in the next car, a few of the boys from the hockey team were dyeing their hair. Three were now blond, or almost, and one was green. A slight teenaged girl had been helping them, and came by to wash the peroxide from her hands. Amy told me she was going to move to Winnipeg next year. She said it was too boring in Churchill. I asked her if she was worried about going to the big city by herself. She was sixteen years old. She wasn't worried.

"You have to be honest to stay in Churchill," Shelley said. "I have to face these people every day. Whatever it is, it's going to come out eventually. In the cities down south, you can wear a mask, even with your friends. You have to. Even now, when I go back there I have to get out my mask again. Sometimes it takes me a while to remember how, but not here. It's too close. No mask is thick enough. If I'm feeling bitchy or lousy or horny . . . that's the way I have to be. Tomorrow I'll be different and these people will let me be different. You can't survive here any other way."

The Honeymooners had arrived and were talking with the Salt-and-Pepper Man. He was staring into the groom's video camera and talking. The groom checked how much tape he had left.

Frank bought more wine, four bottles, and pulled a bag of pistachio nuts from the cooler of plenty. Hands reached in from all directions. The thrum of the wheels at my feet and the wine in my head were warming me into a gentle roast. Across the table, my father, who for so many years had been the mask of reason and restraint to me, was laughing heartily and swapping stories like he'd known these people all his life.

Joan joined us. She lives in Weir River,[1] six hours south of Churchill. Joan came to Weir River from Thompson when her husband was transferred. That's how she got to Weir River. The more interesting question, it turned out, was how she met him.

Joan grew up in England and came to visit her sister and brother-in-law on their farm west of Dauphin, Saskatchewan, some twenty years ago. Joan had just extended her visa for six months when the man she would marry came out of the bush. He'd been working on a fertilizer contract. It was Hallowe'en, his birthday. He'd been on a four-day drunk.

I asked exactly how it was that she came to marry him on those particular credentials.

"I don't know," she said. "He was such a big teddy bear. He's six-foot-six. He's very comfortable and down-to-earth. He was the first six-foot-six teddy bear I'd ever met. Besides, on our first date he let me drive his eighteen-wheeler full of canola seed across the border to the States. I didn't even have a licence. I'd never met anyone who would have done that back in England. I knew a month later I was going to marry him, but we had to wait for a break in the fertilizer business."

---

1. Actually, she doesn't. She asked me not to say where she lives, so I chose Weir River because I wanted to tell you about it anyway. It's called Weir River because the Cree fished there using a weir. It's also called Weir River because the people who lived there decided to change the name from the one a bunch of Hudson Bay Railway workers gave it years before. They called it "Asshole River."

Incidentally, there are other stories about the names of the towns on the way to Churchill. At mile 319.3 you come to the town of Luke, named after a mail carrier and fur trader, Luke Clemens. He was related to that Clemens, Mark Twain.

The other name I like is at mile 236—the town of Arnot. It's named after William Arnot, who was in charge of the railway water supply for fourteen years.

"Hey! I've seen you before. You're from around here."

"Arnot."

"Are so!"

Joan was a police officer in Kent before coming to Canada, but when she got off the plane in Winnipeg and stepped outside into the prairie wind she knew right away she'd come home.

She works with young offenders. She says she'd like to go back to school and do a degree, maybe go into politics. It's been seventeen years since her husband walked out of the bush. He works for Hydro now. That has him in the bush for ten weeks at a time, but none of that's dampened her enthusiasm for him. She didn't say that, but I could see it in her eyes. He might just as well have walked out of the bush yesterday.

There weren't many of us there that night who hadn't come out of the bush in one way or another to end up in Churchill. In some ways, most of us were still in it. Dennis came north after he separated from the woman he'd been married to for thirty years. Shelley was the black sheep in a family so domineering she'd had to go to the end of the railroad line to get away from them. Frank had dragged his family there from Montreal for reasons I never quite understood and wasn't sure I wanted to. Either way, he was still hearing about it four years later, and probably would for the rest of his life.

"Everybody makes mistakes," Frank told me.

It was nice to think that, mistakes or not, we might each find our own Joan one day, waiting for us at the edge of the bush, thrilled at who we are just because she hasn't met us before.

Pete was getting up to go. Frank offered him another beer. "Come on, Pete, have a beer."

"I should go."

"Have a beer."

"I've gotta work tomorrow, Frank."

"Pete . . . have a beer."

"Well . . . ," Pete said.

You're already out of the bush, Pete, I was thinking. You've come out, she was waiting for you and you found her. Get to bed with your beautiful wife and children and be happy. Don't stay out here with us. Don't go back into the bush.

He was still deciding.

I decided to lead by example and said my good nights, leaving my father taking in one of Dennis's northern tales, leaning back and grinning a slow grin.

It was colder than it had been. Snow and frost had blown into the gap between the cars. As I went through the doors, the wind howled away the noise of the party. My bed took a few more minutes to warm up than it usually did. I looked out the window hoping for northern lights.

It was still cloudy.

~

Dawn on the March barren lands is an anomaly—it's the only moment of colour in the day. The *Hudson Bay* arrived in Churchill at 8:30 a.m., the last kilometres of approach giving way to a monochrome world. There was white snow, grey ice, black rock and a few shades in between. Earlier, the sunrise had given us a sliver of pink, but it was gone in less than half an hour. After that, we were on our own.

The *Hudson Bay* was scheduled to spend twelve hours in Churchill before turning back for Winnipeg. The next train came two days later. Dad and I, typical southerners, planned only to stay the day, to spend our cash from the bank machine in The Pas, and go. This had earned us much grief from the

Churchillians the night before. The Louisiana couple, after the disappointment of the thaw that had gripped their trip so far, saw the endless snowdrifts and immediately decided to stay, if only to test the ton of clothing they'd brought with them. As they stepped from the train and hit the frozen ground, the first prickle of cold hitting their faces, they smiled, wide-eyed with satisfaction.

My first impression was of noise. Ski-Doos, vans and taxis raced their engines against the cold as family members waited for their arrivals. Children cried as parents packed them into the train station. The sign hanging from the eaves creaked like a rusty swingset, and above and around and beneath all of that sound blew the howling Arctic wind. It whipped at our legs and our necks. Snow flew as if from a snowblower, horizontal and hard, scraping our faces and turning our heads.

The skyline in Churchill is dominated by the concrete grain-handling facility of the port. It is seven storeys tall and as long as a football field, and stands like an abandoned garrison against the driving wind.

Once the Canadian Pacific Railway began hauling prairie grain east and west in the late 1800s, farmers soon found out what railroad contractors had known all along. The CPR and its directors were not particularly charitable. They had spent decades creating a monopoly, and they intended to use it. Prairie farmers sent up a cry for an alternative. It was the cry of the voter.

The first prime minister to respond to that cry was Wilfrid Laurier, as part of his election platform in 1908. He even began construction on a line heading north to Hudson Bay in 1910. Apparently, though, that wasn't enough. Robert Laird Borden was elected prime minister in 1911, and following the lead of railroad-building politicians before him he continued work on the line without any real idea where it would finish. The first choice was Port Nelson, south and east of Churchill, but still a heck of a long way north.

Port Nelson was well-positioned on Hudson Bay, at the mouth of a delta, but it wasn't the most practical choice if the desire was to have the line finished in anything resembling a reasonable length of time. Before track could be laid and a port built in Port Nelson, the workers on the Hudson Bay Railway had to build a seventeen-span steel bridge, as well as—get this—the island the bridge was leading to. They were well on their way in this task, having created a body of land that was about 185,800 square metres, when Canada decided to fight the war in Europe in 1917 instead of remodelling the nation's Arctic land mass.

Canadian National formally took over the railroad in 1923, waited three years and then worked on the project for two *more* years before it brought in an expert who decided the line should end in Churchill, instead. Nine years later, it got there. The first shipment of prairie grain finally left Churchill for Europe in 1931, seven elections and six prime ministers after it had begun. It seems safe to assume that most of the prairie farmers who'd first voted for Laurier back in 1911 were either retired or dead.

Churchill as a port has never fully lived up to the expectations those farmers held for it. Somewhere in the order of twenty ships went through in 1999, but that was a banner year. Because of the unstable track, the Hudson Bay line can only carry grain cars that are smaller and less efficient than those used further south, and because the port is so far north, the shipping season is only two months long.

Looking at the port when we arrived, it was hard to imagine anything ever sailing there. Hudson Bay was a jagged and endless jumble of ice. Five kilometres from town and you might as well have been five hundred, while the grain elevator, the monument to commerce, prosperity and connection to the south, lay as grey and lifeless as any other rock on the horizon, only bigger.

Dad and I had no plan for our day. We put on every stitch of winter clothing we had, left the rest at the train station and set out into the freeze. A dogsled went by on Kelsey Avenue. I suppressed the urge to hail it like a cab.

At the Visitors' Centre we felt examples of the furs that had first opened the economy of the region to European traders. There were fox pelts, beaver, wolf, lynx and snowshoe hare. The hare pelt was lovely—long, thick and warm—especially warm. Men died for furs in Churchill's early days. I could understand why.

We also heard the sad story of Henry Hudson, who came to the area seeking the Northwest Passage in 1610. It's appropriate that they named the bay after him. His crew mutinied and set him adrift on those very waters. I could understand why.

We watched a video, too, on the history of the region, and of the Hudson Bay Company's giant installation across the Churchill River—Prince of Wales Fort. Like the railroad, the project went a little long. The Hudson Bay Company started building in 1731 and spent the next forty years getting it done. The fort had walls twelve feet thick and held forty-two cannons. It was intended to protect the company's valuable fur holdings against the French, but after all that, when the French came knocking, the fort fell without a shot. That was in autumn of 1782. Winter was on the way. The British simply gave up. I could understand why.

Then, as if none of those lessons of history meant anything at all, scientists and developers caught up in the excitement of 1957 as the International Geophysical Year, decided that Churchill was *the* location for a rocket base specializing in atmospheric exploration. The Churchill Research Range sent thousands of rockets blasting up into space before it closed in 1985.

It opened again in 1989, running launches for the National Aeronautics and Space Administration (NASA) and the Canadian Space Agency.

Lately, the rocket range has been renamed SpacePort Canada. An organization called Akjuit Aerospace is adding launch facilities for larger rockets, with the intention of eventually operating as a commercial polar spaceport.

It was hard enough to get comparative information on the viability of the seaport. How Churchill will ultimately fare as a spaceport is not something I feel particularly qualified to predict.

The Town Centre was impressive, and somewhat space-station-like as well. It housed, in one connected building, the elementary and high school, the library, gym, bowling alley, curling rink, hockey rink, hospital, dental clinic, indoor playground, cafeteria and much else. Walking through it, we passed preschoolers, elders, high-school kids and many others in between, going about their daily rounds within each other's circles.

In larger cities, schools can end up cloistering students from the rest of the community. They spend their days with the kids in their year, with their teachers and parents. Here, there was no choice but to mix. Gangly teenagers had to wait for the basketball court while a line of five-year-olds took their turn. The little kids aimed, tongues out the corners of their mouths, and, one after one, missed wildly. One shot missed by so much that it rolled out the door and down the hall. The teens said nothing. Most likely, they had been in the same line at that age themselves.

On the upper level of the Town Centre, we came across a line of windows overlooking the bay. There was a bench to sit on.

It was precisely what we had seen on the train on the way up. In fact, the line of windows was shaped very much like the windows of a train car. I remembered how locals and tourists alike sat watching from the train, taken in by nothing more than the endless land. It was much the same looking at Hudson Bay. The light and snow were constantly changing with the wind, and there was something enticing about it, the way a waterfall pulls you to its edge, drawing you closer than you really ought to be. The ice was savage. It lay menacingly silent, quite capable of swallowing the entire town. Those windows would act as a safe viewing area for the bears in fall and the whales in summer, but they worked with the ice in winter, too. "This is close enough," they were saying. "You don't really want to go out there, anyway."

We did go out there. We walked across the rock to the edge of the ice. The windows were right: That was far enough.

We stopped in the library and saw what was becoming a typical use pattern for the town—kids of all ages, seniors, workers and tourists. I resisted the urge to use the computers to send an e-mail south.

The museum had ancient Inuit carving, traditional tools and kayaks, and a stuffed muskox the size of a very large motorcycle. I jokingly stared into his eyes through the glass but found that, somewhere deep in my brain, I still half expected him to charge, even though he'd been dead for fourteen years. I suppose my cerebral cortex has a few ancient traditions of its own.

We wrote postcards and bought souvenirs. We went back to the Town Centre. It was late afternoon. The Young Travellers arrived and we agreed to set out together for a lounge the curling skip had told us about on the train. He said it was a good place. On the way out we passed the library and saw the Salt-and-Pepper Man talking to a very busy librarian.

The sun was low enough that most of the streets were shaded. The traveller from Japan had a full-length goosedown parka with a fur-lined hood. He'd bought it in Nagoya and had worn it all the way here, but he didn't have any gloves. It was easily minus thirty degrees Celsius, with the wind as steady as ever. He kept his hands tucked into his sleeves, the cuffs sticking out like empty tubes.

The lounge was no further than two city blocks. Halfway, my father's cheeks and nose had gone white. We ducked into a souvenir shop. Frozen tourists were apparently a common sight—the clerk didn't even look up. We pressed hands to faces, tucked hands back in sleeves and set out again.

The lounge was the last building on the street. I grabbed the door and pushed. We spilled in like ice cubes, and I understood instantly why the curling skip had recommended it. He was the bartender.

"Hi!" he called, grinning. He was behind a panelled bar loaded high with booze. Four men huddled together on barstools, still in coveralls and outdoor clothing, speaking low and smoking, with several empty glasses on the bar. A fifth burst in with icicles on his moustache, his face pink with cold. "Jesus!" he cursed and threw down his mittens. The others nodded.

We ordered coffee and tea, stayed till we were warm and suited up for the big two-block trek back. We were expected at Frank's place for dinner.

In Frank's parking lot I saw Margaret getting out of her minivan. I'd met her that morning on the train. She'd grown up in Kuala Lumpur, a huge, hot, dense and crowded city. Then, when she was a teenager her family moved to Thompson. Margaret said she and her sister cried every day for two years.

Now she was smiling. She held the door for us at Frank's place and followed us in.

It was a subdued version of the dining car from the night before. There was a large, boardroom-style table at the centre of the room. Several locals chatted around it, while Frank boomed out greetings from the counter.

The Louisiana couple came in. "We need more clothes," she was saying.

"Maybe so," he said. "I think we oughta rent a truck."

They took the table beside the Honeymooners, the Young Travellers sat with us, and the Salt-and-Pepper Man was in the corner. All present and accounted for.

It was just over an hour before the *Hudson Bay* would head south again. I'd watched it pull away to turn around after we'd stepped off that morning. It was a desolate feeling to see it leave, even knowing it would be back hours later. I had no urge to stay any longer.

The Spanish Young Traveller was leaving. The Honeymooners were staying, and, a surprise, the Japanese Young Traveller was staying.

He was shy, but resolute. "I will stay in Churchill two more days."

The food warmed us for the hike back to the station. I had Arctic char, just because, before we piled on clothes again, thanked Frank, waved goodbye and opened the door to pressing cold. I looked back one last time. At the Honeymooners' table, his camera was jammed. She was smiling. As the blast of cold from the open door crossed the room, the Salt-and-Pepper Man looked up, and his eyes were momentarily clear.

Cloud cover was blowing across the sky. The darkness was inky black. The wind howled off the bay, the savage ice only steps away. The warmth was gone before we'd left the parking lot.

Something caught my eye from a home on my right. The windows were lit from behind snowdrifts piled up high in front. I could see pictures hung on a living room wall. They were photographs of young children. I looked again. They were Pete's children, the ones we'd met on the train. Then, at another window, I saw Valerie. She was in the kitchen doing dishes and singing to herself.

Pete wasn't there.

I looked again while Dad walked ahead, covering his cheeks.

Valerie put away another plate.

Where was Pete?

I couldn't wait any longer.

The *Hudson Bay* idled, as promised. Our beds were already made. I lay down for a moment and fell asleep with my clothes on, still slightly cold.

Dad woke me later. He'd been in the dining car with the crew.

"Look," he said, pointing through the darkened room to the window.

A turquoise-green veil hung over the sky to the west. It shimmered in layers, lifting and falling, as if it were breathing. Northern lights. We watched in silence as our train crossed the barren lands.

Winnipeg, Manitoba

~

DAD AND I HAD A LAYOVER in Winnipeg on the way back east from Churchill. It was a chance to enjoy a good hotel breakfast and do what we'd been doing for the past five days, anyway: read, write and talk. It was pleasant, but with only a half day to spend there, and except for the March wind, it could have been any Canadian city.

Back in mid-August, though, it was not the same story. When I was heading west across the Shield with a family of four, Winnipeg had been an oasis. It was people and civilization and, finally, something to look at other than rocks and trees. Arriving in Winnipeg was not only a pleasure; it was absolutely necessary and not a minute too soon.

I know, I sound like one of the Complainers I was complaining about. I can't help it. Even for me, for whom the most wretched experience would have been just another good yarn, the last few hours of the Canadian Shield were like the last few cold peas on my childhood plate. There might not have been much left, but there was no telling how long it would take to get through it.

There was also a drunkenness that set in just before the prairies. It was as if the train itself were punch drunk from

having been pounded with granite for the better part of a day. We passengers had no choice but to wobble along.

The one compensation, for those still unwobbled enough to notice, was the tunnels. There were five of them in those last hours before the prairies. They roared out of nowhere and threw us into darkness, the throb of the engine louder from the reverberation of a closet of rock.

The first one was a thrill. We were in the Dome. My son happened to look ahead. He saw it coming and yelled, "Tunnel!" We all turned just in time to see the mountain's jagged maw open up and swallow us whole. The darkness was very sudden, very thick and lasted three or four seconds. The whole car came alive afterward, with stories of what we'd seen, which was, after all, nothing—but still, it was fun. We talked about it a good ten minutes, until someone with a guidebook announced the next one was coming in forty-five minutes and everybody cheered.

That was midday. Four Shield hours later I strolled through the coaches. It wasn't pretty. Most people were asleep, and once again, flung in all directions with limbs strewn about the aisle like trees after a tornado.

Everything suddenly went black. I wheeled around and yelled "TUN . . ." but we were already out of it.

Nobody else noticed.

But they noticed the prairies. The transition from Shield to prairie is almost the opposite to the experience of going into a tunnel. The once mighty and ubiquitous rock shrinks into the earth and all but disappears. The trees taper off so fast that it seems they're running away. The view expands exponentially. The engine's dull throb floats off into the distance, the ride becomes smooth and quiet, and everyone, everywhere on the train is bathed in light.

VIA's timing was thoroughly theatrical on this one, too. Our *Canadian* arrived at the Manitoba border just as the sun had begun to dip below the rocky hills of the Shield and cast shadows over the tracks through the black spruce trees that lined the way. Then, within a matter of minutes, there was literally nothing that would cast a shadow for kilometres.

Even in the sunshine, most of the Shield had been a variant of grey. The lakes were slate. The sky was ochre. The stone was charcoal. Now we were bathed in colour. The wheat fields waved a sunny hello. Canola smiled blindingly, and for one glorious instant we floated past a field of sunflowers that was soaking up the almost-horizontal sunlight and belting out yellow with an intensity that was nearly enough to make you turn away.

No one did.

In New Brunswick, I'd felt betrayed when I saw a shopping-mall parking lot after going through the woods for a few hours. It felt like the fantasy of escape had collapsed. Here, as we rolled into Winnipeg, seeing houses and farm equipment and cars and trucks and people and even a shopping mall was a comfort.

Escape is fine, I guess, if you can still remember what it is you're getting away from. Somewhere in that last four hours of the Canadian Shield, most of us had forgotten.

We even saw wildlife: A deer bounded through the back-yards of a distant subdivision, hurdling chain-link fences as it went.

Then we came to Winnipeg's enormous rail yard—the wrong side of the wrong side of the tracks. There are odd-looking bits of rail gear lying around and decrepit boxcars covered in graffiti, some on tracks as rusted as the cars themselves. There was a railroad junkyard, with smashed-up bits of freight and engine parts all piled up and clambering over each other.

There was also a vacuum car. I don't know if that's what the Railroaders call it, but that's what it was—an enormous hood at the end of a flexible duct that skims along just above the track in front of the car. It's a vacuum cleaner to pick up the stray bits of grain that fall out of the thousands of cars Winnipeg sends on their way, all full of Canada's major export resource.[1] You wouldn't think a transport medium that hap-pily flushes its toilets onto the tracks would be worried about a few seeds, but it's not a matter of cleanliness. The vacuum car picks up what is a big draw for large animals that don't tend to fare well in their encounters with trains.

It's not that the railroads are particularly animal friendly, but a deer and a train can make an awful mess and delay shipments, too. It's a problem all over the prairies. Deer are the most com-mon candidates. They see tracks, smell grain, and because, by definition, they're not the ones who were hit by the train last

---

1. That's grain, not peat.

time, it's hard for the lesson to be passed on. They think they've found one very long food trough.

It could be that the deer we saw bounding through the backyards was the missing link in deer mutation. Maybe she finally understood the horror of it all and was getting the hell out of there to tell the others the awful truth.

A few minutes later we saw a wild beast who looked as though he'd evolved far enough to give any train a run for its money. There was a dirty brown hare hopping menacingly out from under the chain-link fence around the train junkyard. He had long pointy ears and the kind of nasty, slow-moving lope of a neighbourhood thug. He looked at the train as if it were a slug on his lettuce, and for a minute I thought he might take a run at us. Instead he sat up, snorted and loped off under a handcar.

Our service manager told us we'd have thirty minutes off the train in Winnipeg. That may not seem like much after as many hours, but we clung to it as all we had. Passengers poured out of the station, all heaving enormous sighs of relief, faces basking in the late-day sun.

The other delight of Winnipeg is that there is something to see when you get off the train, even if you have only thirty minutes. For one thing, there is a rail museum right in the train station with old cabooses (there isn't any other kind any more) and ancient club cars and steam engines. But even when you've raced through that, which we did, you can still go across the street to The Forks.

The Forks is a kind of civic centre at the confluence of the Assiniboine, the Red and the Seine rivers. The area has been a meeting place for First Nations people for thousands of years. Native people could still meet there today, but if they did, they'd have to meet in the riverfront market and shopping mall, and be surrounded by tourists.

There are waterfront shopping malls in Toronto, Halifax, Vancouver, Boston, New York, Baltimore and Philadelphia and, doubtless, many other places. They house the same stores in the same buildings that sell the same things, mostly to tourists who come from places with exactly the same water-front complexes at home. The strange thing is, people don't go to their own waterfront complex unless they have visitors from out of town. There must be something about being away from home that creates an appetite for tie-dye shirts, wind chimes and fudge.

The shops in The Forks sold wind chimes and fudge, and postcards and T-shirts, but I was in no position to be fussy about my extra-railroad entertainment. Besides, there was also a real fruit market, a real seafood store[2] and, against type, tons of people who looked like real Winnipeggers just hanging out.

The boardwalk along the riverbank was delightful. There were buskers, walking paths and a tented amphitheatre with free concerts. We wandered around the boardwalk and down by the river. We climbed the observation tower. It's only seven floors up, but in Winnipeg that's enough to see a long way.

Then, just as my legs were beginning to stop lurching me this way and that, it was time to get back on the train.

In the 1880s Winnipeg was the gateway to the West on the Canadian railroad. The Shield might have been the biggest obstacle, but once it had been conquered (if, I wonder, still feeling a little wobble-drunk, it actually was) the prairies were wide open and waiting.

---

2. Doubtless capitalizing on Winnipeg's proximity to so many oceans.

Settlers poured into the prairies by train. In Ontario the railroad was built between existing towns, most of them on the shore of a lake or river. From Winnipeg west, the towns and cities treated the railroad itself as the river. It brought work, food, mail, visitors, services and, mostly, people who'd be looking for yet more work, food, mail, visitors and services.

These days the railroad brings a river of tourists, twenty-one cars' worth at a time. They pour out of the train, buy fudge, wind chimes, T-shirts and postcards, and pour their way back on board.

That river's slowed in recent years. Cal noticed that. He started with VIA just out of school, as a porter in 1977. After a while, he took a few years off, and when he came back, things had changed.

"Mostly the service," Cal said. "It was more geared to tourists."

Cal was part of a new crew that boarded with us in Winnipeg. I found him and his colleagues in the dining car after they'd made the beds, served the dinner and cleaned up, and things were quiet for a while. Cal was obviously proud of his railway and his country, and was happy to show it off to people from elsewhere, but he would have liked, at the same time, to help out more of the people who lived along the line.

Gail felt the same way. When she listed the highlights of her years with VIA, she talked about bringing people into their cottages on Lake of the Woods or helping an Innu hunter load a caribou carcass into the baggage car.

Gail and Cal had been on the same training course back in 1977. "It was supposed to be a summer job," she laughed.

"I liked the travelling," Cal said. "It's not the nine to five." He paused. "Still," he went on, "nobody plans a career as a porter."

"It's twenty-two years for me now," Gail said, "so I'm thinking . . ."

"Maybe a buyout," Cal said.

"Might be time."

"Right."

They talked that way, finishing each other's thoughts, the way couples do after years together—the one who wanted to leave and the one who'd come back.

I'd noticed something about the way this crew worked at dinner. Two people waited on each side of the car. Cal had been on our side. He was in his late thirties—a handsome Black man with a strong build, smooth on his feet and very articulate.

Cal worked with Luke. Luke was somewhere just past fifty and built like a linebacker. He puffed as he worked, and by the time he brought us dessert he was sweating.

VIA's sleeping-car service is called *Silver and Blue*. VIA has a lot invested in train elegance, which, considering the passengers have a lot invested in the cost of the tickets, is fair enough. The rooms come with little toilet bags for each passenger, with shampoo and soap and towels. Snacks are served in the Bullet Lounge in the afternoons, and coffee and juice are there for the asking at any time of day. But it's in the dining car that the crew really put on the show. The tables have fresh flowers and linen napkins, and the food usually more than measures up. That night I'd had fresh Manitoba pickerel for the main course. It was as sweet and delicate as any I'd had. The vegetables were fresh and not overdone. I was delighted.

I also liked Luke, but the whole *Silver and Blue* thing wasn't really sticking with him. He was a Railroader. There was no resentment in the way he served us, and anyone could see he was working hard, but when the menu offered a choice of

Tricolour Orzo or *Cajun Frites* Luke asked if we wanted "rice or potatoes?"

My guess was he'd have been a lot more comfortable heaving a caribou carcass into the baggage car.

What caught my eye, though, was that he'd asked only a few of us if we wanted the *Seasonal Fruit Medley* or the *Flatbread Pointes with Brie* ("Grapes or cheese and crackers?"). Cal had covered the rest. Luke would come out and serve the entrees (Clunk!), but before he could move to take another order Cal would swoop in and do it for him.

They never talked about it that I could see, or even exchanged looks. Cal just did it.

That evening I was talking with Cal and Gail in the dining car. Luke trundled out of the kitchen, heaving a sigh of relief at being finished. He was walking right past. I took out my tape recorder.

"You didn't ask Cal what he did when he wasn't working here," Gail said, leading me away, and I saw that I wasn't going to be talking with Luke, no matter what, but Cal had a good story.

Cal was an athlete. He'd run track and field at university and then gone to the Winter Olympics with the Canadian four-man bobsled team, first in Calgary in 1988 and then in Albertville, France, in 1992.

"We won something in bobsledding in Albertville, didn't we?" I asked, not noticing how easily it was now "we" that had been to the Olympics, although my memory of the events was a little fuzzier than his.

"We came fourth," he said, and then I remembered. It was a heartbreaker. Canada did very well in Albertville. It was our best Winter Olympics yet. We won medals in downhill skiing, freestyle skiing, speed skating . . . Bobsled was held later in the games. The press was all over the four-man team. It was practically a sure thing.

They missed the medal round by .04 of a second. Four separate races of 1.6 kilometres each, and the total difference in the Canadians' time and the time of team ahead of them was .04 seconds. You can't even say "four-man bobsled" in .04 seconds.

"Back then it felt like a huge burden," Cal said. "It felt like failure. But it goes away with time."

Cal probably had a pretty healthy sense of time. Between the train, the bobsled and his family, he almost had no choice in the matter.

His father, Cleveland, grew up in Weymouth Falls, Nova Scotia, south of Digby on the French Shore. He served in the army, ended up in Winnipeg and joined the railroad the very day he got his discharge. Cleveland started with the railroad as a porter, when it was still impossible for a Black man to do anything else. But after things changed in 1964, he worked his way up to steward, waiter, sleeping-car conductor and, finally, service manager on the *Canadian*. Cal's uncle, Fletcher, worked for the railroad, too. He ended up in VIA's training department in Winnipeg.

"I worked on the train with my dad for a while," Cal said. "He was my manager."

I asked what that was like.

"Aw, it was OK," he said. "It was just like being at home! No, he gave me lots of room. I think he was worried that if we hung around together too much I'd start to hear all the stories about him," Cal went on, to laughs all around.

Gail was from a railroad family as well, with two uncles in the head office. One of them went out of his way to say hello on her first day. She was impressed, until he took her aside and said, "Listen, if you hear anything about me from these guys don't tell your aunt."

She did hear. She didn't say anything.

But she had a few stories of her own. The first woman to work on the train was hired by Canadian National in 1975. She had quit by the time Gail joined two years later.

"There was no such thing as sexual harassment. You put up with it back then. You put up with each other. If somebody did something to you, there was nowhere to turn because most of the time they were your boss. You learned pretty quickly what to do. One guy grabbed me one time, so I grabbed him back. 'You wanna feel this?' I asked. I was still holding on, tight. 'Next time you grab me it'll be ten times harder.' No problem after that."

"So," I asked, "when did that stop happening?"

"Stop happening?" Gail asked.

More laughs.

"Let me put it this way," she said. "The old-timers aren't the worst thing about this job. I can handle them. Right now my problem is the way the system is set up."

"Yeah," Cal said, "I think maybe it's time for me. Time for a change. I don't know what, but I'll get to something else before too long yet. It's the lifestyle, eh? It jams you up."

Later on, I had to rewind my tape three times to hear where it happened, but right here, where I'm interrupting him, Cal and Gail both took the other point of view. They did it throughout the conversation: two lines saying they would be leaving and two more explaining why they wouldn't.

"We live and work in the same environment and that's what you get attached to. It's the people you meet and seeing the country," said Cal. "I never get tired of a prairie sunset."

"Or watching a thunderstorm from the Dome," Gail put in.

They looked down the car to the back of the dining room and suddenly turned again.

"Headquarters can cut as far as we can go, and we won't be able to stop them, but every year they seem to cut another job," said Cal. "That's my biggest cry. They seem to disregard our aging workforce and the workload they put on them. We work four days straight through now, with no layovers. Seventy-five hours straight is not uncommon. It's hard for an aging worker."

He caught me off guard. There was no question the work wasn't that hard for him. He was in terrific shape and probably would be for a long time. I wondered if he was feeling guilty about wanting to leave because of his family's history. That didn't seem to fit either, though. He loved the train, and he loved serving customers, but something else was bothering him.

Cal looked to the back of the dining car again, and then I saw what had prompted his tirade. It was Luke. He was in the booth at the back, his head back, big square chest rising and falling. He was fast asleep. Not old enough to retire and stuck in a job that was getting younger all the time.

"Look at him," Cal said, "he's got thirty-three years. What more do they want?"

I had to go through three sleeping cars before I got back to ours. Back in our bedroom, my wife was reading. She put down her book and smiled when she saw me. The children were asleep in their bunks. I kissed their foreheads and straightened their covers as the train rolled west, the prairie sun finally dipping below the tracks.

Unity, Saskatchewan

I WASN'T EXPECTING MUCH in Saskatchewan.

Everyone talked about the mountains. I was ready to be swept away by the mountains, to forget reality and get dizzy in the thin air and the soaring heights. The prairies were just supposed to be flat and dull and long—a forgettable buildup to the real stuff the next day. I wasn't expecting slow, breathtaking beauty and warmth. I wasn't expecting romance, and I especially wasn't expecting either from the TV at the foot of the bed.

Strange things happen when you're heading into a prairie sunset. The upper bunk, for example, in a train bedroom stops feeling cramped or claustrophobic. Instead, a cozy feeling sweeps over the bunk and it becomes not unlike a tree fort. There's a net to hold you in, mostly, and the upper bunk becomes a sanctuary of sorts—above the trials of the day.

The lower bunk, because it's sheltered by the upper one, becomes very cozy as well, and it has an added feature: a window. I'm sure if you asked, the service attendant would make your bed so that your feet were toward the wall and your head was by the window. That would be nice. When you woke up, you could roll onto your back and look at the sky. But if you don't say anything, when you come back from your

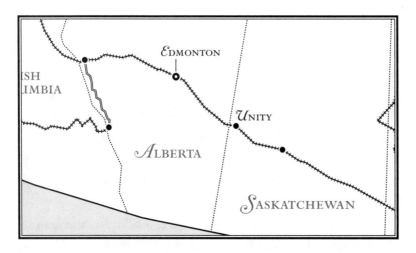

evening trip to the dining room or the Bullet Lounge, your bed is made and your head is at the wall and your feet are by the window.

I do not have a TV at the foot of my bed, never have and never intend to get one, but on the prairies, at dusk, in a bedroom on the *Canadian,* the window at the foot of your bed becomes exactly that—a large and very generous TV. The program it shows is one of the most beautiful things I have ever seen. The oranges and yellows blend and mix, not at all unlike the northern lights, except the colour of fireworks. The farmland scrolls lazily by. With that poignant railroad soundtrack beneath and the tantalizing possibility that the images before you could actually be evolving into something even more beautiful, the effect is both soothing and intoxicating, and it lasts and lasts and lasts.

The night we left Winnipeg, the sunset started somewhere west of Portage la Prairie. There were no mountains or hills to get in its way, and since we were on a train barrelling straight into it, that sunset wasn't only spectacular, it was almost endless.

I am thoroughly convinced of the beauty of what I saw that night. It was, without any embellishment on my part, unforgettable. I am also aware, however, of the temptation to mix in a romantic element and try to make it sound even better. Just as, years ago, I was able to turn a horse ring in Truro into a nightclub in Las Vegas, I'm now resisting the temptation to turn a train bedroom in Saskatchewan into a villa in Tuscany, a château in the South of France or even a honeymoon suite at Niagara Falls.

I wonder about the nature of that temptation. Some of it, I'm convinced, comes from a nationalist sentiment. I know, the state has no place in the bedrooms of the nation, even if they're on the nation's national railroad, but there is something enticing about the Canadian content on the prairie-train TV. It doesn't need to be cropped or edited or puffed up or subsidized. It is Canada—not plain, predictable, dull, flat, polite, insignificant Canada, but deep and luscious and inviting Canada, romantic and passionate, perfectly happy to stay that way for the entire night or until you go to sleep.

This particular brand of nationalism is something we enjoy here probably more than we know. In Canada, the scenes most compelling to the romantic heart are the same ones that, without romance, make us want to take our vacations somewhere else.

A blustery January afternoon in Nova Scotia, for example, is not a big draw for honeymoon travellers, but with the right person, all of that mist and fog and crystal ice can, instead of turning lips blue, bring them together in the most tender and unhurried way.

A walk in the early December snow is much the same. It could be just about anywhere in Canada, but a tree-lined city

street is best. The storm that had commuters late and freez-
ing that morning by nightfall has time drifting as slowly as the
snowflakes that feather through the halo of the street lamps.
Snow-lined sidewalks gather you together. A traffic light at
the corner is nothing but an excuse to lean against each other,
waiting, kissing, missing light after light, waiting and kissing
some more.

I'm starting to smell horse manure.

At any rate, back on our train, crossing the prairie in the
sunset, the reality of the evening was more than enough. My
wife and I were lying close, bathed in the warming light of the
heartland. We'd had wine with dinner. We had no worries of
getting anywhere that night, or missing stops or paying bills,
and our children, both safely above us, were sound asleep and
seemed to be ready to stay that way for most of the night.

I'll keep the rest of the evening to myself, except to say
that when the light finally began to fade, I looked out and
saw we were passing a town called Unity, Saskatchewan.
With the reality of nationalism and romance all in mind,
I turned away from that most private of public broadcasts
out our train bedroom window, kissed my wife, thanked
Canada and said good night.

~

I met Roy and Delores at breakfast. Roy had been born in New
York. He was slightly short, with a round head, permanently
wiry hair that would not do anything it didn't want to, and
glasses with black plastic frames. He wore a white-collared
shirt with an undershirt showing through, and sported a pocket
protector in the breast pocket.

"I fell like a sack of bricks the moment I saw him," Delores said.

She was from Dublin, working in London, England, when Roy was a GI, just after the war. The streets were full of youth and exuberance.

"I was just finished my shift at the department store and he walked in looking for perfume for his girlfriend."

"I just didn't know that girlfriend was you." Roy smiled.

"We celebrated fifty years this year," Delores said.

They sat across from us in the dining car. They chatted, side by side, but it was clear they would rather have been sitting across from each other, looking up between bites to gaze deeply. Now and then Delores would reach across and play with Roy's hair.

"We really fell in love on the trains of London," Delores went on. "Roy was stationed out of town and I would take the train out to see him. Then, after we'd moved to New York and decided to come to Canada, we took the train. Up along the Hudson River to Montreal, then west."

"On this track," Roy jumped in.

"And in a dining car just like this," said Delores.

"I took a job at the university," Roy went on. "I thought I would hate it, but that was a long, long time ago."

"My mother didn't believe I'd married a professor," Delores said. "She thought I was lying. Right up until the day she finally met him."

They'd been on holiday in Montreal.

"So romantic," Delores giggled.

"Yup." Roy blushed.

"But I still love the prairies best."

"Yup."

And then, after at least five minutes of silence while we ate, Roy said "yup" again, and Delores kissed him.

Roy and Delores reminded me of another Canadian railroad love story. I heard it from a trombone teacher.

John Swallow grew up on a farm in upstate New York. He learned to play the euphonium in his high-school band. The euphonium is a smaller member of the tuba family, and as its name[1] might suggest, its sound is mellow and euphonious. John was a brilliant player, but those were the war years and the era of the big band, which use only trombones in the low brass. There were no jobs for people who played the euphonium, and plenty for those who played the trombone.

He ended up, among other positions, as trombonist in the Chicago Symphony Orchestra under the legendary tyrant Fritz Reiner, and later, in the New York City Ballet Orchestra and the New York Brass Quintet.

He was a tall man, handsome in a craggy way. He wore the big, boxy double-breasted suits that had been popular during the war years. I met him in the mid-1980s, when those same suits were enjoying a revival. I think that was a coincidence, but I'm not sure. He had a strong sense of style. I remember peeking into his teaching studio to find out what was making the insistent, high-pitched buzz under the slow, melodic passage an undergraduate student was playing. It was a tiny, portable, battery-operated electric shaver. "Here," Mr. Swallow was saying, while he did his chin, "try that part again."

Still, he was an excellent, dedicated and sought-after teacher. John Swallow taught trombone at three of the most prestigious

---

1. The name is also the source of many cheesy band jokes. For example:
Question: How do you get a hold of a euphonium player?
Answer: Youphonium.

schools in the United States: the Manhattan School of Music, the New England Conservatory in Boston, and between the two, at Yale University in New Haven, Connecticut. I met him at Yale.

There are many train lines connecting those three cities, but this isn't a New York commuter train story. It takes place in Canada, on the prairies.

When I began studying with Mr. Swallow, he was just about to celebrate his sixtieth birthday. There were five of us studying with him at Yale that year. His wife, Wendy, invited us out to their house for a party.

We saw all the requisite sights for trombone students: his studio, his photographs. We heard stories of the devilishly hard trombone concerto he had commissioned from the composer Gunther Schuller. ("He asked how high he could write for me. I told him high F. He wrote an F sharp!") And we admired the ratty old armchair that, it was claimed, had once belonged to Tommy Dorsey. We all sat in it.

Wendy was delightful to us all. She happily played the part of surrogate mom and filled our stomachs with more and better food than any of us had enjoyed in weeks, but she was no hausfrau. She was charming, elegant and poised.

I noticed a poster on the wall advertising a tour of the Sadler's Wells ballet company of England. I asked about it, and a smile crossed her lips.

"That," she said, looking at John, "was how we met."

Wendy had been a dancer with Sadler's Wells. She'd grown up in the Royal Ballet School in London and joined the professional company when she was just seventeen. John was a freelance trombonist in New York. When the ballet came to tour North America in 1950, it contracted an orchestra from New York and John got the gig.

He remembered Wendy from that tour. She remembered him. But John was already married. Nothing happened.

Two years later the Sadler's Wells company came back across the Atlantic. They were to tour, by train, from New York north to Montreal, west to Vancouver, south to Los Angeles, east to Atlanta and back up north again. It was a long tour. The orchestra contractor hired John again. Wendy was still dancing with the company. John, in the two years since the last tour, had been divorced from his first wife. He was available. Wendy was there. It was a long tour. There were long, romantic interludes on the train with nothing to do between shows. There were sunsets and peaceful dawns and long nights on the train with lots of time and nothing to do. It was a long tour.

But Wendy was engaged. Her fiancé was a dancer. He was on the train, too.

It was a long tour.

"It was a great job," John told me. "We got to play the Met in New York for a month, and then we left for the road. The dancers and the crew and the orchestra each had their own separate cars. We were not supposed to be together at all. The only time we saw each other, at first, anyway, was in the dining car, across the room from each other."

The sparks were flying from the moment the company arrived. Those sparks had an entire month in New York to land on something flammable. By the time the company pulled out of Grand Central Station in New York, the fire was fairly crackling. But even that wasn't enough at first. Wendy and the other

dancer had a date chosen for their wedding when the tour
ended. The entire company were thrilled about it. They were
talking about the day, about the party they'd have, about how
lovely the couple would be, about the music, the dresses, the
flowers. Performing groups are notoriously protective and
incestuous societies. Rituals and mores and values and traditions are all set up among the group members, and anyone
who disrupts any of it is not only not welcome; that person is
destroying something very dear to everyone present.

When that disrupting person is disrupting a wedding
between dancers, that person is evil incarnate.

That's not how Mr. Swallow described it. All he said was
"It was very controversial."

It's the only time I can ever recall John Swallow saying anything that could be described as understated. He talked of
secret meetings at night, of curtained berths and private
rooms, but he wouldn't give any more detail than that.

"My grandchildren might read this," he said.

I would like to know the precise moment Wendy crossed
back over that international dating line and decided she
couldn't go through with the engagement and that she had
to be with John. She was still engaged when they left Winnipeg
for the haul across the prairies. John told me that much. He
also said that when they reached Washington, D.C., the
engagement was off. There were a lot of very romantic spots
on the itinerary between Winnipeg and D.C.—Banff,
Revelstoke, Vancouver, San Francisco, New Mexico, the
Carolinas, Chesapeake Bay . . . so many possibilities.

Still, my money is on Unity, Saskatchewan.

John and Wendy did live happily, and they did have the joy
of new, tingling, overwhelming love catching fire on a train

going through the Rockies, but that was also a mixed blessing. The rest of the company were not keen. If any of them
had thought of John as anything but a crook and a scoundrel
(an American one, at that) before the train left Washington,
D.C., they certainly didn't after. Icy disapproval would have
been the rule.

It was a long tour.

That tour ended in January 1953. John and Wendy were
married that April. Wendy left the company and stayed with
John in New York.

John Swallow ended up playing principal trombone with
the New York City Ballet Orchestra for forty years, although
he never went on another ballet tour and never on another
orchestra tour by train. Airfares became cheaper, highways
better, trucking more available and affordable. But that was
all right. The prairie sunset had performed its magic once,
and that was enough. John loved Wendy to the end, and she
him. I could see that in 1983, when she looked at him across
the room at his sixtieth birthday party. She died six years later,
very suddenly, of cancer. Wendy Swallow and her contraband
trombonist were married thirty-six years. They had three children, three grandchildren when Wendy died (now eight) and
still no regrets.

~

I woke at 5:30 the next morning. That TV/window at the foot
of the bed was equipped with an almost-impenetrable vinyl
blind, but I hadn't pulled it. I didn't want to close anything out.
So the sun exploded onto us as we were rounding a corner,
when, for a moment, the window faced slightly east.

It was even more beautiful than the night before. We were beside a huge open valley, with dewy greens that made me thirsty just looking at them.

The usual tourist reactions proved, as usual, futile. Grab the camera!—no camera is big enough. Tell the others! Tell them what, that the sun is rising? I found it odd that the easily packaged moments of Canadian beauty are the ones at the extremes: the most easterly or westerly, the highest, the farthest south, the busiest . . . Western Saskatchewan isn't any of those. It's the middle. It's stunningly beautiful in a way that is too wide or too loose or not packaged enough to fit in a brochure.

Oddly enough, the middle of the country looks best at the extremes of the day.

I stayed awake, quietly watching the gentle hills roll by my feet for I don't know how long, until my family woke up.

A slow breakfast is a wonderful thing. It's denial of a sort. A slow lunch is slothful, because it throws away the rest of the day, and when it's finally over you might as well just keep eating and call it dinner. But a slow breakfast is luxury itself. There is always another thought to play with, always more coffee to drink, always one more memory to linger on and turn over in your mind, like a candy on your tongue. Whatever that was last night, in the dark beneath the royal blue, with the orange fireworks slowly fading away, whatever that was, a long breakfast tells it to pretend it will stay for just a little bit longer.

Breakfast finally ended when we crossed the Battle River, just inside the Alberta border. The trestle is sixty-one metres up at the highest point. The valley stretches forever to the north, as big as a courtship promise, and the span goes all the way from last night's flights to this morning's gentle landing—close to ten football fields long.

We watched each tie tick by.

The romance of the prairies was still shining, like a glow that stays around long after the sun has set, but even it couldn't last forever, and with all of us watching for any last moments of stolen beauty, real or imagined, the credits started to roll.

Jasper, *Alberta*

~

WE WENT TO THE DOME right after breakfast and were already late. We were still well east of Edmonton, and wouldn't be in Jasper until the early afternoon, but no matter. The Dome was full, and it was no longer the Theatre of Contentment, but the Theatre of the Very Excited. The dreamy romance of the prairies and the Alberta hills had been tossed aside. The car was full of laughter and conversation. Some passengers had imported muffins and coffee from the dining car and had eaten breakfast in the Dome just to get the best seats. The mountains were coming. Maybe they'd be huge and imponderable and even more impossible to absorb than anything we'd seen so far, but these passengers had been in absorption training since they'd left Toronto and were more than ready to soak up all they could.

Bill and Margaret were in the front row. They were in their early seventies, on a retirement holiday from their home in Toronto.

Bill grew up on a farm in Groundlet, Saskatchewan. One of his childhood neighbours was an engineer for the local train to Saskatoon. Bill remembered waking up to the sound of the locomotive starting up each morning.

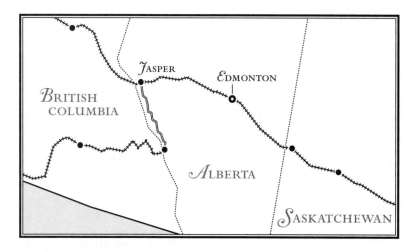

He took that same train when he left home as a young man for college in Saskatoon. He got a part-time job as an upholsterer with a furniture maker and later became a supervisor. From there he served in the air force, in Abbotsford, British Columbia, but the lights of the big city still called, so in 1951 he took the eastbound overnight to Toronto.

His furniture experience got him a job, but he wanted more excitement. He moved on to—guess what?—a job as a yard switchman for the Canadian Pacific Railway at Union Station.

"I had to make up the trains, decide which cars went where, passenger trains and boxcars, and send them off on their way on the road."

I expressed a certain amount of despair at the notion that the person deciding which cars went with which trains in one of the country's largest rail yards might have qualified for his position simply by his abundant skill with a chesterfield, but that was just the beginning for Bill. Within six weeks he'd left the railroad and put his air force experience to work with a job with AV Roe working on the Arrow, Canada's pioneer supersonic jet. He wasn't making seat covers for the cockpit, either.

"I guess I was what you'd call versatile," he laughed. "What the heck, eh? The only way to learn is on the job."

Bill stayed eight and a half years at AV Roe. He loved the work, and the community. He organized the company's bowling team. Margaret's brother-in-law signed up, and one night he brought along Margaret. That's where she met Bill. They were married and, soon after, they bought their first house just west of Toronto.

"It was close to the airport, where Bill worked," Margaret said. "It was a lovely place."

The two of them glowed just remembering the time. They were young and full of promise and surrounded by people just like them. Then, one February morning, Bill went to work and found that his own prime minister, John Diefenbaker, had decided to shut down the factory and the better part of the entire Canadian aviation industry in exchange for some American missiles that never really worked.[1]

What the heck, indeed. Bill and Margaret watched as the planes were destroyed, the factory closed, and their entire circle of friends at AV Roe upholstered the Boeing Corporation of Washington State with the bulk of Canada's young high-tech talent.

"All of Margaret's family were in Canada, and we'd just bought the house, so we decided not to go, but we were the only ones," Bill said. "Boeing came calling and everyone else

---

1. This analysis is a little glib, if I do say so myself. The other side of the Arrow debate was that it had cost six times its American equivalent, and that no one, not even the Canadian Air Force, was prepared to buy it. Canadians love it because it was something we did better than the Yanks, but others say the Arrow was lucky to have been martyred and immortalized the way it was.

we knew went south. It was a very hard time. For a while there, I worked at anything I could find."

For someone who had spent his life learning on the job, it meant that he'd learned all he was going to about supersonic flight in Canada. There were no more jobs at all. Bill ended up going back into the furniture business and finally finding work at DeHavilland, working on airplanes that were content to stay well below the speed of sound.

Bill and Margaret enjoyed a happy life, anyway. They seemed like the kind of unflappable people who'd learned to be that way by flapping so much that it no longer worried them.

"What the heck," Bill said again. "We got here somehow."

I found Brenda in the galley. She was the chef who'd made the delicious pickerel the night before and some customized Mickey Mouse pancakes for my kids that morning at breakfast. She said she loved cooking on the train. She'd been a chef for fifteen years and thought this was one of the most fun jobs of all. She talked about seeing the country and meeting people, but as she was chatting and smiling, I kept noticing the big, very full pot of soup that was boiling furiously just behind her back.

"Yeah," she said, "that could happen if we hit a jolt. But it hasn't. The worst is chopping with the knife. If the train stops suddenly and you're chopping fast then—oops—there go your fingers."

That hasn't happened to Brenda either, and it's obvious she doesn't worry about it.

She's in that tiny kitchen from 5:00 a.m. until 11:30 p.m. every working day. If there's any danger, she just doesn't think of it. Her worst experience, so far, was her very first trip. The grill in the galley gave up and she had to do all her grilling in the train's other kitchen, four rail cars away, carrying sixty people's breakfasts, lunches and dinners back and forth through sleeping-cars and coaches, all day and all night long.

"After that," she said, "it's been easy."

Before coming to VIA Brenda spent a year cooking for one hundred workers at a gold exploration camp at Bathurst Inlet on the shore of Arctic Ocean.

"I would have stayed there a long time," she said.

I asked what happened.

"The price of gold dropped and they cut back everything. There's just a skeleton crew up there now. But it was great— great money, let me tell ya. Great money and nothing to spend it on."

I asked how much she had left.

"Not a penny," she smiled. "But that's OK. I like it here, too."

"Here," at that point, was Viking, Alberta.

My friend Ron once told me about going home from Viking when he was a teenager in the mid-seventies. He'd been vis-iting family and took the train back to Montreal. His rela-tives dropped him off at the station in the early morning. The train appeared on the horizon, just a cloud of dust. As it got closer and closer, he began to realize what an enormous and powerful thing it was. It sent dust for kilometres in all direc-tions. The locomotive was well over twice Ron's height. The train was nineteen cars long. It roared into the station with the engine rolling so far beyond the platform that he began to wonder if it would stop at all. When it finally did, he took a moment to look all the way to the front and along to the back, just to take it in before he climbed on board and saw that he was the only person getting on in Viking, Alberta, that day. This enormous machine had stopped just for him. He climbed aboard with a grin as wide and proud, I'm guessing, as the one he wore when he told me the story twenty-five years later.

As we pulled into Edmonton, the service manager announced a fifteen-minute stop, and told us that if we were going to get off, we should stay next to the fence at the edge and watch out for the people working on the train. I wondered what it was about Edmonton's VIA employees that could be so threatening.

The train took on water in Edmonton. What with showers and all, they were going through a lot of it. Each car had a tank to fill, and the way the stop was configured, the station itself was at the very front of the train, with the platform running some twenty-one cars in the other direction. That's a long way for a small number of workers to go, connecting twenty-one separate hoses to twenty-one separate water tanks in a fifteen-minute stop. Edmonton's VIA managers have found a twofold solution. They use young workers who like to work fast anyway, and they give them Rollerblades.

The platform was very narrow, with only enough room for the golf cart–like vehicle used to bring less mobile passengers back from the back end of the train. The golf carts didn't go that fast, but still, the drivers weren't old, and the way they drove, I figured they'd only just been promoted from the Rollerblades. No one got run over, but there were some close calls. In fact, despite the service manager's warning, most of the passengers strolled blithely down the middle of the platform and took their chances. That could have been their way of making Edmonton's train station an interesting stop.

There were many beautiful train stations built in Edmonton, but most of them have been torn down. Edmonton used to be less a whole city than two halves that didn't quite make a whole. One side of the river had money and the other side had fun, but each side had its own train station—Canadian Pacific Railway and Canadian National, respectively. CN's was a grand château downtown and the CPR's was an elegant, sloping number in Strathcona. When a rail bridge across the river finally joined the two in 1913, the CPR built another station, a classic flat-roofed stone monolith on Jasper Avenue.

You'd think the provincial capital that views itself as far above the arch-rival city to the south would have cherished its oh-so-holier-than-not-just-thou-but-all-of-Calgary heritage train stations—a sign of true standing in the history of this country. It didn't. CN pulled down their station in 1966 and replaced it with an office tower. The CPR (to much opposition, but obviously not enough) ripped down theirs in 1978. The old CPR station still stands in Strathcona, but VIA, in the spirit of train station construction, decided to throw up an imitation strip mall with skinny platforms out beside the airport to save the trouble of going all the way into town. So now, to thousands of tourists, the lovely city of Edmonton is a strip mall at the end of a runway, which is memorable only because of the possibility of being flattened by water monkeys on Rollerblades or geezers in golf carts.

Calgary is quite happy with that.

Still, even the drab station couldn't take all the impulsiveness out of the people there. Two of the New Yorkers who had complained their way across the Canadian Shield were now clearly more at home. They darted back and forth, holding hands and giggling, playing chicken with a golf cart. Another couple whooped as they stepped in the path of a speeding rollerblader and were momentarily spun around like square dancers.

The only place that was remotely peaceful was the cab of the locomotive.

Steve, the engineer who was joining us in Edmonton, said it would be fine if I climbed up for a look.

The first thing I noticed was how high it was. It was a long climb from ground level, which was somewhat comforting. In Toronto, the suv has become popular largely because, on the highway, it's taller than the cars. It feels like a winner.

The second thing I noticed was how spacious it was. It was a General Motors Diesel Locomotive, 3,600 HP, with two big, comfortable bucket seats (Bill, did you do these?), reams of dials and buttons and graphs, a fridge, a hot plate, a door to the engine itself, and lots and lots of room.

Steve started driving a train in 1972, as a switcher in the Calgary yard. In 1991 VIA hired him away from CN specifically to be an engineer on the main line. It was the highest job available to a passenger engineer.

"The only real problem on this job is boredom," he said. "Passenger trains have priority in every situation on this track. Freights have to vary their speed, compensate for the size of the load and generally think a lot more. I don't have to worry about any of that. It's their job to get out of my way now. I just go straight through."

I admired his confidence, but it did occur to me that he might think about it, too.

It was a funny thing. At one point, just west of Edmonton, I left an alarming little memo in my notes.

"I'm aware of a funny kind of fear," it says. "Every now and then it occurs to me that we might be about to hit something and there would be absolutely no way of knowing it was coming and nothing at all I could do about it."

I told myself that Steve wasn't *that* bored. He just needed a little boost now and then. In 1986, just about where we were at that time, at least one train engineer seems to have needed a boost. He didn't manage to find it.

I didn't know many of the details of what had happened in Hinton, Alberta, in 1986. I asked a few VIA employees about it, and as kindly as possible they brushed the question off.

The tourist brochures talk about Hinton, Alberta, as the Gateway to the Rockies. They talk about its impressive elevation on the long railroad climb up to Jasper. They talk about its winter sports, such as cross-country skiing, its canoe trip facilities in the many nearby provincial and national parks. They talk about how close it is to the Park Gate at Jasper National Park.

They don't talk about the one thing Hinton, Alberta, is remembered for most.

It was February 17, 1986. VIA's train No. 4, the *Super Continental,* was on its way from Vancouver to Toronto and Montreal. It was made up of two 1,750-HP General Motors Diesel Locomotives, a baggage car, a Skyline car, two sleeping cars and a coach. In Jasper it had joined up with train No. 6 from Prince Rupert. That added another baggage car, day coach, dining car and sleeping car. Like our train, No. 4 was carrying tourists from Europe and the United States, a few holidaying Canadians and, significantly, in the days just before extensive service cuts, many more Canadians simply using the train as a way to get from A to B.

Unfortunately, some of them only got halfway there.

That day, train No. 4 was rolling easily down the grade from the foothills just sixteen kilometres east of Hinton. The 122 people on board had just been treated to the spectacular sights of dawn in the Rocky Mountains. Many were having breakfast as they left Jasper, and they were settling in for the gentle ride to Edmonton. The train passed through Hinton and through a signal giving it the go-ahead to proceed at seventy-two kilometres per hour around the coming bend. As the locomotive came around that bend, the engineer saw any Railroader's worst nightmare: the 114-car CN freight train No. 413—less than one-sixth of a kilometre away on the same track and travelling at full speed towards an inevitable head-on collision.

As it is with everything about train travel, even train wrecks have been wrapped in the mist of nostalgia. Folk ballads tell of endless heroism, of last-minute leaps to safety, of thrilling speed and noble sacrifices. Of the ninety-three people who survived the crash at Mile 173 near Hinton, I would venture that none of them would describe what memories they have of that morning as nostalgic. What feelings the other twenty-nine people experienced in the horrific seconds before they died will never be known.

CN's freight No. 413 weighed 11,340,000 kilograms. It was powered by three General Motors locomotives and was pulling forty cars of grain, seven flatcars of steel sewer pipe, forty-five cars of sulphur, seventeen cars of corrosive and flammable refining chemicals, a heavy rail-construction car and a caboose.

The power of the collision was astonishing. One loaded freight car was catapulted forty-five metres. It pulverized one of the VIA train's observation domes when it landed. The steel sewer pipes—1.2 metres wide and 15.2 metres long—were scattered like matchsticks. The sulphur cars ruptured, pouring a sickly yellow all over the scene.

The front-end crews of both trains were lost. The freight train not only crushed the VIA engine, it literally stopped the passenger train on the spot and trampled it. The freight locomotives, inexorably pushed by their enormous load, climbed right over the VIA engines and split them open like loaves of bread. Thousands of litres of diesel fuel spilled and instantly ignited into a wave of fire fifteen metres tall. The freight locomotives surfed that wave and climbed on over the passenger train, crushing first the baggage car and then a passenger coach carrying twenty-one people. What was left of the pulverized car was awash in flames as the wave of fire roared through both cars with enough heat to weld the steel carriage to the rails.

The freight locomotives kept pounding through the passenger train, flattening two more cars before they stopped just short of the observation car. The grain cars piled up behind them, strewn and stacked, sometimes three deep.

One passenger saw the freight coming. She was in the cherished front seat of the Dome and screamed, "Oh, my God! There's another train on the track!" just before the impact. No one else had time to look. In the back of the first coach that was crushed and seared by the freight locomotives, miraculously, three young men survived. They were buried in the twisted rubble of the car, their clothes and skin ignited by the wall of fire that followed, but then, seconds later, the fire was doused by a river of grain flowing from the ruptured freight. They swam through the grain, climbed out through a crack in the toppled car's roof and scrambled to safety.

Survival, though, brought horrible sights. They, and many others who lived, managed to save some passengers, but had to stand helpless as many others perished before their eyes.

There were some blessings. The corrosive chemicals were in cars that were far enough back on train No. 413 that they

were not among the seventy-six that derailed. The spilled sulphur could easily have caught fire and produced sulphur diox-
ide fumes that could have taken more lives, but it didn't. The
conductor of train No. 413, who was in the caboose and survived the crash, radioed for emergency help and, within half
an hour, emergency crews began to arrive.

The disaster unleashed another destructive wave, a wave
of political blame that raced through the Mulroney government, the Canadian Transport Commission and the most
beleaguered of them all even before the crash, VIA Rail.

No one will ever know exactly what happened in the cab of
CN's train No. 413 once it passed under the block signal that
should have stopped it on the Medicine Lodge siding. Answers
are still hard to come by all these years later. "Someone fell
asleep" was the best I could get out of the VIA staff, but I have
no doubt the truth gets passed between Railroaders as regularly as trains pass Mile 173 today.

"No one wants to talk about that," one fellow told me. "We
all lost too many friends."

The Canadian Transport Commission conducted an inves-
tigation. They concluded, in relatively little time, that human
error had caused the disaster. The freight engineer could have
avoided the crash. The braking system on the CN locomotive
was a "dead man's switch," a brake that works by default: The
train won't move unless the engineer is pressing it. If the engineer had lifted his foot even for a moment, the freight would
have stopped. Why he didn't is a secret he took with him to
the grave.

One day, when I called the number Cal had given me for
his home in Winnipeg, I heard a voice that sounded like his on
the other end of the line, but it told me that Cal wasn't there.

It turned out to be Cleveland, Cal's father. We chatted about the railroad and about having a son follow in his footsteps. This was a full year after I met Cal, and he still hadn't quit as he'd said he might. Eventually we got around to the Hinton crash, and Cleveland told me that he was the service manager on that train. Working in the sleeping cars, he would have been far enough back that his car wasn't crushed. Cleveland was charming and, long retired, quite willing to talk about almost anything, except Hinton.

"It was one of the last runs of my career," he said. "It was hell."

He would have heard the sickening screech of metal through metal and felt himself thrown into the very thing he and his colleagues, if they admitted it, would have feared their entire working lives. He would have been there, on the side of the track with the bodies and the twisted wreckage, watching as lives slipped away.

"It was hell" was enough.

Whether any monstrous freight trains were lurking near Hinton or anywhere else on our trip, I'll never know. Steve, our engineer, for all his complaints of boredom on the job, must have stayed alert. We went through Edson, Hinton, the Park Gate and into the splendour of the Rocky Mountains without incident.

The mountains *were* splendid—stirring, cold and huge. At times I would forget they were there and then look with a start to see them still watching. Other times when I looked at them, I felt an eeriness that took a while to place. It was like waking up in the darkness beside a sleeping loved one, and realizing that after all the years you've spent together, you don't really know this person who shares your bed at all. There will always be parts of her that stay secret, and parts of you that will always be alone.

I'm not sure if that happens to the town of Jasper when it wakes up in the middle of the night, but it knows these mountains as well as anyone can. It also knows the trains—the ones full of people and the ones full of coal. Jasper is both a gaudy tourist town and a hard-working mountain railroad town. The sound of a passing freight is a constant. The people who live there are far more likely to jump at silence than the hoot of a whistle.

But trains aren't the only way to get there. There are buses, cars, pickups and rvs bringing people there almost every day, just to look around. They're not coming for the town. It could be nothing more than a burger joint and a gas station. The real draw is the mountains and the rivers and, to a certain extent, the fact that every other tourist train and bus stops there, too.

Still, the town is a town. People live there and work and send their children to school and meet in the grocery store and, likely, complain about the tourists. It's a real place with a real life, and it's the rail industry that allows it to hang on to any kind of integrity at all. The trains don't care if it's high season or low, or if the skiing's good. They're too busy working.

The train station in Jasper reflects that. It's a tourist stop, full of pamphlets and gewgaws, but it also sees enough traffic to get a little dirty and employ the kind of harried staff who aren't rude, but let you know you're not the only person in the world.

To the people on our train who were convinced that they were, in fact, the only people in the world, this was a mild irritant. They tapped their feet, paid redcaps to hump their bags and paraded away as if once they'd left, the place might collapse without them.

It didn't collapse, not even after I tried to squeeze out the quaintly narrow doors with a mule train's worth of bags strapped to my shoulders. We were down to eight bags, plus the ubiquitous laptop, but they were not the kinds of bags that you'd want to carry for more than a long city block, especially Jasper's city blocks, which are very, very long.

Jasper is even shaped like a train. It is long and skinny with stuff to look at on both sides: mountains on one and the Athabasca River on the other. Each of those long blocks of the town is like a car. There is a "dining" block, an "outfitters'" block and several "hotel" blocks, which range from first class down to coach.

The residential blocks are the *real* coach blocks. That's where the only affordable accommodation is. People may hold a variety of jobs in Jasper, but if they have any unrented space in their house during the summer or the ski season, they're throwing money away.

We stayed in the cheapest place we could find. Naturally, the train station is closest to the more expensive hotels, so the most important people in the world don't have to walk very far. The rest of us, that is, my family and I, had to schlep all the way to the other end of town. My daughter even asked if I would carry her on my shoulders along with all the bags. After a second block, just to bring a little quiet back to the freight-rumbled streets of Jasper, I relented—giving new meaning to the words "Travel Atlas." If Jasper were a train, I started thinking, I wanted to get off.

Part of the trouble was the altitude. Jasper starts way up there and gets higher. We were lowlanders, and our paltry little heart-and-lung systems let us know in short order that short breaths would be all we were getting for a while. We huffed to our B & B, thudded onto our beds and huffed back into town.

Then we went to a family restaurant and ate like hogs. Either we had been doing nothing but sitting and eating on the train for three days and we'd got used to such gluttony, or we had just expended huge amounts of energy simply walking up the street, or maybe both. By the time we got back to our place, we'd both eaten and exercised enough to fall asleep.

Except that we didn't, not right away. Somehow, the long, slow climb to slumber was fraught with derailments for all of us.

It wasn't what I'd pictured when we began to talk about this trip so many months earlier. It wasn't the idyllic family peace of mutual joy, of united thought and purpose, of happiness and love and fulfillment and pride. It just wasn't. It didn't matter that we were almost across the country, or that we were surrounded by awesome mountain splendour. Right then, we were squished into a small room with hard beds in a little house too far from the train station, and we were all tired and grumpy and not falling asleep.

I did finally fall asleep, but I woke again in the middle of night. I sat up and found I had to steady myself against a wall, not because the floor was moving, but because it wasn't. I wasn't sure I liked not being on the train. I felt lonely. I wondered if that was the one thing none of the crew had told me yet—the reason they all talk about quitting the railroad, yet never do. On the train, you don't need to figure out where you are, or even who you are. There's no point in asking. The second you do, the answer isn't true any more.

As a system, it works fine, unless you get off.

I crawled along the bed and looked out the window and up. The stars were gleaming and a freight was rumbling by, probably had been all night long. My family were folded up around me, not clobbered by sleep but held in by it, wrapped tight in arms and blankets, bound so tight that nothing inside them was even close to getting out.

I looked out the window again and my eyes began to adjust. I could make out the shape of the mountain behind the house, a still, giant Buddha. I waited, listening for answers, but none came—just a cool breeze rolling down from the peak and spilling in the window, saying, "Go back to bed."

Banff, Alberta

⁓

No train runs directly from Jasper to Banff. There is a highway. There are things to see along that highway, but if you don't have a car you must travel by what the rail fans of the world surely think of as the Transportation Antichrist: the motor coach.

We were overfed, underslept losers from the cheap end of town who were schlepping, yet again, our load of bags the length of Jasper's endless blocks to the bus stop. It was early morning. We were already tired. It was no time for any pretense of Higher Transport Thinking. We took the bus.

It wasn't just a bus. It offered a guided tour and a stop to visit the Columbia Icefields along the way. The driver gave a mostly interesting commentary on what we were seeing as we went—animals and raging rivers and dizzying peaks that used to be wild and threatening and distant and are now, well, a bus ride away.

That threw us into an interesting conflict in position. From the moment we'd arrived in Jasper, we'd taken our place at the bottom of the great hierarchy of tourists. The number of high-end accommodations, attractions, food and sheer beauty that we were not going to able to enjoy was simply staggering. By

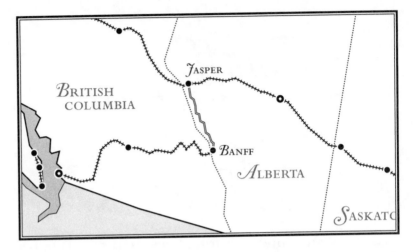

consequence, then, whatever we did see had to be thought of, by tourist standards, as pretty mundane.

It wasn't. The Columbia Icefields inspired great awe. The patch of ancient, rotting ice we stood on, the Athabasca Glacier, was huge and stunning. It was truly the edge of wilderness. All of the glacier we could see was still just a toenail on the sprawling sea of ice that stretched out beyond the peaks above us. At the same time, it was no more wild or inaccessible than a suburban shopping mall. Get on the bus and there you are. The Athabasca Glacier was also speckled with "SnoCoaches" (buses) that were specially designed not to destroy it any further than they and their ancestors already had. They drive up the glacier and park in rows just like at a shopping mall. You get out, walk, gawk and get back on. If the SnoCoaches are too wild for you, you can still eat in the food court in the Icefield Centre[1] and, as it were, window shop.

---

1. Bus terminal, Brewster tour ticket office, Glacier Gallery, licensed cafeteria, souvenir shop, themed clothing boutique, information desk, thirty-two-room Icefield Chalet, wheelchair accessible, smoke-free.

It's true that there were helicopter tours and backcountry expeditions. But in the shopping mall of the icefields, they were Holt Renfrew. We were in the Bay.

What distressed me most was this: The one force that had proved itself even more awesome than all of the ferocious natural power around us *was* us. We, the proles in the buses, simply by our numbers and our money and our outrageous consumption, were clearly winning the war. Time after time, even in the protected regions of Canada's oldest national parks, we saw glaciers that used to be bigger, rivers that used to be wilder and, mostly, places that used to be completely out of reach to anyone even remotely like us.

The day we went from Jasper to Banff, there were lots of people like us—busloads.

I found myself secretly cheering when I heard of losses to our side. The week before, a mudslide had erupted out of a flash flood from the mountains just outside town. Sudden rains hit the mountain above and a quaint little creek took about five minutes to rage itself into a torrent of mud more than four and a half metres deep. It closed the Trans-Canada Highway for an entire day.

Hurray!

Our driver also told us about the time, years ago, that a herd of elk loitering in the highway in the middle of the afternoon ran him right off the road. No one was hurt, but it wasn't an isolated incident, and the park authorities didn't like that sort of thing, so they eventually built a series of animal overpasses to accommodate the wandering herds.

Elk are everywhere in Jasper and Banff—much like squirrels in other towns, except they're as big as other towns. They've also, apparently, adapted quite well to tourist-town life. They walk around, eating the lawns, the golf course, the hedges, flopped here and there like enormous hood ornaments. They give birth all over the place and attack you if you come close to their calves. In Jasper, when it's rutting season, the males have been known to charge just about anything that moves, sometimes right down the main street if they feel a threat to their chances with a potential mate.

Tourists pummelled by rutting bull elk! Hurray!

There have also been, over the years, hundreds of people mauled by black bears and, in recent months, a few who have fallen victim to cougar attacks. People died. I'm not going to cheer, but I'll bet the elk would.

However, those incidents are anomalies at best. For the slice of wilderness sandwiched between two tourist towns, two railroad lines and two very busy national parks, the war is largely lost.

Along with the victory of the human proles in this place has come the victory of the bus station. The train station in Banff, once a gateway to beauty and the public cathedral that a train station should be, is now a restaurant, gift shop and boutique that is a long way out of town. It handles train passengers when they happen to arrive, but it wouldn't care if they didn't.

The bus station, by contrast, bustles. It's run by the Brewster company, the name on almost every bus in town. The Brewsters started in Banff in 1892 with a dairy operation that sold to the Banff Springs Hotel. Successive generations of Brewsters worked as hunting and fishing guides. Jim Brewster gained the distinction of being the first cottager in Jasper after he built a chalet on Maligne Lake in 1925. I'd like to report that a cougar ate him for that, but I don't think that happened—another of nature's lost opportunities.

It was Fred Brewster, however, who really put the bus on the road. Fred was working for the family dairy in 1916 when it dawned on him that the real money wasn't in milk, but in *cheese*. He bought the first overland coach and started giving sightseeing tours. The company's never looked back, not even to see the site where, in 1883, three rail workers building the Canadian Pacific Railway line stumbled on hot springs at the base of Sulphur Mountain, which is on your left.

Al, our bus driver, in his even and well-modulated tones, welcomed us to Banff. The Brewster terminal hummed with people and vehicles coming and going, but he took the time to talk to us about the place.

"Development's gone a little crazy here in the past ten years," Al said. "There are hotels everywhere and no place to stay. You wouldn't believe the number of young people I bring here every week. They come looking for work and end up sleeping five, six to a room while they try to find a place. Sometimes they never do find anything. They end up going back home. Getting a job here is easy. Getting an apartment is impossible."

I thanked myself for the planning I'd done before the trip. I had booked us rooms in a dormitory.

Only as a last resort, though. The first thing I did, months before, when I began to plan our accommodations, was to call the Banff Springs Hotel. I love the Banff Springs Hotel. I had been to Banff a few times as a student, but never to the hotel. I'd only marvelled at pictures. There is one view, you probably know the one I mean, that literally took my breath away the first time I saw it. It is shot from the south, with the grand old spires of the hotel rising from the evergreen forest. It almost looks as if the building's towers are mountain peaks themselves. I just couldn't imagine a more thrilling building in a more thrilling place.

The Banff Springs Hotel was the first of CPR's truly grand hotels, built in 1888 by the CPR's president, William Van Horne. It was initially put there for a very pedantic reason: The grade into the Rockies on the early transcontinental runs was so steep that, for the steam engines of the day, pulling up a full dining car, along with all of those well-heeled passengers, was right out of the question. The CPR's first solution was to build restaurants in Field and Rogers Pass. The train would lumber up the hill, everyone would get off, stuff themselves and get back on, presumably creating even greater braking problems on the way down the other side.

Van Horne himself, in addition to being a brilliant manager, financier, practical joker, conjuror, painter and architect (he had a significant voice in the design of the hotel) was a legendary eater. At Covenhoven, his palatial estate on Minister's Island in the Bay of Fundy, the kitchen was filled with every delicacy and never, ever out of stock. In their excellent book on the history of the CPR, *Lords of the Line,* authors David Cruise and Alison Griffiths tell the story of a guest at Covenhoven who had to extend his visit because of a storm. After three extra days of Van Horne's hospitality, the man exclaimed, "Thank God the storm let up! I was beginning to hear the angels sing. Van [Horne] was determined to feed us all to death."

That business of riding up a hill and eating proved to be enormously popular. It wasn't long before Van Horne decided to give his bloated guests a place to sleep off their indulgence, and charge them for it, too.

Van Horne selected the site for the Banff Springs Hotel himself, and like him, it was a huge success. There is a statue of him at the centre of the vast circular driveway at the entrance. The statue stands on a stone pedestal that puts his giant head at a height of at least four and a half metres, and he is pointing as if issuing a command, which would be either "Work!" or "Eat!" depending on your reasons for addressing him.

The hotel took eighteen years to build. It has 770 guest-rooms, including a Presidential Suite with eight bedrooms, a library, a lap pool, a private glass elevator[2] and a grand piano. There are seventeen restaurants in the hotel, fifteen specialty shops, a twenty-seven-hole golf course, a bowling alley, boutiques, beauty parlours, ballrooms, boardrooms and a spa with fifteen private treatment rooms and an indoor waterfall.

When I knew I'd be going through Banff, a successful author bringing the best there could possibly be to his family, I naturally assumed we would stay at the Banff Springs Hotel. I even assumed that we would stay there gratis, seeing as the public relations department would be eager to pounce on the vast possibilities for increased profits presented by the publicity they would receive from this book.

It was difficult, however, to alert the necessary agents to this impending boon when they wouldn't return my calls.

I tried. Oh, Lord, I tried. I phoned, I faxed, I e-mailed, I— yes, I did—I begged.

Nothing. The Banff Springs Hotel did not think there was any need to give me a room. In fact, the Banff Springs Hotel did not have a room for me, paid or not. I was eventually told, in essence, that it might be possible for me to stay there alone, for a minimal charge, in a very small room somewhere near

---

2. This is the kind of oxymoron you can live with when you're president.

the stables, if they still had stables, in the middle of November, if there weren't any conferences booked.

At the time of writing, by the way, the cheapest room in the Banff Springs Hotel in November is three hundred dollars per night—hardly prole territory.

I called that dormitory I mentioned before. It was where I'd stayed twenty years ago as a student at the Banff Centre for the Performing Arts.

I only had to call once.

I was a little distressed when no one else from our motor coach was going to the Banff Centre. There were courtesy cabs and shuttle buses to every other hotel, it seemed, but none for ours. We took a cab.

I saw the dormitory, Lloyd Hall, looking exactly as it had in 1979—three floors, white brick, dull but satisfactory. With a sigh, I pointed it out to all present as where we'd be staying. But I was wrong. The administration, bless them, had put us into a new building that wasn't there the last time I'd been through. The Professional Development Centre was airy and clean and beautiful. It had high ceilings, a sculpture garden, and was made of cedar logs the colour of vanilla ice cream. Not only that, our room turned out to be a *suite* (for crying out loud!), with a *fireplace,* with windows that *opened* and had *views.* From the bedroom I could even, if I leaned out, see one of the spires of the Banff Springs Hotel. I stuck out my tongue.

The Professional Development Centre was built to house delegates and professors who come for various conferences and seminars. The Banff Centre, in addition to housing performing artists who don't make any money, brings in thinker types who do. They come to its Centre for Management and

Centre for Conferences.[3] In other words, it's supposed to be nice. Big companies pay lots of money for it to be that way. It wasn't built for authors whose books don't sell hotel rooms. We just happened to show up when there weren't any business thinkers around. We lucked out.

The other great thrill about the Banff Centre was the pool.

Since taking this trip, I've often thought about writing another book called *Where to Swim in Canada*. My children, I discovered, would sneer at, nay, would blow their noses into, a reservation confirmation telegram from the finest hotel anywhere if it didn't have a pool. Their memories of this trip will be directly tempered by how much swimming they did, and where. They could easily have been standing before the majestic beauty of Banff's Mount Rundle, Vermilion Lakes or even the indoor waterfall in the Presidential Suite at the Banff Springs Hotel and still ask, "Where's the pool?"—which is exactly what they did.

We were in the Banff Centre's pool mere minutes after dropping our bags. Then we ate dinner and retired to our beautiful suite, feeling very much the recipients of good fortune and luxury.

The next morning's breakfast was wonderful. The Banff Centre has a dining room with one wall of windows that is a giant wide-angle lens. Our waitress, Barb, who was twenty-one, lithe, fit and living with four other people in a three-bedroom flat,

---

3. B.F. Skinner is just one of the famous thinkers to attend a conference in Banff. He celebrated his eightieth birthday there in 1984, on the occasion of the sixteenth annual Behavioral Science Conference. Skinner is the one who could teach a pigeon to walk in circles using a system of rewards. He believed the same principles could be applied to humans. He must have liked Banff. The other fifteen Behavioral Science Conferences were held there, too.

recommended that we spend our morning hiking up Tunnel Mountain.

It's not really a mountain by Banff standards, but it's a nice hike, and you can see a long way from the top.

"It takes me half an hour," Barb said.

It took us two. It gave us great views of Mount Rundle's stunning lift, and of Dall's sheep, bighorn sheep and elk, lazing about the valley below—especially on the golf course, where one bull elk had discovered the tempting sweetness of the tenth-hole green. None of the golfers asked to play through.

We also met a family from Ohio. They ignored the many signs about not disturbing the flora and fauna; their petulant daughter was scratching her name in the rock, while their petulant sons chewed salted sunflower seeds, the shells dribbling out of their open mouths. We later found the discarded empty bag. The product was called "Spitz."

After the hike, we walked through town on the way to lunch. We squeezed our way through the crowds in front of the art shops and sweater shops and golf shops. There were branch offices of expensive stores from around the world, carrying many of the same items they did back in London, the only local content of the venture being the size of the receipt.

It was hard to imagine where all of these people came from. If the forces of economics in Banff were anything like those in the rest of the world, there should have been many, many more proles like us who couldn't even think of buying most of what was for sale. But commerce was booming. People streamed in and out of shops, through turnstiles and past security gates, with armloads of packages piled high as the mountains.

Conversation was booming as well. At least, talk was. I found an amazing shamelessness about the place. Even as we plunged through the seething masses, surly and sweaty and hungry as we were, the chat floated easily around us in snippets—the kind of talk that the privileged throw away like furniture that no longer matches the drapes.

"Get one of those. Have you got one yet? No? Get one."

"I'm about money. I don't give a shit where I work as long as it pays."

"Ooh, I love that! That's what J.F.K. Jr. was wearing!"

Lunch was surprisingly peaceful. We found an upstairs place that was hectic but had a refreshing laziness about it, too. The staff were so frazzled that they couldn't be bothered with any kind of attention. I had to ask for a menu, for our food and even for the bill. Our waiter, Skip or Chip or Freshie, I forget which, had either gone on a break or gone for good. The manager was leaning on the bar staring into space for a good ten minutes while we waited, forks neatly placed across our empty plates, none of us eating or even talking any more. I finally got up and said, "We'd like to go."

"Oh," he said, struck with the quaintness of the idea, "OK. Have a great day."

I left some money by the till.

We were trying to have a great day. We really were. The hike had been wonderful, but the longer we walked through town, the more the place just felt wrong.

It reminded me of returning to New York City as a tourist after having lived and worked there a while. New York was *about* work, and sweat and stress and swearing at cabs who cut you off, and now you were going to be late and, damn it, get the hell out of my way! Being part of that was thrilling, but watching it was awful. Once that driving stress was gone, the whole charade collapsed.

Somehow, for me, Banff was the same. It wasn't that work was there and we weren't in it. The only work in Banff comes from the people who go there to do what we were doing . . . *looking.* Banff has built an entire society all around the business of that looking. Thousands of people spend and earn millions of dollars fuelling the search, but it's got nothing to do with the soul of the place at all. It's all stuck on like the faux-Tudor Styrofoam beams on the slapped-together shopping quads downtown.

Banff isn't about money, or shopping, or even Presidential Suites with private glass elevators and grand pianos. For all its exclusivity, it might as well have been a campground full of people with portable stereos and coolers full of beer—peace and serenity that nobody notices unless it comes with a big piece of meat.

The price tags didn't matter. Once through that turnstile, the proles and the high priests were exactly the same. They were all going to paradise and turning it into the Slough of Despond because it felt more like home.

If Banff was going to be about anything, it seemed to me, it shouldn't have been about how much money we could spend. It should have been about how poor and tiny we are compared with the thundering peaks and the sheets of glacial ice, the avalanches and mudslides, the savage cold, the teeming life and the cougars, which see us as just another snack that won't fight as much as an elk.

Banff is a little foothold on the roaring, savage peak of nature. We should be lucky to get out alive.

We went to a New Age shop with incense and soothing music. We bought fancy candles and cuddly stuffed puppets for the kids—black bears and timber wolves. We went back to the Banff Centre and sat in our room. We went swimming.

The swimming must have washed away some of our discontent. The day was waning and we were ready to head out into Banff again for dinner, but the swimming must have also washed away our common sense. There were hundreds of restaurants all fairly close by, but I called the Banff Springs Hotel.

The operator told me what was available, which, remarkably, since it took about ten minutes to go through all the options, was nothing. All seventeen restaurants, it seemed, were as stuffed as the patrons spilling out of their seats.

I called the public relations people who'd been so glad to ignore my calls in the past. They still were.

After much cajoling I got us reservations at the Koffee Haus, which didn't take reservations, but it wouldn't be busy because it was the kind of place that catered to geezers and little children, and would be empty by nine o'clock. They told us to come at eight-thirty.

A busload of seniors was pulling in just as we arrived. The service was slow. Our kids practically fell asleep at the table before our meals arrived. The food was dull and shiny at the same time. It cost a lot of money.

We walked out onto the terrace and watched as the sun set on Mount Rundle, and then, as we walked back, on the hotel and Banff itself.

Our room at the Banff Centre was still as wonderful as before, but we were considerably less so. We were tired and grumpy, and the kids, the same ones who'd nodded off in their butter-soaked beans an hour earlier, wouldn't go to sleep. What seemed like hours later, I crawled into bed.

The proles lost to the monied, nature lost to both, and in the battle that was Banff we lost to them all.

Kamloops, British Columbia

~

BANFF'S TRAIN STATION WAS ALIVE again the morning we left town. No longer just a gift shop and restaurant, it was full of people about to board a train.

The first time *anybody* boarded a train in Banff was July 1886, when the Canadian Pacific Railway's train No. 1, the *Pacific Express,* pulled through on its maiden voyage from Montreal to Port Moody, British Columbia.

The transcontinental railway was hailed as both a political and corporate success. The promise of its construction was a cornerstone of the Confederation agreement that joined the country together. Its completion saved the political fortunes of at least one prime minister (Sir John A. Macdonald) and made a few bold men very, very rich in the process. The railway's construction had also killed hundreds of workers, but nobody seemed to worry much about that. Soon enough, more bold men were eager to get filthy rich building more railroads, further prime ministers were eager to earn political favour, and more workers were willing to risk their lives.

Within twenty years of the CPR's transcontinental track completion, Prime Minister Wilfrid Laurier, at the beginning

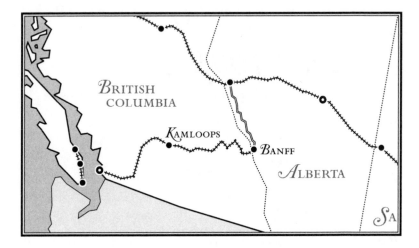

of what he said would be "Canada's Century," granted char-
ters to two more railways bent on building lines from Central
Canada to the west coast. The Grand Trunk Pacific and the
Canadian Northern Railway both built their tracks through
the Rocky Mountains by the Yellowhead Pass via Jasper. The
Northern's tracks arced down to Kamloops and then along
the banks of the Thompson and Fraser rivers, opposite the
CPR line. The Grand Trunk went north and west from Jasper,
along the Skeena River to Prince Rupert. Both completed
their tracks, but financially speaking, both got soaked. In 1917,
with a dual railway bankruptcy crisis on its hands, Robert
Laird Borden's government began the process of joining the
two together, along with some two hundred other smaller
railways. It took until 1923 to complete the amalgamation,
but in the end the result was Canadian National.[1]

---

1. As you may recall, Mr. Borden and his involvement in the railways, or lack
thereof, have come up before. He's the one who built just enough of the line to
Churchill, Manitoba, to get re-elected, and still managed to put off its completion
for another fourteen years.

The Canadian Pacific Railway wasn't particularly happy about that.

The CPR liked the competition much better when it either wasn't there at all or was occupied with infighting and not enjoying a federal subsidy. Still, the two railways, operating both freight and passenger services, co-existed civilly, if not happily, until 1960. By then both were enjoying a steadily strengthening freight business, but the passenger service was quickly running out of time. With improvements in airplane travel and highway and car travel taking their toll, the CPR began cutting back its passenger service—a logical choice, given the circumstances. Except the CPR was bound by a contract signed by its founders and Sir John A. Macdonald in October 1880.

The contract was a sweet one for the CPR—land, money, power—the whole deal. In return it had to operate the railroad for the rest of time. Actually, the CPR agreed to "maintain, work and run the Canadian Railway *efficiently*" for the rest of time.

Those are my italics, but you get the point. In most Railroaders' minds, running empty passenger trains wasn't efficient. In the minds of the people waiting on the platform, cancelling the train wasn't running the railroad.

There are many, many other sides to this argument, some still being argued today. The pro-industry types see it as corporate treason that any government should be able to dictate what any free-standing corporation should and shouldn't do to balance its books. The pro-regulation types say that the CPR was running, after all, on tracks that were largely donated to them at the taxpayers' expense, and since they were making money on freight, why couldn't they use some of those profits to cover their losses on the passenger side?

Back in the sixties, while the CPR was arguing, CN gave the rail passenger business one more try. It began a very ambitious program and cashed in big with Montreal's EXPO '67 (despite leaving its go-go boots on the *Turbo*). The program was such a success that even after EXPO, CN's ridership was well up from where it had been. But by then the government hadn't done anything with the railroad for such a long time that it decided to mess things up a little bit more, anyway.

It did this by creating the National Transportation Act. The Act, in turn, created the Canadian Transport Commission, the forming of commissions having long been established as an even more thoroughly Canadian pastime than building railroads. However, presumably caught up in the rebellious ways of the time, the Canadian Transport Commission decided that, instead of building the passenger railroad, it would destroy it.

Greg Gormick, in his 1986 CBC Radio documentary *Ribbons of Steel,* quotes Jack Pickersgill, the former Liberal minister of transport and president of the Canadian Transport Commission: "We'd laid down in the National Transportation Act a program for getting rid of passenger service. It wasn't just to reduce it, it was eventually to get rid of it."

They failed, but they did do some significant collateral damage. The commissioners told CN and the CPR that they might, indeed, be able to dump a passenger line that wasn't paying for itself, but they had to ask first. If the commission, in its wisdom, thought Canada needed that line and that it shouldn't be cut, it would pay back the railways the money they were losing on that line. Well, not quite. They would pay back most of the money—80 percent of it.

The railways, being peopled by Railroaders instead of commissioners, couldn't get themselves to see past that 20 percent they were spending and never getting back. From there on, if it hadn't been true before, the word "service" on those regional rail lines became a highly relative term. Trains were few and far between, and not happy to be there in the first place.

The Canadian Transport Commission, meanwhile, having failed to restore the service or destroy it, did the thing it knew best—it formed another committee, and called it VIA Rail.

Pierre Trudeau's government created VIA Rail in 1977 with great optimism for the future. VIA took over both CN's and the CPR's passenger lines, and was thereafter Canada's only national passenger railway. You could almost hear the sighs of relief exploding out of Montreal's Windsor Station and CN headquarters just down the street. They were now free to play in the hugely profitable freight industry, using their taxpayer-funded tracks, which they would subsequently charge VIA to use. VIA had trains going through both Jasper and Banff, using the CPR and CN equipment, stations and maintenance facilities and, in some cases, employees. Naturally enough, VIA (and its taxpayers) had to pay for all of that, too.

VIA managed at first, even succeeded, but not for long. In the summer of 1981 VIA had just finished the last step in its transition to running all of what used to be CN and CPR passenger trains. The Trudeau government kept up the standard of meddling established by all previous governments. VIA was told it had done a great job and would now have to do the same job for the same money, except it was going to have to buy all of its equipment with that money, too.

The result was the first of a series of massive cutbacks to service. One thousand jobs were lost that summer. Twenty regional routes were cut, to great but futile protests from many smaller communities.

Banff, though, was still covered. It lay on the original CPR line and was one of the most popular stops. The only complaint VIA ever heard about Banff was that when the train went through, it was the wrong time of day.

VIA's transcontinental trains worked, as they still do, on a Toronto-to-Vancouver schedule that had minimal stops and took about three days. The trip through the Rockies, starting in either Edmonton or Calgary, took about twenty-three hours and posed a scheduling problem.

Back in the heyday of rail travel, the ridership would have been made up of a fairly even balance of people who just wanted to get to their destination as quickly as they could and people who were interested in sightseeing. For the let's-get-there types, stopping was out of the question. For the sightseers, without any stops, that twenty-three-hour trip across the Rockies meant there was never enough daylight to see it all. If they were awake for the Kicking Horse Pass and the spiral tunnels, they'd be sleeping through Spences Bridge and the Fraser Canyon.

Unless they were from Kenora.

In hindsight, considering the number of sightseers on board, a daytime train that took two days to cross the Rockies and stopped in the middle seems an obvious answer. That it took so long for VIA to try it has to do with the old Railroaders' devotion to getting there on time, and perhaps a reluctance to admit that what was once the country's transportation backbone had become a sightseeing bus on rails. Oddly enough, that wouldn't have bothered William Van Horne one bit. To him, the tourists were just as good as the business travellers, as long as they were paying full price.

VIA did try a two-day tourist train service in 1988 and 1989. It was the first sign that VIA was beginning to recover from the cutbacks of seven years before. Employee morale was high. Service attendants learned to be even more customer-friendly, and to act as much as tour guides and entertainers as service people. They arranged hotels in Kamloops, halfway there, with entertainment and dining available. They knocked themselves out.

The result was the only new, truly profitable Canadian passenger train in fifty years, the *Rocky Mountaineer*.

Enter the prime minister.

In 1989–90 the Brian Mulroney government was well on its way to becoming the most hated administration of the second half of the century.[2] There were so few trains running that hardly anyone was using the service any more, so what difference was the tiny number of voters who still took the train going to make? That Mulroney had campaigned on a platform of improving rail service didn't appear to make any difference either. The government and VIA—and it is always hard to tell where one leaves off and the other begins—sharpened their axes and went to work. They cut even more regional lines, isolated more communities and slashed even more jobs. They chopped the transcontinental on the CN line to only three trains per week, chopped the transcontinental on the CPR line altogether and sold the line's only promise of a new money-maker, the *Rocky Mountaineer*.

---

2. At the time of writing, Mulroney is still one of our most hated political figures. In recent months some of his allies, and even his adversaries, have come forward to say that his work on free trade will eventually earn him a place of honour in our history, which may indeed be true, but it hasn't happened yet.

I talked to a VIA employee who helped to develop the *Rocky Mountaineer.*

"That was our train," she said, still bitter some ten years later. "We built it, made it work, made it pay and got it all figured out, just so they could take it away from us."

VIA still runs a transcontinental train, the *Canadian,* three times per week. It stops in Jasper, then takes the CN route that bypasses Banff and runs across the river from the CPR line to Vancouver. Some of the good stuff still goes by at night, but the train usually gets there on time.

The *Rocky Mountaineer* is owned and operated by the Great Canadian Railtour Company Ltd. It runs only in the summer and for a week at Christmas, and it's a huge success. That's the train that we, and everyone else but the waitress in the coffee shop, were lined up for in the Banff train station that morning.

It was, I have to say, exciting.

The trip we were about to take is said to be one of the most beautiful in the world. It's that same amazing ride that Lady Agnes Macdonald took on the cowcatcher. The train was huffing impatiently and so were we when the gates to the platform opened, three service attendants sang, "All aboard!" in three-part harmony, and we were off.

We stowed our bags (carefully sorted as those we'd need for the overnight in Kamloops and those we wouldn't), found our seats, and felt the chug and lurch of the adventure begin.

Each car, we discovered, had its own service attendant. Cameron, a decent fellow, was ours. As we rolled out of Banff he did what a good host always does and told us what was going to happen. We'd see lots of great stuff. We'd get to Kamloops in nine and a half hours. We couldn't go to the other cars, unless we wanted to smoke, and then we had to go to the vestibule space between our car and the next one. There was an open window and we could use it for pictures, too, but we could only have four people there at a time, and we could only stay for fifteen minutes, in case someone else wanted it. If we caught anyone from any other car in our vestibule, we could tell Cameron and he'd get rid of them. We'd eat our lunches in our seats. They'd be cold meals, in the kinds of trays that airplanes use. Lunch today was turkey or ham. Tomorrow it would be salmon or chicken. He'd start serving lunch at the front of the car today, and the back of the car tomorrow. We might not get the meal of our choice today, but depending on where we were, we probably would tomorrow.

We went through the spiral tunnel, and Cameron told us about it. Cameron told us about Lady Agnes on the cow-catcher and about the work crew that was almost squished by the runaway locomotive. He told us about the Kicking Horse River, and we went by it. Then Cameron told us he was going to serve breakfast, and he did. Everything was happening as it should, and that was because Cameron made sure it did. Cameron was *working*. We weren't.

On VIA, no one had told us where to go or not to go or what to do and how long to stay. It was all up to us. It wasn't as if I'd noticed putting out any significant effort to entertain myself on the VIA trains, but here I didn't have to do anything at all. A thousand workers had spent two years blowing off 725 tonnes of dynamite to build this tunnel, and all I had to do was sit and watch it go by.

The only niggling want I could identify anywhere in my body was my urge to see the Dome car.

The Dome on the *Rocky Mountaineer,* as you might have grasped from Cameron's detailed instructions, wasn't available to everyone on the train. We were travelling in what is called "Signature Service." They won't call it coach, but there are two levels of service on the train, and Signature Service isn't the upper one. "Gold Leaf Service" is the upper one. When you travel Gold Leaf Service on the *Rocky Mountaineer,* you don't have to leave your copy of Proust on your seat in the Dome. The whole car is the Dome. It's where you sit for the entire trip—an assigned seat right there under an almost completely glassed-in roof. The Gold Leaf car is a double-decker. Downstairs is the dining area—there are linen table-cloths, sterling service and great food. And the coolest thing is that there's not only an open window at the back of the Gold Leaf car, but an actual balcony with a little railing, where you can smoke cigars and drink port, just as Sir. John A. did.

I wanted to see the Dome.

Doug, the manager of Gold Leaf Services, showed me around.

It was very, very nice. The kitchen staff, three of them per car, were preparing lunch, and it looked like excellent food. The attendants, four of them per car, were charming and attractive. The view from the Dome was spectacular. We rolled over the Stoney Creek bridge (ninety-nine metres above the creek bed, one of the highest in the world), and it was jaw-droppingly great.

When I went back to my seat in the coach, the place was abuzz with the excitement of the bridge we'd just crossed and the view we'd just seen. My only thought was "But you *didn't* see it." The coach windows were suddenly tiny and dull. The seats were skinny and the whole car plain and cramped.

The coach trip wasn't cheap by any means, but it was noth-ing compared with the Dome. Yet all of the advertising for the

Rocky Mountaineer was about Gold Leaf Service. The Gold Leaf people got their own line in the Banff Station and got to board before we did. They had red carpet (true!) at the entrances to their cars, and uniformed employees standing by like royal guards at the doors.

After my diatribe on the evils of luxury in the previous chapter, I'm not going to say much about that, but interestingly there was only one Gold Leaf car and fifteen of the others. You'd think all those coach folks would look around and get upset. Cameron had gone to such pains to make sure everything was fair in our car—that everyone had just as much chance to have salmon for lunch, that no one got to stay too long at the window. Then—and it was a strange moment, I have to say—he told us all about the Dome and Gold Leaf Service, the great food and the view and the seats and the balcony. His comments were greeted with absolute silence. I half expected someone who wasn't going to get salmon that day to stand up, grab his plastic fork and lead an intra-train uprising right then and there.

Nobody did. If they said anything, it was that they really wanted to come back again and do the trip in the Dome. They said it with a misty-eyed hope in their eyes, as if to say they knew they didn't deserve any better than they had, but still, people can dream, can't they?

~

The couple sitting in front of us were from Dallas, Texas. They were on their honeymoon. He was clean-cut and almost pretty, and she was sultry and slightly surly, with big hair and a steady, downward gaze.

I talked to him. Mostly, we talked business, politics and weddings. They had had a big one—two hundred guests, which was a lot of work for her, he said, so he arranged the honeymoon.

"You planned the entire trip without her input?" I asked.

"Yup," he said. "She was sure I'd do a good job."

She looked up and smiled flatly. Yikes. When we talked work, the Groom told me his job was as a paramedic nurse in an emergency helicopter, dealing with accident and tornado victims with only seconds to live.

"Good," I said, "that's good."

Behind us was a pair of middle-aged women from the U.S. Midwest, Catherine and Beth. They weren't on a honeymoon. In fact, I'll be honest, after meeting the Newlyweds I knew I had to talk to Catherine and Beth. I'd noticed the book Beth was reading almost the moment we got on the train. It was a paperback titled *What If I Married the Wrong Person?*

I talked with Catherine first. The old rule about people saying what's important to them in the first few minutes held true. I asked why she'd chosen the *Rocky Mountaineer,* and she said:

"Well, originally I was just looking for someplace to go and I didn't have a travel partner. So I thought someplace for a single lady, I mean, I'm not single, but someplace for a lady to go alone and feel safe, travel, get off and go home."

Those were her first words. No partner. Single, er, no, not single. The next words said that Beth and she were friends from church, that they were both married and that both of their husbands didn't like to travel.

"We used to travel when my daughter was young," Catherine said. "But he became interested in a hobby and was consumed by it. He's a target shooter. He shoots at these heavy metal silhouette targets—chickens, turkeys, pigs and lambs, at outdoor shooting ranges. He's very good. He's won championships. He's been to South Africa and Ireland. He's going to Australia in a couple of years."

"I thought he didn't like to travel?"

"He needs a reason. Sightseeing isn't a reason."

Beth's husband, she said, if he went anywhere, just zipped there and zipped back.

I asked what he did like to do.

"Football and golf, and golf and football," she said. "But even for them, he won't travel. He just likes them on TV."

"It would be preferable to travel with your husband," Catherine said, "but when he's no fun . . ." They both began to laugh.

We talked about their trip, and it came out that Catherine was the one who organized all of the details for each stop. She picked the route and she booked the hotels.

I glanced back at the Newlyweds. All was quiet.

I asked Catherine if that was what she had done with her husband when they used to travel together. I guess I wanted to know what had happened.

Catherine said that no, she hadn't organized their trips when they took them. They just got into the car.

Was she more comfortable with everything planned out in advance?

"I kind of like to know . . ." she began.

"Kind of," Beth said, tongue-in-cheek. Catherine looked at her in silence, and then they both burst out laughing.

Catherine, it turned out, really likes being organized. When she and Beth go travelling, she books a minimum of five hotels in each city and cancels the others only when they are actually checked in to the one they like best. She gives credit card numbers for all of them, too, just to be sure.

She'd done that for this trip, as well. They were near Whistler, British Columbia, just a few days before, on a hiking trail that was supposed to be a ten-minute walk. Signs were stapled to the trees, warning that bears had been seen in the vicinity and to be cautious. They took a wrong turn, walked and chatted for a while, and found themselves alone in the woods, a lot farther than ten minutes from anything. That's when Catherine realized she still had rooms booked at two hotels, and that she still had to cancel one. It was 5:30 p.m., and she was going to be charged for both rooms at 6:00 p.m.

"I left Beth and ran back to the car," she said.

"Alone," Beth said. "In the woods. She left me. With a bear."

Catherine got her money back. Beth made it out on time. No one saw the bear.

I thought about Beth's couch potato husband and wondered if he'd ever seen that side of his wife. Had he always been the way he was?

"Oh, no," she said, "he was real exciting and fun."

"When did he change?"

"About the second week after our marriage."

Big laughs.

Beth's stick-in-the-mud husband was her second. Her first marriage had broken up when their three children were in their late teens and early twenties. This marriage was in its fifteenth year. That's a lot of televised golf.

I asked Catherine if she had ever considered going along with her husband on his target shooting trips, even if she just tagged along on the flight and then did her own thing when they got there.

"I don't think I'm welcome any more," she said. "He's just kind of cut off. He lives in his own world. I'd just be in the way. His shooting is his main focus in life."

By that logic, she'd be in the way a lot of the time.

"Hm-mm," she nodded. "I've gotten used to it."

Catherine began to talk about their earlier trips, when they were first married. It was just the two of them. They'd decide to take off on a Friday afternoon. He'd call home from the office and she'd get the camping stuff ready. He'd finish work early and off they'd go into the mountains.

Beth said it wasn't until you saw a couple in their older years that you could really tell how they were together. She said she enjoyed watching an older couple travelling together, holding hands.

They both looked out the window a while.

Catherine had been to a lot of marriage seminars and relationship workshops. He wouldn't go, but she went anyway to help her learn how to cope.

"I guess I have learned how to cope," she said. "We're just married and living separately in the same house."

Why not just live separately in different houses, then?

She waited a long time. The train carriage creaked along beneath us.

"Biblically, we can't get divorced. Scripturally, there are only two reasons why you can have a divorce—adultery and abandonment."

A person could abandon another person and never leave the house.

"Right," she said. "I don't know where that line is. Leaving is a frightening thought. It's a huge thing, the house, the money . . ."

"That's where I am," Beth said. "I'm fifty-nine. Moving is a huge thing. He's OK. He's just a stick in the mud. Some parts of my life are fulfilling and others just are. It's OK."

Beth really was at peace, as far as I could tell. She'd come to terms with whatever it was. But still, I looked up the car at the Newlyweds again. Fifteen years, twenty years, thirty, maybe, and all you get is "OK"?

Catherine wasn't OK.

"I have a daughter. She's thirty and she's married," Catherine said. "I don't want her to be from a broken home, although I've been told she already is."

So what if her daughter ended up in a similar marriage, would Catherine want her to stay?

"No. No. No way. There are so many times I've thought, 'Get out now.' I don't say that out loud, but I think it. I find myself alone in the kitchen and suddenly it's in my head without any warning at all. 'Don't live like this forever,' it says, and I know I can't. But I still am. Time's running out and I'm still here. It's hard. I could die soon and I'll take this with me. I'd like to say I could find peace, but I'm not at peace. I do miss companionship. I do."

Cameron came around with the lunch orders. He was out of turkey. The Newlyweds got the last one.

The afternoon rolled along. We went through tunnels that lasted forever and saw peaks and rivers that dwarfed and drowned anything we'd passed so far. And just to remind us that some things in Western Canada are exactly the same as they are anywhere else, on one of those rivers, at a calm little pool, we saw a group of whitewater rafters. They stood when we waved, turned around and, in unison, mooned the train.

After lunch, I wandered to the front of the car and ended up talking with Kevin and Pauline. I noticed them because of the mountain scene he was sketching onto the pad on his lap. It was lovely work.

They were from northern England, and both were retired. "I taught kindergarten for thirty-three years," Pauline said. "I loved it. I loved seeing little children every day."

"She was very good at it," Kevin said.

"I still am," she laughed. "But I'm quite enjoying retirement as well. Our grandchildren keep me in practice."

Kevin had taught, too, and then moved up to an administrative position as head of the art department at a community college, overseeing a staff of twenty-five. He did that for eighteen years before taking an attractive early-retirement package at the age of fifty-six, five years ago.

"But I'm really just starting to get into work again as an artist," he said. "I couldn't paint very much as an administrator. Now I'm painting again and it's an absolute joy. It wasn't instantaneous, of course. I imagined myself picking up my brushes the day after I left the office, but in actual fact it took almost six years before I truly found my hands."

As we talked, I was watching Pauline. She seemed very content. It was a remarkable thing to see someone taking such a completely supportive role without diminishing herself in any way.

I looked back down the car at Catherine and was still looking that way when Kevin said something that brought me right back.

"What I did do while slowly working back into painting was something that ended up satisfying many of the artistic needs.

I took up field archery, which I'd left alone for twenty years, competitive field archery. I started competing all over the place. It became obsessive."

"So . . . ," I asked Pauline, "did you lose him there for a while?"

"Oh, no," she said, "it was only on weekends."

"I've slowed down on that now," Kevin said. "It was a means to an end. Now I'm painting and we find we have quite a lot of time together as well."

"It's lovely," Pauline said, and she took his hand in hers and patted it. They both smiled.

I had to wait a few minutes to get by Cameron and back to my seat. He was pushing a trolley down the centre aisle, offering drinks.

"Would you like a coffee or tea, or a soft drink? I have some cookies, too," he was saying, over and over again, all the way down the train. He even kept the inflection of his voice the same for every passenger.

He'd promised it would be fair.

I finally squeezed by and went back to my seat. The Newlyweds were sleeping, cuddled under a blanket. My family were asleep. Beth was reading her book. Catherine was sitting still, looking ahead and thinking.

~

There was nothing fair about our arrival in Kamloops. We, the Signature Service passengers, were shuttled out of our cars and onto the dusty platform, through the station and into waiting motorcoaches, with drill team precision. We'd been sorted by hotel, with our bags loaded on as well. Within three minutes, all fifteen train cars' worth of people had found their seats and were ready to go.

I noticed the Gold Leaf passengers as we were leaving. No one was hurrying them. They were being guided, literally by the arm, past the waving members of a local re-enactment troupe who were on horseback, dressed in chaps and big hats and red bandanas. The Gold Leaf passengers, while making sure they didn't trip on the wrinkles in their red carpet on the way to the limousines, didn't appear to notice them.

Meanwhile, our bus sweltered in the heat. It dripped sweat on the inside ceiling. It was mid-August, and we were in a semi-arid desert on a sunny day. As our bus groaned and puked up the hill to our hotel, we began to bake.

The only thing not suffering from the stifling heat was our bus driver, Sally. From the moment we were on the bus she was speaking to us, telling us stories about Kamloops and its history. Well, no . . . she wasn't telling us the history of Kamloops.

It took a few moments to realize, in all the heat and the shuttling here and there, that Sally wasn't really saying anything. Her story ran from the hot-rod show that had been in town last week to the shopping mall we were passing and how a Great Canadian Superstore is there now and it has great prices and anything you want but you don't have to buy that much if you don't want to (the underpass is coming up and Everybody Duck! and there it goes) and Kamloops has grown to a population of eighty thousand people living in forty-four square kilometres and the old house with the wonderful gardens that used to be on the corner was the most important place in town but it isn't now because the gardens aren't there and the house isn't either since they put in the drugstore on the corner.

The twenty-minute cattle call lineup at the Comfort Inn was delightful by comparison. The hotel was about as long as Jasper. Our room was at the end.

There was only one thing to do.

We went swimming.

Vancouver, British Columbia

WE HAD THE PLEASURE of Sally's company once again the next morning, when at an ungodly hour she herded grumpy busloads of us back to the station. The Superstore was still there. Kamloops's population was still eighty thousand. The house that used to have the beautiful gardens still didn't have them. The only change in the routine came when the bus broke down. We sat for ten minutes waiting for another bus to take us the rest of the way. Sally talked to us a little more to keep us from getting restless.

Even Cameron, our ever-smooth service attendant, had a slight edge in his morning greeting that day once we'd been herded into our seats. His words were cordial, but there was a distinct "don't mess with me" quality about them as well.

When he reminded us that he'd be starting from the back of the car this time and that he might not have enough salmon for everyone at lunch, I decided I would have to weigh the consequences of mentioning that if I was the one who lost out.

His tone softened once we got rolling. He had plenty to talk about for the first few hours—including a few cameo appearances by Mother Nature. We saw bears (two), osprey (two), Dall's sheep (one) and coyote (one). The osprey caused

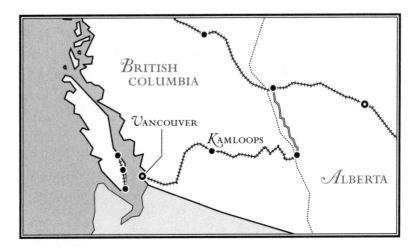

him a bit of consternation. It appeared for a few seconds on the port side during Cameron's history of the treacherous bit of riverside track known as Avalanche Alley. The fish hawk floated by and the entire car's worth of passengers surged to one side to see it. Cameron stopped his story while the bird disappeared, only to be a line or two back into it when one of the kids on board yelled, "There it is!" and the tide of passengers lurched across the car to the other side.

Cameron waited as patiently as he could, but I'm not sure he ever finished the story. My attention span began to slip. It was a funny thing—there was nothing to shorten it. I had nothing to do but sit and watch and listen, but as the day and the trip and Cameron all rolled on, I became more and more impatient. It wasn't that I didn't want to know what he was telling us. I just would rather have been left to discover some of it for myself.

Idly, I began to cast my increasingly cynical eye about the car to see if I could categorize the members of this train community. I looked for Noble Patriarchs and Den Mothers, but didn't get very far. It's not that we weren't a community, but by appointing Cameron to the roles of Mayor, Entertainer and Den Mother, among others, there didn't seem to be the same competition among the townsfolk to win a position for themselves beyond Mere Citizen.

In one way, Cameron's stories gave us historical figures to play the roles for us. Lady Agnes Macdonald took over as a better-living Bonne Vivante than any of us could hope to become. William Van Horne was at once the Noblest of Patriarchs, the toughest Jock and, evidence of his amazing diversity, Aesthete (Van Horne was a respected collector— he bought up many Impressionist pictures long before they were popular), Artist (he was a painter himself) and Despot (they didn't call him "The Terror of Flat Crick" for nothing).

The track we were travelling was also built by one character who lived almost more roles than can be listed—Captain of Industry, Mover and Shaker, Opportunist, Knave, Dandy, Weasel and Devil, and, it must be said, Genius, Brain and Winner. But strangely, the track doesn't carry his name.

Andrew Onderdonk was a young, smart, handsome, rich American engineer who cruised into Ottawa in November 1879 for a meeting with Andrew Tupper, the minister of railways and public works. He walked out with four contracts to build one of the most gruelling sections of rail line in the country. Not coincidentally, the contracts were some of the richest. That fall Tupper announced the government had contracted to build 200 kilometres of railway track in British Columbia—a first step toward honouring the Confederation promise of a transcontinental railway.

He didn't trouble anybody with any of the details of the deal, like, for example, where the track was going to go. There was consternation over that. More than one community had been told the railroad was coming its way. When the minister of railways was so unsure of where his railway was going that he couldn't make any promises to constituents, while being simultaneously so sure about where his railway was going that he could pay a builder upwards of five million dollars to build it, people got upset.

None of that bothered Andrew Onderdonk. He paid $250,000 for contracts to blast a railroad out of the solid rock on the banks of the Upper Fraser and Thompson rivers between Yale and Kamloops, and was rewarded with multiple millions.

Onderdonk had several factors working in his favour. For one thing, the railway was such a political issue that every delay or setback equalled a nasty kick in the pants to the powers that were in Ottawa. No one told Onderdonk to finish this thing no matter the cost, but that was the message, and that's what he did.

He arrived in Yale, British Columbia, to a thirteen-gun salute in April 1880. Construction started a month later and continued day and night for five years under horrendous conditions. Within six months the hospital at Yale had to be expanded. A year later, editorials appeared in the local paper complaining about the deplorable condition of the cemetery, due to overcrowding caused by the bodies of dead railway workers. Workers died in rock slides, tunnel cave-ins, accidents with blasting powder or nitroglycerine, and many more died simply by losing their footing and falling into the treacherous river below. Onderdonk had agreed to complete the job regardless of cost, and that included the cost of human life. Hundreds died in the first eighteen months of construction, yet in that time the crews had laid a grand total of only 3.2 kilometres of track.

Not surprisingly, Onderdonk began to experience a labour shortage. He solved that problem by importing Chinese workers by the boatload to do the work the Canadians wouldn't touch. In 1882 Onderdonk brought between six and seven thousand Chinese workers to build the railroad. All of them came from Guangdong Province, the area surrounding Hong Kong.

White people in Canada weren't happy about it.

The *Winnipeg Times* said: "It is an established fact that dealings with the Chinese are attended with evil results."

Onderdonk's thirteen-gun salute in April 1880 wasn't his only welcome. When he came into Victoria, delegates from the Anti-Chinese Association were there to greet him. He promised them that he would hire white people first, and only when he ran out of them would he move on to French Canadians and finally, if necessary, Chinese.

Our politicians showed no more insight.

"Well," John A. Macdonald told a political gathering in Toronto, "they do come and so do rats. I am pledged to build the great Pacific Railroad in five years, and if I cannot obtain white labour, I must employ other."

One could argue, quite accurately, that Onderdonk was no more Demon than any of the other power-brokers in the rail business. Also, that the Chinese workers knew well the danger they were getting into, and Onderdonk gave them a chance at a new life here that they otherwise wouldn't have seen.

To paint the immigrant workers as frail and helpless would be inaccurate at best. They might have been non-voting, underpaid labour with few rights and no language skills, but they also possessed remarkable solidarity and confidence.

Pierre Berton's *The Last Spike* tells of Onderdonk's Chinese workers' very first payday. There had been an error in the accounting department and each man was paid one cent less than had been agreed. The workers stormed the company store and would not move until the matter was resolved. It was. In another tale, a work gang's white boss refused to allow the men to build fires to make afternoon tea. The men dropped their tools and walked as a group to the head office in Yale. They got their tea.

All the pluck and determination in the world, however, wouldn't take the grim reality out of the numbers involved: Six hundred Chinese died completing the 200 kilometres from Yale to Kamloops—almost one in ten workers, or five deaths per mile of track.

Those that survived, generally speaking, weren't facing an easier life once the line was finished. Many didn't have enough money saved to get back home, and had to stay and fight an even more dangerous fate than what they'd just come through: Canadian winters in rural British Columbia, with rampant racism and no way of earning a living.

Andrew Onderdonk met his obligations to the CPR and completed the track on time. Facing a rural British Columbia winter was never an issue for him. Onderdonk quietly went on to other projects, including, eventually, the westernmost section of the CPR railway, from Yale to Port Moody, and the last section of track from Eagle Pass to Craigellachie, the site of the famous "last spike."

Onderdonk's British Columbia track was paid for with public money. When the CPR agreed to build the transcontinental railroad, it did so on the condition of its notorious contract with Sir John A. Macdonald. The contract gave the CPR, among other things, twenty-five million acres in land grants tax-free for twenty years or until sold. The CPR could write up to

$25 million in bonds against that land and would still enjoy a twenty-year monopoly on railroad-building anywhere south of the transcontinental line west of Winnipeg. This prevented any (further) invasion by American railroads. The contract also handed over all track built with government money.

You'd think the CPR would have been happy with that. One of the big sticking points when the line was complete was that the CPR wanted compensation from the government because the Onderdonk lines were in such bad shape. There was a public outcry over the shoddy inspection of the Upper Fraser sections, paid for, naturally enough, with public money. The CPR said it was almost completely impassable and would have to be totally rebuilt. They were right.

Of the Chinese workers, some might have managed to save what was needed to buy a comfortable life back home, but not many. The workers were paid a dollar a day in Canada, half of what their white counterparts earned. From that they had to pay room and board, tools, taxes and other expenses. It was estimated that the most any Chinese worker could save would be forty-three dollars per year, not including whatever debt he still carried from the cost of his initial passage to Canada. For most, that debt would have been considerable.

Meanwhile, Andrew Onderdonk had already cashed his cheque. His client was not the CPR, but the federal government. He took his millions and went on to major railway projects in Buenos Aires, Chicago and New York, where he built the subway tunnel under the East River in 1905.

Cameron didn't tell us all of that as we rolled along the banks of the Fraser on the *Rocky Mountaineer*. He told us about the loss of life and the hard living conditions. He didn't tell us much about Onderdonk, but since another of the known community roles from turn-of-the-last-century Canada was Railway Baron, perhaps he didn't have to.

There was an American family sitting across from us, a late-thirties husband and wife with a three-year-old son. They lived in California, where their child was born, but the parents were both originally from Hong Kong, now part of Guangdong Province. Both were dressed very elegantly. She had a large diamond on her ring finger and more on her earrings. He was wearing a Rolex watch and the kind of sunglasses you don't leave on a train.

It was an odd dynamic. Jasper and Banff had been full of Asian tourists, but on the *Rocky Mountaineer,* the family from California were the only people in our car and, as far as I could see, on the entire train who could remotely be called "ethnic."

The young family watched and listened with interest as Cameron told us about the Chinese workers while we passed the places where so many of them had died. There was Jaws of Death Gorge, Avalanche Alley, Indictment Hole (where, it was said, anyone who tried to build a railway ought to be indicted) and Hell's Gate. Just after one of those points, Cameron was serving drinks from his trolley, and the man with the Rolex asked for a soft drink and some juice for his son. Cameron had to lean over quite far, as if he were bowing, to hand the child the juice he'd asked for. The man smiled.

~

The scenery along the Fraser and Thompson rivers was stunning. As happened so often on this trip, it wasn't what I was expecting. I had thought the big thrills of the trip would be over by Kamloops, but this was scenery like none I have seen anywhere else. The mountains looked like the baking south coast of Crete, while the river below foamed as though it had just left the Arctic. The mountains were not as tall as in Banff, but were sparse and remote and somehow even more humbling.

At least, they should have been.

I'm sure if I had been actually *on* a mountain that afternoon, with the prospect of a night ahead with the rattlesnakes and the coyotes, I wouldn't have needed silence to be duly awed. As it was, I was in a mostly comfortable train, sitting behind a pair of cuddling newlyweds, digesting my salmon lunch. There was little austerity in my life. Not that I wanted hardship, but a little quiet to appreciate my luxury would have been welcome.

That just wasn't going to happen. The kids were rangy. I want to say, in their defence, that they behaved very well for children of four and six years old. My wife was an organizational genius when it came to their entertainment. She brought games, tapes, puzzles and books, and the children enjoyed them all. To be fair, they did listen to Cameron's historical anecdotes for quite a while, as well, but they would have had to be miniature saints to politely listen for as long as they were expected to that day. On the VIA train, when the entertainment ran dry, it would have been time for a stroll to the Dome with the hope of seeing other children or something of a distraction. Here, we were stuck.

I looked out at the mountains, trying to capture the distance and the isolation, but it was as if they were pretending we weren't there.

Cameron was talking again. I realized that he talked to us any time the train stopped. It must have been company policy to smooth over the number of hours a train spends waiting on a siding for a passing freight. This time he told us about the ginseng crop along the Thompson River and how it is sold all over the world as a natural stress reliever, which, at that point, was irony of the highest order.

The kids were wiggling because their legs were stiff. My legs were too stiff to wiggle. The kids were thirsty. I was thirsty. They wanted drinks. I didn't want them to want drinks. Wanting drinks meant bothering Cameron in the middle of a story at the end of his "don't mess with me" day. They wanted to ask Cameron for drinks anyway. I wanted them to forget about their stupid drinks and listen to Cameron just because everybody else was, even though I myself didn't want to listen to him ever again.

If he gets wind of my griping, he'll probably say I'm still ticked off that I lost the poetry contest. Cameron invited us to write poems about the salmon that spawn in the Adams River, one of the spots on the tour commentary. The prize for the best poem was a *Rocky Mountaineer* T-shirt.

I do have a British Columbia river poem in my repertoire.

Chris Barry wrote it in our grade-five class at Elizabeth Ballantyne School in Montreal West.

Miss Chaffey taught grade five that year. She was a diesel who'd been teaching grade five since before there was steam. By the time we came along, she did things the way they'd always been done and wasn't prepared to stop for anyone or anything. That meant she really liked children who did what they were told. That meant she really liked sweet little girls. That meant she really didn't like boys.

The only male she had any good words for, as far as we could tell, was her nephew, who flew a helicopter in the Lower Fraser Valley.

The *Rocky Mountaineer* went through the Lower Fraser Valley. I looked.

No helicopters that day.

But back in grade five, we felt his presence. Any time any of us got on Miss Chaffey's wrong side, which was all the time, she would tell us, by way of instructive comparison, about her wonderful nephew. He never would have committed such an egregious crime as we had. And because of the depth of his virtue, while our fathers were slogging it back and forth to their jobs in slushy Montreal, he spent his days flying a helicopter in the Lower Fraser Valley.

There was a garbage collectors' strike in Montreal at the time. As one of our English assignments, Miss Chaffey asked us to write a poem about it. I wrote one, but the one who should have won the T-shirt, if there had been one, was Chris Barry. Here's his poem:

Garbage here, garbage there,
You can smell it everywhere,
You can smell it in the streets,
You can smell it in the alley,
You can even get a whiff of it
In the Lower Fraser Valley. [1]

Miss Chaffey gave him a C.

Anyway, I wish I'd read that poem, but I didn't. I couldn't think of a pithy bit of verse to save my life.

Struggling with my tiny attention span for a stupidly long time, I wound up scrawling two pages of doggerel. It was so

---

1. Copyright Chris Barry, 1972. Used with permission.

messy that I became the only entrant to read his own work to the car.

I sucked. A teacher visiting from New Zealand wrote a poem that was funny, warm and, above all, short. He got the T-shirt. I got five minutes of mike time in which to humiliate myself.

The kids were mortified, but that was just one more spike in the railroad holiday coffin. We were nearing three weeks away from home and it was taking its toll. At about this time a kindly older woman was walking by and was drawn to begin a conversation with my apparently cute little children. The conversation went like this:

"Hello. Where are you from?"

"Toronto," my daughter answered.

"Oh, and how do you get here from Toronto?"

"You have to take a million trains."

The woman decided to find her seat.

Cameron was talking again. It was a bit like sitting in church for a very long time, with impressive scenery going by the windows. Whatever freight we were waiting for must have been waiting for the sermon to end.

I began to think very uncharitable thoughts about our service attendant, which wasn't fair. He was just doing his job, and doing it very well, but after eight hours it stopped mattering. Despite all his grace, smarts and training, at a certain point he might as well have been Sally telling us about the Kamloops Superstore all over again. It was just too much.

I wondered if anyone else was going through what I was, or if there might be some clue as to how to deal with this problem, some community system I had missed. I looked around the car, but saw only the backs of heads. It did occur to me, though, that I hadn't looked for a flagitious poltroon on this train, yet. The Nobles and Den Mothers might have been absorbed into the service and the stories, but in every other train there had been an F.P., even after all of the other roles had faded into the carpet, the poltroon had prevailed.

I couldn't find one.

"There's always one," I said out loud.

"What?" the kids said. "What? What is it? What?" People turned around to look at us. Cameron stopped his story of the Skuzzy Creek Bridge mid-span and threw us a look.

Then it dawned on me.

It was me.

~

We'd passed Salmon Arm, British Columbia, the day before, but this seems like a good time to talk about it.

Salmon Arm is one of the places where Prime Minister Pierre Trudeau distinguished himself in a distinctly flagitious manner. During August 1982, the Trudeau sons, Justin, Sasha and Michel, and father Pierre went from Vancouver to Jasper, and then on to Ontario. It was the family's summer holiday. They travelled by train, in a pair of luxurious private rail cars that were on loan from the governor general. The cars were already in the west. Princess Anne had used them the month before, as had the (then) West German chancellor, Helmut Schmidt. The cars had to be brought back east, anyway. The Trudeaus simply rolled along for the ride.

But things were not simple in Western Canada in August 1982. Inflation rocketed with every passing month. The Canadian dollar plummeted almost as dramatically. Trudeau was in his last term, having pledged to retire before the next election. Many Canadians were trying their damnedest to make sure he did.

In the weeks leading up to the trip, one disaffected westerner began a campaign to raise enough money to bribe Trudeau out of office. British Columbia was in the midst of a provincial workers' strike, and Alberta's and Ontario's civil servants were almost ready to walk as well. The Liberals put a 6-percent ceiling on wage increases to the public sector, with inflation running well into the teens. To the general public, they preached restraint and asked voters, for the sake of the country, to live within their means.

Then the prime minister, the man who had personally been talking about the importance of belt-tightening among the masses, decided to take a two-week rail holiday in the mountains in a pair of private luxury cars, all paid for by the public purse.

Trudeau could be impulsive and arrogant. It's safe to say that arrogance eventually cost him his job. It was also among the qualities that made sure Trudeaumania, if it ever reached the West, never took hold in the same way it did in the East.

That being said, any footage of his appearances from the time are now thrilling to watch. He didn't joke and back-slap his way around the issues. He didn't speak in twenty-minute circular paragraphs that were droned with the "uhh" pauses of an old prop plane with nowhere to land. If you've listened to any of the ministers prime who followed him, you'll recognize those techniques all too well. Trudeau didn't use them. He said, simply, through much of his conflicted career, variants of his most famous challenge "Just watch me." It is a pleasure to see someone still in touch with the fire that got him where he was.

But the only thing it got him in Salmon Arm was trouble.

On August 8, 1982, the Trudeau family luxury cars, hooked up to the back of a VIA train heading east from Vancouver, pulled into Salmon Arm. There to meet the train were three constituents who had voted for Trudeau in the previous election, but who, like much of the country at the time, were not happy with the results. They were all British Columbia government workers, and all on strike. They greeted the prime minister with signs saying "Practise what you preach" and "Fly Economy Class," holding them up to the Trudeau cars when the train stopped.

Salmon Arm is not a big town, and the train station does not have wide platforms. When the train pulled to a stop, the signs were right in front of the three windows in the Trudeau sleeping car. An aide pulled the blinds down. Then, to the everlasting surprise of the protesters, Trudeau lifted one of the blinds back up. He read the placard in front of him, smiled at the woman holding it, gave her the finger and closed the blind. Then he went to the next window, raised the blind and did the same for the female protester's husband and again for the third in the group, a friend. Three windows, three protesters, three fingers—a just society.

TV camera crews that were travelling in the VIA cars had seen the placards and began to film the confrontation. It was a story with legs, and the prime minister's fingers did the walking. For many, Trudeau's salute was proof of his party's disdain for the West.

The hubbub followed the train east like a political sonic boom. Newscasts broadcast Trudeau's unmistakable gesture. Mere hours later, when the train emerged from the giant Connaught Tunnel under Rogers Pass at the Alberta border, protesters were waiting with a supply of very ripe tomatoes.

The protesters weren't sure which car Trudeau was in, so they pelted the entire train.

In Canmore, Alberta, people threw eggs. One of the eggs, to the cheers of the crowd, struck a window just behind where Trudeau looked out. More protesters met the train in Calgary, still more in Winnipeg.

When the train pulled into Sudbury, Ontario, things got ugly.

Sudbury, at the time, was suffering the highest unemployment rates in North America. Forty percent of the adult workforce was not working. That number was a full 14 percentage points above the Trudeau administration's current standing in the national polls.

Five hundred people were waiting when Trudeau's train pulled in to Sudbury at 11:15 p.m. One enterprising fellow showed up with ten dozen eggs, each painted with a little blue fist complete with extended middle finger. He charged fifty cents a piece and sold out in minutes. "What are you reading to your children?" one angry man shouted. *"Humpty Dumpty?"* Those who hadn't brought eggs or tomatoes threw rocks. One rock smashed a window on the car where the Trudeau children were sleeping.

The train was scheduled to stop for thirty minutes in Sudbury. It left after fifteen. VIA passengers who missed getting on in Sudbury were sent by taxi to Parry Sound and met the train there.

Pierre, Justin, Sasha and Michel Trudeau left the train in Orillia, Ontario, and continued by car. Justin was ten years old that summer, Sasha, eight, and Michel, six.

There really isn't any excuse for what Trudeau did in Salmon Arm. By all accounts, the three protesters were not rude or even noisy. They were doing precisely what Trudeau had consistently encouraged every Canadian to do: making their voices heard. He might have been on holiday with his children, who had only recently suffered the pain of their parents' separation. He might have been beleaguered and frustrated with the demands of his job. None of that excuses his blatant failure to see, at that moment, that he was a wealthy and privileged man who'd lost his connection with the people he was supposed to be leading—people who were not wealthy or privileged at all. He turned his back on them and suffered the consequences.

On the other hand, no one person could have rescued the economy that summer. Most people today, in hindsight, accuse Trudeau of vastly overspending on the public sector during his leadership, not spending too little. In Sudbury, Inco Ltd.'s massive layoffs weren't due to federal policies, but to a combination of a glut in the nickel market and a severe recession that stretched well beyond Canada's borders. In the end, Inco had to share a good portion of the blame for what happened that night in Sudbury, as well. The day before the train arrived, the mining giant had announced that within six months it would be cutting another fifteen hundred jobs.

The impression that stays with me, though, isn't one of big business woes, government economic policy, or of arrogant leaders and raging workers. What I keep seeing is three school-aged children who were awakened in the middle of the night by a shower of rocks smashing into the windows above their beds. Everyone, no matter whether they were throwing the finger, the rocks, the tomatoes or the layoff notices, had to get his or her conscience around that.

~

We arrived safely in Vancouver. The classic 1915 station welcomed us with the kind of nobility only a grand train station can muster. I said goodbyes to Catherine and Beth, and wished them well. Kevin and Pauline walked past and said goodbye, too. They held hands as they walked. I looked for the Newlyweds, but they had disappeared. I felt a shudder for the Groom, but decided he would have to face whatever came on his own.

I looked for Duffy, the quizzical joker with no long-term memory who had been on the train in northern Ontario. I realized he'd gotten off the VIA train in Jasper at the same time we did, and I'd forgotten to say goodbye. I decided that was all right, since he'd have forgotten, too.

In the end, there were no incidents. My children had not exploded, my wife and I had only smouldered. Cameron had managed to finish all his stories. Everyone got lunch, even if it wasn't exactly the one he or she had hoped for.

We took a cab to our hotel. We ate dinner and went for a walk. Vancouver was cool and foggy. It was good weather for sleeping. Our hotel was a tall one and we were up near the top. I stood out on the balcony for a while, hoping to watch the sun set over the Pacific, but the window faced north, and it got cold before it got beautiful.

I came in and found my wife looking at the children with a mixture of love and relief. They were sleeping, their hair still wet from their swim after dinner.

~

Sixteen years after his cross-country train trip in the governor general's private cars, on November 13, 1998, only 150 kilometres from Salmon Arm, Michel Trudeau, the youngest of the three Trudeau boys, was swept into Lake Kokanee in an avalanche while backcountry skiing. His body was never recovered. He was twenty-three years old.

Pierre Elliott Trudeau died two years later, at eighty.

In the outpouring of emotion that followed, there were several lasting impressions, but two will likely remain sharper than others. One was of Justin Trudeau at the state funeral in Notre-Dame Basilica in Montreal, delivering his father's eulogy.

The other enduring image was of Pierre Trudeau's casket being taken the 187 kilometres from the Parliament Buildings in Ottawa to Notre-Dame in Montreal by train, in a two-level car draped in black.

Reporters who travelled with the train recalled solitary farmers standing at attention, caps across their hearts, surrounded on all sides by empty fields as the train rolled by. Construction workers stopped work and took off hard hats. At level crossings, others held out books and campaign posters. One woman lifted up a canoe paddle wrapped with a scarf. Justin and Sasha Trudeau were on board. When the train passed through towns, they asked that it slow to a crawl as mourners leaned close and handed them roses and flags. In many towns people reached out to touch the train as it passed. Other times, even if the Trudeau sons weren't looking, people stood silently, and as many still do when a train passes, they waved.

first ending

Victoria,
British Columbia

$\sim$

WE DIDN'T REALLY THINK it through before we went on the westernmost passenger train in Canada.

There were a couple of prime ministers who didn't really think it through, either.

On July 20, 1871, Prime Minister John A. Macdonald brought British Columbia into Confederation with the promise of a railway that would link it with the seats of power in the East and provide a viable shipping route from the Atlantic to the Pacific. He promised British Columbia that construction would begin on the railroad within two years, and that the job would be finished in ten. A kind of land-speculation lottery sprang up around Vancouver Island, based on predictions of where the prime minister planned his railroad would meet the Pacific, and how it would get to the island.

No one considered that Macdonald might have been talking out of his not-so-deep hat, and that he had no idea at all of the answers to any of those questions.

By July 1872, though, they were beginning to wonder. There was nothing even close to the beginning of a railroad connecting with the West. British Columbia had near to 1,000 kilometres of coastline and Macdonald had said, and

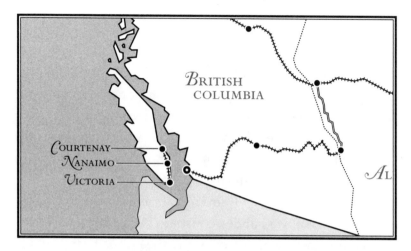

done, precisely nothing about where the all-important Pacific terminus would be.

Nevertheless, he kept his promise by pulling the name "Esquimalt" out of the foggy, coastal air and arranging a sod-turning ceremony there for July 19, 1873, one day short of the promised two years.

Esquimalt was a naval base outside Victoria. Even if there had been a railroad to the Pacific at the time, which there wasn't, before it could have reached Esquimalt, it would have had to cross eight thousand feet of fictional train trestle between the mainland, the Gulf Islands and Vancouver Island. So far, one piece of sod had been turned.

Then Macdonald got caught in a nasty influence-peddling scandal and resigned. His replacement was Alexander Mackenzie. Mackenzie called Macdonald's railroad commitments "a promise meant to be broken." Folks in Victoria, especially the land speculators, were not keen on that kind of talk, and they made a fuss. Mackenzie knew too well that there was plenty of time for delay tactics before the next election, but very little time for results. He also knew that no prime minister could afford to disregard an entire province, no matter how far away it was.

In 1875 Mackenzie introduced a bill to start building the Esquimalt railway as compensation for not having started it yet, if that makes any sense. The Senate decided it didn't. They struck it down. Later that year Mackenzie gave up on results and simply bought himself some voter patience, giving British Columbia $750,000 instead.

Then on July 22, 1878, seven years and two days after the promise of a railway under construction within two years, Mackenzie finally announced where the railroad would reach the Pacific: Burrard Inlet, near Vancouver, not Esquimalt, on Vancouver Island.

His response to indignant Victorians was a political variation on "That's the way it goes."

He was out of office within two months, while Macdonald, with help from his old sod-turners in Victoria, turned electoral sod all over the country and won a landslide victory.

So knowing where his friends were, John A. Macdonald promised, again, to build a railroad to Esquimalt. He just wasn't very clear on where the other end of the line would be. Doubtless, there were still plenty of speculators who were sure he'd said the railroad would be the western end of a continuous track that was to start in Halifax.

It took eight more years and yet another election, but a train did finally roll into Esquimalt in 1886. It had come all the way from . . . Nanaimo, seventy miles away. In another two years the Esquimalt and Nanaimo Railway (E & N) reached Victoria—seventeen years late and right on time.

One local businessman who was willing to wait for the E & N and never complain about the delay was a coal baron named Robert Dunsmuir. When the feds finally got around to really wanting to build the island railroad, the CPR said it really had done enough railroad building for the time being, thanks very much. So the feds hired Dunsmuir to build it and paid him $750,000 plus two million acres in land grants. That's more than ten thousand dollars, plus land, for each of the seventy miles from Esquimalt to Nanaimo.

The CPR did eventually buy the line, in 1905, netting Dunsmuir even more cash. Nine years later the CPR extended it north to Courtenay. There still is no track linking Vancouver Island to the mainland.

The *Malahat*, as VIA now calls the train, leaves Victoria every day in the early morning, arrives in Courtenay for lunch and then heads back, getting to Victoria in the evening. Victoria gets a lot of tourist business through the ferryboats that dock there for the day and return that night. The charming city is a popular day-trip destination from Seattle.

Courtenay is a charming place, too, with a nice shopping district, a music festival in the summer, the picturesque town of Comox not far away, and a lovely beach. For tourists who arrive from Seattle, it would be the perfect way to spend an extra day out of Victoria, maybe stay overnight, do some shopping, see some of the island and be back in time for the boat home.

Except the *Malahat* leaves Victoria before the ferryboats arrive in the morning, and it returns mere minutes before they leave, when it's on time.

That's the way it goes.

We picked it up in Nanaimo, heading south to Victoria.

From the street, Nanaimo's train station is old and dull, but it would have been a warm and welcoming building in its day. Its roof has a gentle slope, the walls are covered in cedar shakes with a stucco facade that houses three ticket windows. The day I was there the pansies in the flower boxes were in full bloom, but the ticket windows were boarded up. The waiting room was abandoned, except for a rack with a few pamphlets.

The men's room was the proud possessor of the biggest urinals I've ever seen—like vertical bathtubs. I'm assuming they were put in when the station was built back in 1920, when space was cheap. They were made by the Twyford Corporation in Henley, England—model name "Adamant."

The stairway leading up to the second floor was boarded up with a single plank and a messy sign saying "no entry." Like apparently hundreds of others, I ignored it.

The door to the main room upstairs was held shut with a broken padlock. Inside there was a damp and smelly mattress lying on the floor and graffiti explaining in no uncertain terms how it might best be put to use. The floorboards were rotting at the north end of the building, the roof was collapsing, and the whole place was suffused with creepy decay. I went back downstairs.

In the main lobby, I noticed a map tacked onto the plywood wall. It had "VIA Rail Nanaimo, B.C." and some train times written in black marker across the top. Another note explained that VIA would no longer accept reservations for seats on the train by phone, but only at a VIA sales office.

Clearly, the station wasn't one of them.

There was a list of travel agents. At the top of the list was Eaton's, Nanaimo. It had gone out of business earlier that year.

I walked around Nanaimo a few minutes. It is the only Canadian city I've been to where you can leave a decrepit train station and, within a single city block, pass a battery factory, a tire manufacturer, an industrial glass dealership and arrive at an organic bakery where heavily pierced young people will sell you a latte and a muffin for far too much money and take a very long time doing it.

It occurred to me that the train schedule tacked up in the lobby looked as if it had been there since the mid-1970s. I wasn't sure I trusted it, so I ran back to the station.

John was on the platform, getting set to water the window boxes. He was the reason they looked good. He's a volunteer.

"It's not too good these days," he said. "I've been doing this fifteen years since I retired. It's gone downhill. The cars are continually breaking down. It runs late most of the time. Sometimes they'll go two or three days without a train and they'll just put the people on a bus. You know, people who come here want to ride the train. They're disappointed but nobody seems to care. I hate to see it.

"I've lived here beside the tracks all my life. It was a busy freight line. They were offloading and onloading from the time it came in till it left again. We had a steam train coming from the north and another from the south every day. Now the freights are once a week—nothing, really. The lumber companies use trucks. It used to be a busy place."

I asked about a room off the lobby that I'd noticed. It appeared to be a kind of shrine.

"That used to be the main office where all the freight went through and the messages went out from the old guy with the Morse code. There used to be fifty or sixty people working here. It was quite a place. Now they rent it out for a yoga class."

The *Malahat* tooted as it approached. A few more people had gathered on the platform and they began to pick up their bags. The train was made up of two dayliner cars—the kind with the engine built in right under the passenger section.

John unlocked a little door on the side of the station to get at the faucet to water the window boxes.

The padlock on the faucet door was a big, old brass lock, about the circumference of a softball, with "CPR" in raised letters across the body. The key was big, too, and brass. It weighed as much as a small rock.

"I found it on the platform one day," John smiled. "They used to be all over the place."

The train tooted that it was time to leave.

The track from Courtenay to Victoria is owned by the CPR, and the *Malahat* cars are owned by VIA, but I found out talking with the conductor that a shortline company called RailAmerica runs the train, as well as what little freight remains on the line. The track and the train were in rough shape. The cars had the same upholstery that was standard thirty years ago, the deep maroon of my high-school trips to Truro, Nova Scotia, but there was little fantasy left to them. The back of the car had holes along the floor that were plugged with duct tape. The ride was bumpy enough that we held our drinks in our laps.

The conductor's name was Brent. He explained that he didn't work for VIA. VIA just provided the equipment. The CPR just provided the line. RailAmerica leased the cars and track from both of them and kept the difference. That's who Brent worked for. Brent got his clearances every morning by cell-phone from a branch office in Vassar, Michigan. His boss was in Florida.

I asked how any of them could make any money on a two-car train that was falling apart.

"Well, that's the thing, eh?" he said. "When there are three fingers in the pie, nobody eats much."

Brent started working for RailAmerica after he was fired from the CPR. He started at age seventeen in Hamilton as a hostler with a local freight yard. The title of hostler is a throwback to equestrian times—the fellow who cared for the horses. From there he moved up through the railroad ranks to the position of switchman for the CPR. Then, in the early eighties, he was a steward on the most famous and respected passenger train ever to run in Canada—the *Canadian*.

I didn't want to ask how it felt to go from the *Canadian* to the *Malahat*, so I asked how he thought the train fit into the communities it served. To me, that was what gave the people who worked on the trains a sense of purpose and value. Brent thought a long time.

"We bring a lot of kids back and forth," he finally said.

"Kids?"

"Yeah. The parents split up and one lives in Courtenay and the other somewhere else along the line. They put the kids on to get back to Mom or Dad. They're supposed to be twelve, the kids, but most of 'em aren't. I always look out for that. Every kid you ask is always twelve, 'cause they're supposed to be twelve. That's what their parents teach them to say. It puts you in a situation. It's happened that you're supposed to leave a kid off in Duncan, say, and his mom or dad ain't there. So you gotta take him with you. And then when you get to Victoria you get his name and someone has to come and get him. You can't just leave him there. You know you can't."

I have not come across any account of Sir John A. Macdonald expressing an opinion on joint-custody parenting after divorce. I suspect, though, back in 1871, he would have had higher goals for his little pet project of a country that stretched from the Atlantic to the Arctic and Pacific oceans, and the railway that would bring it together.

The train rolled along. We ran beside the highway for a while, with fleets of RVS, the fat and lazy Pullman cars of the twenty-first century, passing us by the dozens.

We pulled into Victoria slightly late. It took us about ten minutes to get sorted out and leave the station, and by then it was empty and the train had rolled off for the night. It was as if it hadn't ever been there in the first place.

The most memorable sights of the trip were the very high trestles we crossed before we reached Victoria. At one trestle, over a narrow river canyon, people were bungee jumping off a second platform slightly upriver. The train slowed down so we could watch. A young woman, all smiles as the cord was belted to her ankles, waved at the train while we waited. She swung her arms back and forth, took a deep breath and became very still, arms by her sides, eyes closed. Her skin seemed to pale. She tipped forward, almost limp, and plunged headfirst down into the chasm below.

That's the way it goes.

second ending

Prince Rupert,
British Columbia

~

*W*HEN A COMPOSER WRITES OUT a piece of music for a group of musicians to play and there are parts of the piece that are repetitive, he or she can use a repeat sign—:‖. It tells the players to go back and play the section again. When it's time to move on to the next bit, sometimes the ending that worked for sending everyone back won't work for sending every-one on. That's when a composer uses a second ending. The players go through the whole thing, but when they get to the end of the repeated part for the last time, they take the second ending.

I'm going to go back to Jasper and take the second ending.

There is still more than one way in Canada to take a train to the Pacific coast. In Jasper, you have a choice of going to Vancouver by VIA Rail or, in the summertime, by the *Rocky Mountaineer,* or you can take VIA's train No. 5, the *Skeena.* The *Skeena* has no sleeping cars. It goes by the Yellowhead Pass, past Mount Robson to Prince George, and stops there for the night. The next morning it continues along the Skeena River to Prince Rupert and the Pacific Ocean.

There has been talk for years of scrapping the *Skeena* from the VIA schedule. The summer I travelled, there was talk of

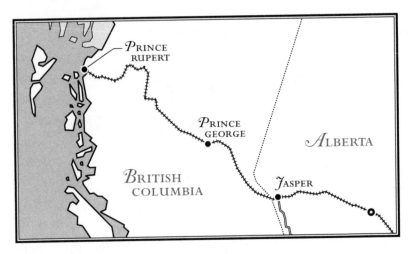

selling it to the people who run the *Rocky Mountaineer*. There has also been talk that the only reason it hasn't been scrapped is the same alleged reason for VIA's switching to the Canadian National route in 1990. That would be the one I mentioned earlier without quoting anyone who didn't want me to use his or her name or to say anything very specific about the voting patterns of certain constituencies, as well as certain prominent members of the Progressive Conservative Party.

But that's just talk.

There's only one certainty—at the time of writing, there is still a VIA train that follows the Skeena River to Prince Rupert. You can pick it up in Jasper, which is what we did.

As befits a second ending, Jasper was much better this time. Some of it had to do with Magoo. Magoo was the dog at our B & B. She was part husky, part wolf—a big, lovable monster with paws like baseball gloves. She loved playing "keep away" with us, but it was mostly a social pursuit. Everybody knew she wasn't really trying. She tolerated us, with a slackjawed half smile.

The walk wasn't torture this time, either. The baggage had become just part of the deal, as baggage, both literal and metaphorical, generally does.

There were only about ten people in our car. We were told a bus-sized tour group would be joining us the next day, but to begin with, we had a coach, an empty first-class car (being held for the tour group), our car and a Dome at the back, mostly to ourselves.

All of that space set the tone for the trip. The crew were kind without being fawning. Now and then they'd point out something worth seeing, but they weren't afraid to show that they'd seen it all many times before, and there was no reason to panic over missing a little spectacular beauty.

Our crew was made up of seasoned veterans and very young summer help, while the ten passengers joining us were mostly in their mid- to late sixties, with one British couple well beyond seventy. Somehow, though, nobody felt the need to, well, act their age. I saw it again and again in the two days we travelled the *Skeena*. For the British couple, the trip was a celebration of their fiftieth wedding anniversary. They had met on a train in London after the war. Just the sound of the wheels seemed to fill them with giddiness. They spent much of the trip huddled together, giggling. Now and then one of the young crew members, all of twenty-four, would look down on them and tut-tut while passing by.

The kicker for me was that I felt as if I were enjoying more luxury than I had anywhere else. The food was good, but it wasn't great. There were no linen napkins. The attendants weren't waiting on us hand and foot. We weren't being treated or acting like millionaires, or even flagitious poltroons. The

real luxuries were space and time, and we had tons of both.
We saw Mount Robson, and the headwaters of the Fraser, and
hour after hour of stunning scenery, and I realized over and
over again how lucky we were to be there.

Canadians pay horrendous taxes. We are choked by bureau-
cracy. We worry about doing the right thing and hesitate, while
others help themselves. We try. We try. A national trying and
hoping and *just doing our best,* and for what? For this. This was
the payoff—our space, our land, our beautiful, endless land.
The train was simply allowing us to see it. For that day, on that
train, I couldn't have asked for more. Luxury, for a Canadian,
as we experienced it that summer, had nothing to do with the
extras and everything to do with enjoying what we already have.

The town of Penny, British Columbia, would qualify as
something that we already have. Penny is west of McBride,
which isn't saying much to a lot of the rest of Canada, but it
means a lot to Penny. Twelve people live in Penny, sometimes
ten, depending on the time of year. One couple goes on vaca-
tion. Penny is a mail stop. There are a few communities on
this route that are accessible only by rail or by river. In the
not-too-distant past there were many such stops, and the train
was their only consistent contact with the outside world. VIA
has a contract with Canada Post to deliver mail to and from
those towns that rely on the train. Penny is the last one.

We stopped, and Terry, our service manager, stepped out
and walked to a small square building flying a Canadian flag.
His jobs in Penny are to collect the mail, feed the dog, Jesse,
bring the mail back with him and drop it into the main system
in Prince George.

We watched him from the Dome. He did an admirable job,
but he came back empty-handed.

"Nope," Terry said when he climbed back in. "Dog's away, too. Maybe tomorrow."

I could see our engineer, Jerry, through the window of the cab on the locomotive. He was leaning on the sill, his elbow on the ledge, as if he were driving a sports car. He gunned the engine and we rolled on.

Jerry likes working the *Skeena*. He lives in Prince George. He drives to Jasper one day and back home the next. That gives him one stop at home on every run. His day is twelve hours long, not eighteen. For a Railroader, it's as close as it comes to nine to five.

Except that it's not nine to five. I watched Jerry and his conductor that day, Eddie, while they worked. Jerry was leaning back. He had his feet propped up on a ledge on the console. He and Eddie talked. They watched.

I asked what they were watching for.

"You never know until you see it. Sometimes you're lucky if you see it at all," Jerry said.

He told of one day when the train had passed a view of Mount Robson, slowing down so passengers could take photographs. If he hadn't slowed down, the rockslide that was waiting around the bend would have derailed the train and sent everybody into the gully below.

"Sometimes you see it in time, sometimes you don't, but if you're not watching," Jerry said, "you never do."

Eddie talked about the time he rounded a bend and saw a farmer on a tractor stopped across the track at the level crossing ahead. The tractor had a large hay wagon behind him. The farmer had his back turned to the train. Eddie hit the horn. The farmer's tractor was so loud he didn't hear it. The wagon was still right across the tracks. They were going to hit.

Eddie jammed on the brakes. The train groaned and lurched. The farmer ahead still had no idea what was coming. Eddie hit every braking device he could find. He couldn't stop the train, but he slowed it down enough that the farmer, in his own methodical, unhurried way, got across the track in time. The locomotive missed him by about a foot. Eddie, his lungs in his throat and his heart in his ankles, whooped for joy when they cleared. He looked out the window to see the farmer blithely bobbing away. There had been a giant diesel monster breathing down his neck and he just hadn't looked.

Eddie and Jerry knew a lot of the farmers alongside the track. They honked the horn and waved hello to many of them. One farmer, Floyd, went into Jasper with them now and then. There really wasn't an easy way for Floyd to get into town from where he was. Jerry and Eddie viewed it as their job, not as Railroaders, just as people. They acted the way neighbours do when they know they'll be seeing a lot of each other.

At one point Eddie heard on the radio from the control centre that a freight would be coming in the other direction, and the *Skeena* should take a siding to get out of the way and wait for it. It was impressive to see how smooth and technically efficient the whole thing had become.

But when we got to the switch, things proceeded in an entirely non-technical fashion. Jerry stopped the train. Eddie climbed down to the track, walked to the switch and heaved it across where it was supposed to be, not with remote control or a fancy mechanical system, but with his hands. He was the conductor. That was part of his job.

A shovel hung on the pole beside the switch. I asked what it was for.

"Snow," Eddie said. There was also a tank of propane with an attached heater that could be switched on by a remote control radio in the locomotive. In winter, when the train was approaching, they could radio ahead and start the propane heater in time for it to melt the snow before they got there. Very high-tech.

"That's the theory, anyway," Eddie said, hefting the shovel appreciatively. "But it's still good to have a shovel around. We get a lot of snow."

Eddie waved Jerry through onto the siding, then he pulled the switch into place for the freight, jogged back to the locomotive and climbed in. There might have been hundreds of people depending on him for their safety every day, but that didn't mean he was above a little shovelling.

~

It would have given Charles Hays a great deal of pleasure to see a train full of contented passengers on the Skeena line.

Charles Melville Hays was an American brought in by a British company to make things happen in Canada. Remarkably, he did.

Before Hays, the Grand Trunk Railroad was a conservative business that took few chances and even fewer actions. The company's Canadian division was founded in 1852. Once it had established an eastern rail network in Canada, its most industrious effort was an aggressive smear campaign in England against the fledgling CPR. The Grand Trunk tried to scare away investors so that things would stay just the way they were.

When the CPR reached the Pacific in 1885, the Grand Trunk realized things were not going to stay anything close to the way they were. The company called Hays.

Charles Hays became general manager of the GrandTrunk in 1896. He spent a few years trying to hang on to the Grand Trunk's holdings in the East while the CPR grew by leaps and bounds. Hays decided the only way the GrandTrunk could survive was by coming up with something even bigger and better than what the CPR had done. He envisioned a new route through the Rocky Mountains with a new community at the end of the line—a bustling industrial metropolis on the British Columbia coast, teeming with industry and dispatching Canadian rail-linked freight lines in steamships to "China, Japan and the Orient." This new western terminus wouldn't simply be a port, however; it would also be a cosmopolitan centre of sophistication and class. A Venice of Canada. He even announced a contest to name the great city. One of the nieces of Manitoba's lieutenant-governor came up with the winner—Prince Rupert.

OK, so Charles Hays might have been the only person in history to think of Venice and Prince Rupert in the same breath. No matter, as the building began through the Yellowhead Pass and on, north to Prince George, it became clear that he fully intended to make all of the hopes and dreams for his railroad's western terminus a reality. The GrandTrunk Pacific Railroad ran its track-laying operation with precision and attention to detail. Hays insisted on the highest-quality materials and the finest craftsmanship and, most important, a straight and level track that would easily tolerate the vast amount of cargo he was sure would be heading towards his northern El Dorado.

After scoffing at his grandiose schemes for years, and by 1912, when the line was against many, many odds beginning to near completion, investors, Railroaders, and even the bean-counters at the CPR began to wonder if he might just make it happen.

But money was running low. Hays had never been afraid to put his own name on the line for the project, so he packed off to England to hustle up investors for more capital. If only he had come home just a little later . . . If he'd been just a little bit less keen . . . If he had, today the average business traveller would be landing at Western Canada's premier international airport, the gleaming and space-age Prince Rupert International.

The Grand Trunk Pacific hammered home its last spike near Fort Fraser on April 7, 1914. Two days later the line's first westbound train from Winnipeg reached the west coast in record time.

Then the First World War broke out in Europe and everything changed. Transportation and tourism all but died. Building debts climbed higher and higher. Canada suddenly had fifty-five thousand kilometres of very expensive track and barely anyone to travel it. Three years later the Grand Trunk Pacific was merely part of a new government railroad bailout called Canadian National, and Prince Rupert, the little fishing village with the big train station and even bigger dreams, stayed a fishing village.

Charles Melville Hays wasn't there to see it. Two years less a week before his precious line was complete, he'd gathered all of the investment money he could find in England. He wasn't finished, though. He wanted the fastest and most exclusive ship home, one that would give him access to plenty of potential investors for his new City of Light in British Columbia. He boarded a brand-new ocean liner that guaranteed him both. It was the *Titanic*.

Now, here's a strange one. In the year 2000, almost exactly eighty-six years (two days short) after the completion of the doomed Grand Trunk Pacific Railroad, and almost eighty-eight years (three days short) after the sinking of the *Titanic*, Canada's transport minister, David Collenette, announced a $400 million capital investment in VIA Rail.

I don't mean to sound cynical. If nothing else, my trip on the *Skeena* was ample evidence that the only thing the Canadian railroad really needs is space and time and good people on the trains who love their work. The land will do the rest. It's just that, in Canada, there seem to be an awful number of things to get in the way of the railroad before it even leaves the station.

That being said, a big chunk of money can only be good news for passenger rail in Canada. With the long-awaited money, VIA is refurbishing stations (ten million dollars on Toronto's Union Station—maybe they can get rid of the "Please"), upgrading track and, best of all, buying and running more trains.

The first addition was to bring back the Montreal-Toronto overnight. It's the opposite of the *Metropolis*—it takes a long time and stops everywhere. But it's perfect for business travellers who don't want to battle traffic to and from the airport. They can get on a train late at night in one city, enjoy that gentle rocking sleep that you only find on a train, shower, have breakfast and walk out of the station right downtown.

VIA's biggest news with the new money was the "Nightstock" luxury rail cars bought from the British rail manufacturer Alstom. The Alstom cars were mostly sleeping-car models intended for rail service through the Chunnel from England to France. They cost £2 million each to build, and VIA picked up 139 of them for a total of CAN$125 million.

That's less than half price.

The wily customer might have asked, "What's wrong with them?"

VIA said, "Nothing."

They may yet turn out to be right on that, although the Council of Canadians with Disabilities didn't think so. They were upset the cars were not handicapped accessible.

"So?" VIA said. "We can fix that."

There were also many unhappy people back in England who said that British Rail spent way too many taxpayer salaries for the cars in the first place, and that they never worked.

To that VIA said, "They'll increase our fleet by 30 percent."

For a nation first brought together by the railroad, which now found itself with almost no trains, it was a compelling argument.

The only persisting public relations problem around the Alstom cars stemmed from an unsubstantiated Web site rumour about the toilets. The Nightstock cars were to be used in the Chunnel, with one locomotive and several cars. Apparently, if everyone on the train had flushed all of the toilets at once, the train would have lost all power and completely shut down just from the shock.

You'd have to wonder how anyone figured that out. It doesn't sound like the kind of thing that would happen by coincidence. At least, you'd hope not—especially in a tunnel.

Still, my CBC Radio colleague Erika Ritter put the situation to a rail expert who knows these cars and their capabilities, and he wouldn't say it *wouldn't* happen.

If the rumour proves correct, it would carry on a Canadian tradition. Toilets have been an issue on VIA's trains for a while. It's not that flushing them stops the train. On the contrary, the train pays no attention at all. Most of the older passenger cars in VIA's fleet have toilets that flush very effectively—right onto the track below, making the stainless steel art deco sleeper cars into a line of shining mobile outhouses. It's hard to believe, especially if you're, as the old song goes, a workman working underneath.[1]

VIA has pledged to use some of its new money to clean up that little problem and build retention tanks on all of its trains. Any passengers who actually prefer the rolling out-house system will have to content themselves with getting a few friends together and, with one great whoosh, watching a streaming intercity express turn into a limp and darkened cesspool.

If you're walking by the rail line one evening and you see a train full of brand-new cars suddenly stop in the middle of a level crossing, I'd suggest you turn around and walk the other way.

~

You don't get much out of the city of Prince George when you ride the *Skeena*. It's just a place to stop with a few hotels. I honestly don't remember anything about our hotel except that it was a five-dollar cab ride from the station and that it had a pool.

We went swimming.

---

1. As heard in 1972 in Bryan Leece's house in Montreal West, from the LP *Songs for Gay Dogs*:

> Gentlemen must please refrain
> From flushing toilets while the train
> Is standing in the station, la, la, la.
> The workmen working underneath
> Are apt to get it in the teeth
> They don't like it; nor would you.

The next morning we had to be back at the station at
7:15 a.m., which was a little early, but our cab driver didn't
say a thing the whole way, and we were back on the *Skeena* on
time and with most of our sensibilities intact.

Eddie, our engineer, was back with us that day. VIA gave
the older, more experienced service attendants to the tour
group that had joined us, which left us with the younger ones,
Domenic and Karine.

Domenic was suave and articulate. His father was a New
Yorker who was placed in Canada for his work with the United
Nations. His mother was a Parisian. Domenic grew up in New
York and Montreal, and went to school at McGill. He was
going back to study genetics at the University of British
Columbia in the fall. We talked about classical music, culture,
language, and about football and trains. The most telling part,
though, was a short while in the afternoon when he was on a
break. He took a seat right across from us, but we were all so
relaxed that time slipped by for a good twenty minutes while
no one felt the need to say a word.

Karine was from Trois-Rivières, between Montreal and
Quebec City on the north shore of the St. Lawrence. She
was pretty, with dark hair and bright eyes. She was in her
fourth month with VIA. Before that she'd studied design at
a community college back in Trois-Rivières, and worked as
a window dresser for a swanky women's-wear chain.

She was very easy to talk to. I could easily see her dealing
with the upper-crust women of Trois-Rivières, Quebec's
answer to the girl next door.

I asked how often she got back home.

"Not too often," she said. "I don't know if the van would
make it."

The van?

"I live in a van—a Volkswagen," she said. "It's great. You don't have to pay rent or taxes . . . My boyfriend and I moved out here and we've been living in the van for two years. It takes us ice climbing in the winter and kayaking in the summer. I love to kayak. We used to park near the river we were going to kayak so that when the cops came to tell us we couldn't park there, we'd tell them we were just kayaking the next day and they were nice to us. When I have to work in Vancouver we park further out, in Squamish or on the North Shore. My other friends who live in vans are out there, too."

There are others?

"Oh, yeah, many of us. We just move around. I don't have a shower every day, but I'm clean. We don't have TV or cellphones. We don't need that much money. We all quit our jobs in the winter, anyway. It's great."

She had to go. One of the older men from the tour group was calling for her. He was a Baptist minister in pressed white slacks and a short-sleeved shirt with a tie. He wanted a ginger ale. He had to switch his Bible from one hand to the other to take it. Karine smiled and chatted with him a while. He was charmed.

We stopped in Fort Fraser. A boy and his grandmother stepped off and walked away on a dirt trail. They were the only people in sight.

Terry, the service manager, told me that on the *Skeena*, that happens all the time.

"In the winter the roads are really bad up here, and it's very cold. A lot of the people in the communities along the line use the train like a taxi. They just come to the track and flag it down. I've been working this route off and on for almost twenty years. I know a lot of the people that live along here pretty well, and that's the way it is with this line. It always has been, even back to the Grand Trunk days. It was created for and run for the people who live here."

I wondered where the tour groups fitted in.

"Tour traffic went up a lot a few years ago after an American documentary made it to TV about this being the last true local railroad in North America. We get a lot of Americans now, and a lot of Germans and British people, too."

What about Canadians?

"I honestly have been trying. I've fought like hell for years to get Canadians to travel these trains and just could not get them to do it. I think a lot of them would just rather get in their car and go. They don't realize how important it is. We've won awards all over the world as the best passenger train in North America, sometimes in the world, but Canadians just don't seem to notice us."

This was the same man who brought the mail from Penny every week. His professional life was built around being relevant to Canadians, even twelve at a time.

"There are so many people who live here that most Canadians think of as being from another century, but they're not. They're here. We get prospectors up in the mountains all winter long coming down and taking the train in to Rupert for a restaurant meal. There's a fellow who used to be a concert pianist and he came up here to get away. Now he tunes pianos to make a living. We pick him up and drop him off at the next town— an itinerant piano tuner.

"I look at this country trying to hold itself together and I think we must have forgotten what brought us together in the first place. This land and these people are what it's about. I keep thinking if I could get people from the East who have never been out here, give them to me for a week on the train and you'd never hear another word about national identity ever again. This is it. It's here. I just can't get them to see it."

Fifteen school-aged Native kids got on in Burns Lake with two adults, a young woman and an older man. The woman was mother to a couple of the kids. The older man, Ted, was grandfather to some of them, although I was never clear which ones. Ted took the train from Burns Lake, British Columbia, to Antigonish, Nova Scotia, in 1965 to go to school. He said he'd never forget it. I asked why he was bringing the kids on the train, and he said he wanted them to know what a train was like. He also said Status Indians get half fare on VIA, and the kids were all going free.

They were going to Houston, one stop and an hour down the line. Houston is the home of the world's largest fishing pole. It was almost twenty metres tall, towering over the convenience store. There was a fleet of cars waiting for the school kids and adults at the level crossing to drive them home.

Further on we came to a Gitksan village called Kitwanga. We were told the town had totem poles that were prominent and important for the local culture. They turned out to be a lot harder to see than the big fishing pole in Houston, but both totem and fishing poles were dwarfed by a towering cluster of mountains called the Seven Sisters. Kitwanga had its share of decay, too. A few houses were falling over, and the graffiti at the side of the rail yard would have made a cab driver blush.

But not the Seven Sisters. You could tell just looking at them that they'd already seen much worse, and weren't particularly worried about it either.

~

It was raining in Prince Rupert the morning after we arrived, apparently the normal state of affairs. That was OK, I decided. We were in the dreamt-of western terminus, and we were going to explore it as it was, without the glossy finish and the pithy brochure anecdotes.

We went for breakfast at a local restaurant instead of staying in the compound that was our hotel. I was picturing a quaint local spot with great breakfasts, you know, like the one my friend Dave Wadley discovered back in Ontario, where the locals would pretend we weren't there?

That's not what it was. The place was full of smoke and fishermen and, mostly, smoking fishermen. They all literally turned around when we came in. I asked for a seat in the non-smoking section and the guys at the counter laughed out loud. There wasn't one.

The only member of our family who wasn't uncomfortable was my son, who was mesmerized by the TV. It was a Sunday morning at eight o'clock. TSN was showing super heavyweight boxing. A fat bald guy named Butterball was throwing repeated left hooks to a fat, hairy guy named Farley, who was losing badly.

We ordered pancakes. Four huge orders came. We barely finished two.

They laughed at us again when we left.

It was still raining.

The need for an agenda lowered us to the predictable tourist fodder and, I'm embarrassed to say, we caved in to it—we went to Prince Rupert's waterfront shopping area and bought stuff we'd never think of buying anywhere else. The place is called Cow Bay. It's not a glassed-in complex and no one was selling wind chimes, but there was fudge, of course, and we bought a heap.

We walked through the rain until our fudge was gone, then to the museum, along the wharf, past an astonishingly smelly fish cannery, all through the rain, until we stopped at an empty street corner wondering what to do. It was midday at best, and despite our slickers we were soaked to the skin.

"Hey!" my daughter said. "I know!"

Prince Rupert has the best pool on the Canadian rail swimming itinerary as we experienced it. It has a swinging rope, a hot tub, a very warm wading pool, a high-diving board and a deep end that goes down so far that it hurt my ears to touch the bottom.

We were the only tourists there. The kids played with the local kids. We chatted with local parents. It was completely new, tons of fun, totally different and just like home.

The swimming pool has towering totem poles by the door. It's next to the performing arts complex. We stayed all afternoon. Charles Melville Hays, I decided, was right all along. In the pool, anyway, Prince Rupert *is* Venice.

Our hotel room was only on the fifth floor of the building, but it was at the top of a hill, and we could see clearly across Seal Cove to the far shore. Back from the pool, I went out on the balcony with my binoculars. I was looking for seals or osprey, but what I saw was train passengers.

My eyes were sweeping the shoreline and caught the edge of a motel room below us and across the street. The curtains were open. I felt guilty spying, but I couldn't turn away. It was the older British couple we'd been with since Jasper—the giggly septuagenarians celebrating fifty years of marriage.

They were sitting on chairs, side by side, looking out the window, not speaking, hiding nothing, at the end of their day, near the end of their lives, trusting the world going by to keep their secrets.

⁓

Back on the train the day before, when we were first approaching Prince Rupert, there hadn't been any signs of rain. With only the Pacific between us and the sun, the sunset was quite like the ones on the prairies, filtering long and slow through the Skeena's misty haze.

The feeling of luxury I'd had that afternoon only intensified the closer we got to the end of our trip. We saw cliffside petroglyphs in the rock next to the track. We saw eagles and ospreys and one court jester of a seal that popped his head out of the water and got a big laugh out of the Dome crowd when he seemed to stick out his tongue.

We also saw the mountains, always, in almost every direction. I had a crick in my neck from looking straight up out the top of the Dome. They soared beside and above us, never giving up, all the way to the sea.

⁓

As usual, we and our bags were the last ones out of the train. We were clumping along the platform, eyeing the hill we'd have to climb to reach our hotel, when our daughter announced she had to pee. The bathroom was in the station. My wife and I exchanged looks, and she took her in, and our son, just in case. I stayed outside on the platform.

I was looking out over the water, feeling my train legs, when a snort behind me wheeled me around. It was our train, backing away from the station for the night, to the end of the line. The sun on the windshield was so bright I couldn't see who was driving until the train jolted to a stop with a hiss, and Eddie climbed out of the cab.

He walked back along the length of the engine, the baggage car, all the way to the Park car, peering around the back of the Bullet Lounge, and then walked all the way back, looking at the wheels, the couplings, the doors, while the engine idled evenly beside him. Satisfied, he stood back for a moment, hands on his hips, and stayed there, looking, for just a moment more. Then he picked up his bag and shuffled out of the train's long shadow, into the glow of the sunset, and away for the night.

Credits

The following served as both resources and inspiration while I was writing this book:

Books

Berton, Pierre. *The Great Depression*. Markham, ON: Penguin Books Canada, 1991; Toronto: McClelland and Stewart, 1990.

————. *The Last Spike*. Toronto: McClelland and Stewart, 1971; Markham, ON: Penguin Books Canada, 1989.

————. *The National Dream*. Toronto: McClelland and Stewart, 1970; Markham, ON: Penguin Books Canada, 1989.

Brown, Ron. *The Train Doesn't Stop Here Anymore*. Toronto: Lynx Images, 1998.

Conrad, Margaret, Alvin Finkel, and Veronica Strong-Boag. *A History of the Canadian Peoples*, Vol. III. Mississauga: Copp Clark Pitman, 1993.

Cruise, David, and Alison Griffiths. *Lords of the Line*. 3rd ed. Toronto: Penguin Books Canada, 1996.

Lees, Gene. *The Will to Swing*. Toronto: Lester & Orpen Dennys, 1988.

Love, J.A., and J. Norman Lowe. *CN Coast to Coast*. Calgary: The Calgary Group of the British Railway Modellers of North America, 1980.

Mackay, Donald, and Lorne Perry. *Train Country*. Vancouver: Douglas & McIntyre, 1994.

McDonnell, Greg. *Passing Trains*. Erin, ON: Boston Mills Press, 1996.

Mitchell, David J. *All Aboard!* Vancouver: Douglas & McIntyre, 1995.

O'Hara, Jane, from *In the Face of Disaster*, Michael Benedict, ed., Toronto: Viking Penguin Books Canada, 2000.

Thompson, M. J. *The Banff Centre*. Banff: Altitude Publishing, 1993.
Uys, Errol Lincoln. *Riding the Rails*. New York: TV Books, 1999.

Articles

Burke, Monte. "Good Salmon Water." *Forbes Magazine* (December 11, 2000), p. 364.

Ninjalicious. "Exploring Subway and LRT Tunnels." *Infiltration*, no. 5 (1999).

Whyte, Kenneth. *Alberta Report*. With Tim Gallagher, Donald Campbell, Gavin Fitch, Barbara Henker and Brian Bergman (February 1986).

Broadcasts

Guettel, Alan, and Greg Gormick, producers. *Ribbons of Steel*. CBC Radio's *Ideas*, 1986 series. With Lister Sinclair.

Schriever, Beatrice, and Greg Gormick, producers. Five-part series on the passenger trains of Canada. CBC Radio's *Morningside*, 1983. With Peter Gzowski.